PRAISE FOR
Secrets Savored

"I highly recommend Secrets Savored as an effective reproducible model of Titus 2. The combination of discipleship through biblical devotions and practical home management skills have strengthened our young couples' marriages and thus their families."

Donna Gaines
Pastor's Wife

"When my husband and I moved to a new city, not knowing anyone, Secrets Savored gave me the opportunity to connect with other women also seeking to grow closer to Jesus and discover His purpose for our lives. This ministry brings together women of all ages, backgrounds, and stages of life in such a sweet way that has blessed me."

Sarah Sherlock
Secrets Savored Participant

"Before I knew about Secrets Savored, I prayed that God would allow me to learn from godly women as it says in Titus 2. I am so grateful that He answered my prayers. I have learned so much from the discipling leaders about God's Word and how to be a godly wife and homemaker. I have also learned to follow Christ through the example of the leadership. I cannot thank them enough for showing me how to love Christ supremely and to love my husband."

Jenny McKay
Secrets Savored Participant and Pastor's Wife

"The most important ministry a Christian can have is discipleship, and Secrets Savored is an excellent tool in carrying out that biblical mandate. In a warm and inviting home setting, young women are led to discover and practice godly living. I have enjoyed being a discipler in a program that balances both the practical and spiritual needs of women. As we talk, eat, study, and have fun together, we develop strong bonds that will last a lifetime. What a blessing!"

Elisa Skinner
Discipling Leader

SECRETS Savored

Creating Community Through Simple Hospitality

Book Two

DIANNE DOUGHARTY

Leader Guide

HIGH BRIDGE BOOKS
HOUSTON

SECRETS SAVORED
Book Two Leader Guide
Copyright © 2021 by Dianne Lynn Dougharty
All rights reserved.

No part of this publication may be reproduced, stored in a retrieval system, or transmitted in any form or by any means electronic, mechanical, photocopying, recording, or otherwise, without the prior written permission of the author.

Scripture quotes are taken from New Living Translation Second Edition, Tyndale House Publishing Company, Carol Stream, Illinois, Copyright ©1968, 1989, 1990, 1991, 1993, 1996, 2004 by Tyndale House Publishing Incorporated. *** Charles Stanley Life Principles Bible Copyright © 2005 by Charles Stanley Holy Bible, New King James Version, Copyright 1982 by Thomas Nelson, Inc.

New American Standard Bible: Ryrie Study Bible, ©1986, 1995 by The Moody Bible Institute. The New Living Translation Parallel Study Bible, ©2011 by Tyndale House Publishers. The Message: The Bible in Contemporary Language Copyright © 2002 by Eugene Peterson. The NIV/Message Parallel Bible Copyright © 2004 The Zondervan Corporation, Grand Rapids, Michigan 49530.

Library of Congress Control Number: 2012945608
ISBN: 978-1-954943-10-0

Graphic Design by *Studio B Print and Design*, Tyler Bedwell

Cover Photography: Jo Laura Bell Photography

Printed in the United States of America U.S. Printing History

First Edition: August 2012

Requests for Information should be addressed to:

Secrets Savored, Inc.
P.O. Box 2257
Cordova, Tennessee 38088

High Bridge Books
Houston, TX

For purchasing the Secrets Savored Book Two Leader Guide complete with weekly lesson plans or the Book Two Workbook for participants go to www.secretssavored.org/curriculum/shop.

You will need one Leader Guide per discipling leader.

You will need one Workbook per participant.

TO MY MOM, DR. BEVERLY CLECKNER
TO MY MOTHER-IN-LAW, MRS. NELL DOUGHARTY

You both impacted my life and gave me a deep desire to be the best wife, mom, and homemaker that I could be. Mom, you sacrificed so much to raise four children and complete your education in the process; always making sure we were well fed, clothed, and lovingly cared for. Your faithfulness, devotion, and commitment to the Lord, your husband, your family, and others have been an example to me. God has abundantly blessed me with being your daughter!

My mother-in-law, Nell, treated me like a daughter from the day Mark brought me to Florida in 1973 to meet his family. I am grateful for the beautiful example she set for me of a modern-day Naomi. Her love of family and home, as well as ministry, was a wonderful example to me. Her years of teaching and investing in young women as a home economics teacher in the public school system was a gift to many. She is dearly missed!

"A gracious woman retains honor."
Proverbs 11:16a NKJV

"Strength and honor are her clothing; she shall rejoice in time to come.
She opens her mouth with wisdom, and on her tongue is the law of kindness.
She watches over the ways of her household, and does not eat the bread of idleness.
Her children rise up and call her blessed; her husband also, and he praises her."

Proverbs 31:25 28 NKJV

WITH GRATITUDE

I am afraid if I try to list the names of all those I owe gratitude, I would neglect someone. So, let me begin with the One without whom none of this would be possible, my heavenly Father. I am grateful to the Lord that He knows best. I would have never dreamed that out of life's most difficult hardship, this ministry would be birthed! Thank you, Father!

> "The Lord says, 'I will guide you along the best pathway for your life.
> I will advise you and watch over you.'"
>
> Psalm 32:8 NLT

I want to thank my church, my pastor, and his wife for their love, encouragement, support, and prayers. Thank you to our Women's Ministry staff, who were very helpful as we launched Secrets and continue to be a great help to the ministry. Thank you to the Secrets discipling leadership who have believed in this ministry and the value of using this material in reaching young women for Christ.

To the many young women who participated in the Secrets ministry around the country these past several years, I love you! Thank you for letting us pour into your lives all the secrets we have attained over the years. I pray this study and the lives of the discipling leadership have profoundly impacted your life and home.

A word of gratitude goes to Jo Laura Bell of Jo Laura Bell Photography for our cover and Tyler Bedwell of Studio B Print Shop for designing our logo and formatting the books. I owe you girls a huge thank you for your service, incredible creativity, and patience!

My dear friend and mentor has joined our Savior in Heaven! I am incredibly grateful for her tireless hours of editing, and for the days and nights spent in my office trying to meet a deadline. Throughout her years of service, Marge honored our Lord and did all things well. I will always be grateful for her—and indebted to her!

To our board, thank you for your tireless work and commitment. My heartfelt appreciation goes to the Harry Smith Foundation for the funding to publish the original curriculum material; you were a direct answer to our prayers!

Thank you to those in the body of Christ who gave to Mark and me in so many ways. You believed in this ministry and prayed for us as God led us down a dark road and through deep waters. Your continued support upon Mark's death has been a blessing to me. To my sweet sisters in Christ—thank you for your love, prayers, listening ears, timely hugs, girl moments, the supplied Kleenex, and the laughter, which at times along this journey were much needed and appreciated—I love you!

I want to thank my parents for their encouragement and belief over the years that I could do anything. I never doubted their love or support! To my siblings and Mark's family, I am grateful for your love, support, encouragement, prayers, and belief in God's calling upon my life. Last, but not least, I am very grateful to my daughters, Angela and Kelly, my sons-in-law, and grandchildren for their patience and sacrifice of time away from Mom and Mimi, while I was doing what God had called me to do. How grateful I am for you. You are treasured and loved a bunch!

CONTENTS

Weekly Recipes XI
Introduction to Secrets Savored XIII
Book Two Schedule XV
Structure for Secrets Savored Study XVI
Components of Weekly Session XVIII
Components of Weekly Bible Study XIX
Understanding the Bible XXI

WEEK ONE
Organizing Your Home (Workbook page 21) 25

WEEK TWO
Organizing Your Closet (Workbook page 39) 49

WEEK THREE
Tips on Laundry, Ironing, and Sewing (Workbook page 53) 69

WEEK FOUR
Etiquette (Workbook page 73) 95

WEEK FIVE
Children's Etiquette (Workbook page 97) 123

OPTIONAL WEEK FIVE
Shower and Party Etiquette (Workbook page 115) 147

WEEK SIX
Tips on Cleaning (Workbook page 135) 167

WEEK SEVEN
Decorating Made Simple (Workbook page 159) 199

WEEK EIGHT
Tips on Gardening, Flowers, and Canning (Workbook page 181) 227

WEEK NINE
Woman to Woman (Workbook page 199) 249

Time in Kitchen Recipes (Workbook page 211) 263

Weekly Recipes

WEEK THREE | 71

Powdered Laundry Detergent
Liquid Laundry Detergent

WEEK FOUR | 112

Valentine Recipes:
Red Velvet Cupcakes
Cream Cheese Icing
Heart-Shaped Cookies and Icing
Linda's Old-Fashioned Sugar Cookies
Peppermint Ice Cream
Chocolate Truffles
Strawberry Cupcakes
Lover's Midnight Spiced Hot Chocolate

OPTIONAL WEEK FIVE | 151

Wedding Shower Recipes:
Hope's Coffee Slush
Refreshing Punch
Baby Carrots with Herb Dressing
Pesto and Turkey Pinwheels
Bacon and Cheese Dip
Chocolate Hazelnut Dipped Strawberries
Mini Almond Cupcakes
Baby Shower Recipes:
Hope's Coffee Slush
Sorority House Casserole
Fruit Kabobs
Lemon Blueberry Mini Muffins
Party Recipes:
Cajun Grilled Beef Tenderloin
Oven-Roasted Squash

WEEK SIX | 169

Homemade Spray Cleaner
Homemade Household Cleaner

WEEK EIGHT | 235

Canning Recipes:
Peach Preserves
Heirloom Tomato Salsa
Olita's Sweet Pickles
Bread and Butter Pickles
Spaghetti Sauce
Green Beans
Barbeque Sauce

TIME IN THE KITCHEN RECIPES | 263

Whole Wheat Yeast Rolls
Sweet Cream Chocolate Cake
Chocolate Cream Icing
Yeast Doughnuts and Glaze
Whole Wheat Orange Muffins
Sour Cream Blueberry Muffins
Six-Ingredient Granola Bars
Christine's Fabulous Coconut Smoothie
Peanut Butter Coconut Power Balls
Whole Wheat Pita Chips
Cheesy Almond Spread
Pan-Seared Cod
Creamy Salmon Filets
Trout Amandine

INTRODUCTION
to Secrets Savored

As a child, I attended church, but unfortunately, I grew up believing that I had to keep a certain set of rules in order to be a Christian. I was always breaking the rules; therefore, I never felt "good enough" or accepted by God.

My husband, Mark, grew up in the same church. Once we were married, we did what most people do who feel that they can never be acceptable to God—we ran from Him. The first few years, we ran hard after the world and away from God. Although our lives were full of things and stuff, we lacked meaning and purpose and peace and joy. We had much, yet we had nothing because we did not have Jesus Christ—who is everything.

> In Romans 11:6 it says, "And since it is through God's kindness, then it is not by their good works. For in that case, God's grace would not be what it really is—free and undeserved." NLT

God tells us that salvation does not come as a result of anything we do, nor because we deserve it, but because of His mercy and grace through the shed blood of His Son, Jesus. It is a free and undeserved gift.

> "For by grace you have been saved through faith. And this is not your own doing; it is a gift of God." Ephesians 2:8 ESV

God intervened in our lives after eleven years of marriage, and Mark was saved. As he studied God's Word, he began to see that it was not by our works or in keeping a set of rules that we are saved, but by the shed blood of Jesus. It was in his accepting Jesus as his personal Lord and Savior that his life was drastically changed. Just a few months after he was saved, I gave my heart and life to Jesus. Thus, my life was forever changed!

The relationship Mark and I had with Christ over the years *determined* the trajectory of our lives, marriage, and family. That relationship sustained me over the eleven years of journeying with him through a dreadful disease called Multiple Systems Atrophy. And, that relationship sustains me now as I adjust to living life without my soulmate and best friend.

In the midst of our journey, God led me to begin a mentoring ministry called Secrets Savored. This ministry is based on the verses in Titus 2 that encourage older women to teach younger women by giving them encouragement and strength for living out the life before them. Often, people ask me why the name Secrets Savored? What is the secret? Would you like to know the secret of Secrets Savored?

The *secret* of Secrets Savored is ***Jesus***!

In this fatherless, iPhone, Facebook, Twitter, self-driven world, Jesus is the only way to true peace and joy. He is the answer for discontentment, insecurity, depression, anxiety, and broken hearts. Secrets Savored is God's tool for reaching young women with the message of relationship versus rules. Through the lives and examples of older godly women and practical and biblical teaching, young women can grow to understand that there is no true peace, joy, contentment, or meaning in life apart from a personal relationship with ***Jesus***. I want them to know they are valued by Him, and what they do in life for Him will count and reap a grand reward in the end.

> "Therefore, since we have been made right in God's sight by faith, we have peace with God because of what Jesus Christ our Lord has done for us." Romans 5:1 NLT

I am excited that you, as discipling leaders, are joining this community of women who desire to create a spirit of hospitality and Christlikeness within their lives, homes, and relationships—for the glory of God!

Book Two SCHEDULE

WEEK ONE: *Organizing Your Home.* Women desire to have their homes and their lives in order. In this week's lesson, you will discover great *how-to* ideas for organizing your home and your life!

WEEK TWO: *Organizing Your Closet.* Lesson includes great ideas for getting your closet organized, shopping your own closet, and etiquette for dress. Consignment sales, Thrift Stores, and on-line shopping can also be discussed.

WEEK THREE: *Tips on Laundry, Ironing, and Sewing.* Instruction will be given in how to make laundry detergent, how to iron, how to sew on a button, and other tips to make the dreaded work of laundry and ironing less dreadful!

WEEK FOUR: *Etiquette.* Some of the topics discussed this week are: Note writing—thank you and condolence notes; table manners and social manners—R.S.V.P., arrival times, how late is too late?; appropriate dress for social gatherings; social media and cell phone etiquette; dressing for a job interview, and other special occasions.

WEEK FIVE: *Children's Etiquette.* Instructions will be given on children's table manners, dining-in and dining-out manners, telephone and social media manners, as well as how to play well with others. Note: Not every class will involve young women with children, when this is the case, consider the optional Week Five on Shower and Party Etiquette.

OPTIONAL WEEK FIVE: *Shower and Party Etiquette.* Some of the topics discussed this week are: invitations: how many, when to mail them, and whom to include on the invitation list. Games and activities are included as well as great recipes to ensure a successful party.

WEEK SIX: *Tips on Cleaning.* Great tips for doing the thing in your home that absolutely has to be done—cleaning! Instructions will be given on making homemade cleaners, how to organize your cleaning projects, and helpful hints for the tough cleaning areas in your home, such as the kitchen and bathroom.

WEEK SEVEN: *Decorating Made Simple.* This week you will discover some simple and practical ways to decorate your home, the basics of decorating, where to start, and much more. Choosing the right colors for your home and other painting tips will be discussed—and all on a budget!

WEEK EIGHT: *Tips on Gardening, Flowers, and Canning.* Invite a professional gardener/landscaper to teach on English Gardens and creative potting, landscaping, growing your own garden, growing herbs, canning, and shopping your local Farmer's Market. Note: Guest may not be necessary if the leadership is experienced and equipped to teach on this topic. Either way, the participants love this week!

WEEK NINE: *Woman to Woman.* Create a panel consisting of three to four women at different stages of life and with different life experiences. Begin class with introducing the guests serving on the panel. Those serving on the panel will address questions on relationships and spiritual and life issues previously submitted by the class participants. Schedule a break half way through the class time for light hors d'oeuvres and drinks. Use the remaining time for additional questions prompted by today's discussion. End with asking each panel participant a couple of questions determined by the leadership. Samples of possible questions to end the session are given in the practical lesson for this week.

STRUCTURE FOR SECRETS SAVORED STUDY

Secrets Savored Curriculum:

BOOK ONE: Provides eight weeks of lessons filled with recipes and practical instruction related to the kitchen, cooking, baking, meal planning, and hospitality. Note: An additional two weeks are provided if the leadership chooses to offer these lessons.

BOOK TWO: Provides nine weeks of lessons filled with additional recipes, and practical instruction on caring for a home, laundry/ironing, proper etiquette (for adults and children), party etiquette, shopping your closet, hospitality, and the art of gardening.

BOOK ONE AND TWO BIBLE STUDY: Take an up-close look at the women of the Bible. Each week the biblical principles found in their life stories are applied to the lives of the women participating in the study.

BOOKS THREE AND FOUR: These books were written due to the desire of young women for a follow-up study to Books One and Two. This curriculum includes additional practical instruction, along with an in-depth Bible study. As women maneuver through life, they face many issues, such as contentment, fear, anxiety, worry, difficult relationships, etc. In this study, the young women look into God's Word for biblical principles concerning these issues. Those principles, when applied, strengthen their walk with Christ and enable them to live purposefully and victoriously. In addition to the Bible study, there are unique practical tools for helping simplify their daily lives through receiving weekly meal plans, a variety of great recipes, short-cuts for meal preparation, and tips on healthy eating.

- Time allotted for each class should be 2-2½ hours per session.

- The cost for each course should be determined by the organization offering Secrets Savored.

- A fee of $25-$30 is recommended and should cover the expense of the workbook, and a portion of the supplies purchased by the leadership for the baking and cooking activities each week. Note: To purchase the Secrets Savored Book One Leader Guide complete with weekly lesson plans or the workbook go to secretssavored.org/curriculum.

- A discipling leadership team of three to four is recommended for each Secrets Savored class of eight to twelve participants. You will need one woman to serve as the teaching leader, one or two assistant leaders, and a home hostess.

Secrets Leadership Responsibility:

- **Teaching Leader:** Each week, the teaching leader will have the overall responsibility of teaching the Practical Lesson and providing all the materials and supplies needed, with the help of the home hostess and other leadership. She and the leadership team will make contacts outside of class with the students as necessary.

- **Assistant Leaders:** These women will fill in for the leader when necessary and will contribute to each of the lessons as determined at the weekly meeting prior to the upcoming class. The Assistants will be called upon to give input, especially in the areas where they are knowledgeable, and to help in teaching the devotional lesson each week (optional for those who are not comfortable). As needed, the assistants will share the responsibility of contacting the young women outside of class. Example: If a young woman were absent, a phone call or text would be made or a note written.

- **Home Hostess:** The home hostess is a part of the leadership team. She should be willing to provide coffee/beverages and some supplies from her kitchen as needed for the Practical Lessons.

- **The Leader Guide:** Available on-line at secretssavored.org/curriculum/shop. It is complete with a Weekly Introduction, Lesson Plan, Practical Lesson Sheets, an Equipment List (necessary for kitchen activities), and a Weekly Devotional Lesson. The participant Workbook, also available on-line, includes a Weekly Introduction, Practical Lesson Sheets, and a Weekly Devotional Lesson Sheet.

- **Team Meeting:** It is recommended that the team meet several weeks prior to the start date to plan the nine lessons and divide responsibilities. This makes the sessions run smoother. If this is not possible, meet weekly prior to class either in person or via email or text. An option for a daytime class would be to meet over lunch following the Secrets Savored class; this is a good time to plan for the coming week's lesson and to divide responsibilities.

COMPONENTS OF WEEKLY SESSION

DEVOTIONAL LESSON:

Each week's lesson is a study of a woman in the Bible and is designed to be 20-30 minutes in length. Practical and biblical life lessons are taken from the lives of the women studied and then applied to the lives of those participating in the study. The weekly teaching time may vary based on the topic. The devotional is located in the back of each week's lesson in the Leader Guide and participant Workbook. Note: A biblical principle to be drawn from the life of the woman studied is included in each week's lesson.

PRACTICAL LESSON:

Each week's practical lesson will cover 1 hour. The curriculum on the home provides activities that include an ironing demonstration, a cleaning demonstration, preparing homemade laundry detergent and cleaners, etc. Guests may be brought in to teach if the leadership feels inadequate to teach on that week's topic.

WEEKLY LESSON SHEETS:

This is a list of the Lesson Sheets for each week's practical lesson found in the participants workbook. This list is included in the Leader Guide weekly lesson plan.

EQUIPMENT LIST:

A detailed list of all the items and equipment required for each week's lesson is provided. The responsibility for providing these should be divided among the leadership. This list is included in the Leader Guide weekly lesson plan.

HELPFUL HINTS:

The Helpful Hints sheets are found in various chapters and are filled with tips for making life easier. These sheets are provided in the Leader Guide and the participants Workbook.

SNACK TIME:

The Leadership will provide a snack each week and the home hostess will provide the beverages. When offering an evening class, make sure the snack is substantial since young women come from work and have not had dinner. Note: On the weeks food is prepared, a snack is optional.

VALENTINE RECIPES:

If you begin this book in the winter following the holidays, special Valentine recipes are included in Week Four should time allow.

TIME IN THE KITCHEN:

Recipes are provided in this section located in the back of the book. Book Two focuses primarily on the home, so this section offers the leadership kitchen activities that can be taught in addition to the practical lessons should time allow. Note: Due to the length of the subject matter covered each week, cooking time may be limited.

COMPONENTS OF WEEKLY BIBLE STUDY

The main purpose in studying the Bible is so that we will know God.
If we know the Bible, we will thus know the God of the Bible.

The Bible ...

- **INFORMS US**
- **INSTRUCTS US**
- **GUIDES US**
- **CORRECTS AND CONVICTS US**

In Psalms 119:11 it says, "I have hidden your word in my heart that I might not sin against you"(NIV). If we hide scripture and biblical truths in our hearts, it will protect us, and we will always have a word of encouragement and instruction to draw upon.

Women are relational, and women relate to other women. God made us that way. Because of that, we will be studying women in the Bible. We will learn biblical principles from each of their lives for living that if followed and applied will protect us from harmful thoughts and actions. Example:

- In studying Sarah, Abraham's wife, we learn about the biblical principle of waiting on God and the consequences of not being willing to wait on Him.

- In studying Rahab, we learn the biblical principle of obedience equals blessing. Her faith led her to trust that God would take care of her and her family. Because she trusted God, He blessed her by placing her in the lineage of Christ.

Many of the women we will be studying over the next few weeks made good choices, but then, others made bad choices. In life, we all make some good and some bad choices. In our study, we will see the blessings of good choices and the consequences of bad choices. God has placed each one within His story so that you and I might relate to them and learn from their lives.

In the workbook participants will find a question sheet to complete prior to class each week. The questions will relate to the passage of scripture read for that week's lesson. The study time required should not exceed thirty minutes.

We will only receive what we are willing to put into the devotional study each week. Remind the participants that hiding God's Word in our hearts means we will always have a word from Him for any circumstance we face. May each woman be blessed as a result of her obedience to study God's Word!

LEADERSHIP RESPONSIBILITY:

The responsibility of the leadership team is to teach the devotional lesson each week.

TEACHING TIME:

Each lesson should not exceed 20-30 minutes and has ample material for the time allotted. The leader who is teaching has the discretionary freedom to use as much or as little of the material, as she deems necessary. Note: When teaching, follow God's direction. He may choose to direct you away from the written lesson given, but be sure to include the biblical principle.

BIBLICAL PRINCIPLE:

A principle taken from the study of each biblical woman's story and applied to the lives of the participants.

BIBLICAL HISTORY SECTION:

This section is placed within the lesson for the purpose of giving the teacher biblical background and information. It is not to be read aloud and is strictly a resource.

DIANNE'S PERSONAL TESTIMONY:

This section is placed within the lesson in order to share personal life experiences related to the day's lesson. Note: Do not feel that you have to use what I have written. Please feel free to use your own stories as to how God has worked in your life related to the context of the lesson.

DISCUSSION QUESTIONS:

Questions given to promote discussion among the participants.

EXAMINING THE HEART:

These questions may promote time in sharing from the heart as to how the biblical principle studied affected each young woman—they appear only in selected lessons.

Understanding THE BIBLE

Each week, we will be studying women in the Bible. The Bible is a large book covering a lot of information and many topics. Let's get familiar with the books that are found in the Bible—66 in all!

BOOKS OF THE BIBLE:

Old Testament: An account of a Nation: Israel (Jewish people)

Genesis	2 Chronicles	Daniel
Exodus	Ezra	Hosea
Leviticus	Nehemiah	Joel
Numbers	Esther	Amos
Deuteronomy	Job	Obadiah
Joshua	Psalms	Jonah
Judges	Proverbs	Micah
Ruth	Ecclesiastes	Nahum
1Samuel	Song of Solomon	Habakkuk
2 Samuel	Isaiah	Zephaniah
1 Kings	Jeremiah	Haggai
2 Kings	Lamentations	Zechariah
1 Chronicles	Ezekiel	Malachi

New Testament: An account of a Man: Jesus

Matthew	Ephesians	Hebrews
Mark	Philippians	James
Luke	Colossians	1 Peter
John	1 Thessalonians	2 Peter
Acts of the Apostles	2 Thessalonians	1 John
Romans	1 Timothy	2 John
1 Corinthians	2 Timothy	3 John
2 Corinthians	Titus	Jude
Galatians	Philemon	Revelation

Three Easy Steps for Studying the Bible…

As you read the Bible, consider these key steps, and you will gain a better knowledge of what you are reading:

STEP 1: Observation—What does the passage say?

- Look carefully at what it says and how it says it.

- Pay attention to the terms, words, etc. Words can have many meanings, but terms are words used in a specific way in a specific context.

- A paragraph is a complete unit of thought.

- The amount of space or the number of chapters or verses given to a specific topic will reveal the importance of that topic.

- *Repetition* is used to demonstrate that something is important. So, watch for repeated words or topics.

- Pay close attention, for example, to certain relationships that appear in the text.

- Be sure you notice the atmosphere, mood, tone, or urgency of the writing.

- *Ask* Who? Who are the people in this passage?
  Ask What? What is happening in this passage?
  Ask Where? Where is this story taking place?
  Ask When? When in time (of day, of the year, in history) is it taking place?

STEP 2: Interpretation—What does the passage mean?

- Ask yourself what is the author's main thought or idea.

- Consider the entire context, verses that come before and after the one you are reading.

- Purchase a good Study Bible and do a cross-reference—look at other scriptures in the Bible noted beside the one you are reading. These verses will help you understand the context of the verse being read. (Example: The NLT Parallel Study Bible or the Ryrie NAS Study Bible.)

- The Bible was written long ago, so when you are trying to figure out what it is saying, you need to understand it from the writer's cultural context. In the front of each book of the Bible, you will find a page informing you of all the details related to that book: The time in which it was written, location, author, etc. Reading this page will give you a better knowledge of what you will be reading.

- Read commentaries by Bible scholars. These books can help you understand scripture. Example: *Matthew Henry's Commentary on the Whole Bible*

STEP 3: Application—What am I going to do about what the passage says and means?

- We study the Bible for the purpose of application. Applying what we have learned will change our lives. Obedience to God's Word will assist us in growing more like Jesus Christ.

- After we have observed a passage and interpreted it to the best of our ability, we must then apply its truth to our own life.

- Asking the following questions will help you to better apply what you have learned:
  How does the truth I have read affect my relationship with God?
  How does this truth affect my relationship with others?
  How does this truth affect me?
  How does this truth affect my response to the enemy, Satan?

- The key to applying what you have read is putting into practice what God has taught you in your study. You may not be able to daily, consciously apply everything you have learned in Bible study, but you can consciously apply *some* of what you have learned.

- God blesses our efforts to apply His truth to our lives. Through our application of those truths, we will be conformed into the image of Jesus Christ.

Week One

ORGANIZING YOUR HOME

Week One

LESSON PLAN

I. GETTING ACQUAINTED

- Greet each young woman upon arrival. Hand out name tags and books.

II. LEADER OPENS IN PRAYER

- If continuing from Book One to Book Two, introduce new class members and have them share a few facts about themselves. Have the participants who attended the Book One Study introduce themselves.

- Have each new participant fill out the Secrets Savored Participant sheet in the back of their workbook (page 221) and turn it into leadership before the end of class.

III. DEVOTIONAL

- This is the first devotional lesson of Book Two, therefore the participants will not have a page in their workbook for this week, but they will in the weeks to follow.

- For help in preparation refer to lesson outline in Devotional section of Leader Guide titled Mary and Martha—*Women with a Choice*.

- Each devotional lesson will contain a **Biblical Principle**. This week's principle is: As Christian women, we must choose to place God first if we desire to experience order and peace in our lives.

- **Leader's Introduction for Devotional Lesson**: We want to take a few minutes to talk about how we can create order in our personal lives and our homes through choosing to spend time with God each day. The word order means a condition where there is a logical arrangement or disposition of things. Having order truly brings a peace and calm to your life.

  The word organize means to arrange or assemble in an orderly manner; to arrange by planning. Organization brings order, and order brings calm and peace. Let's talk about how choosing the way in which we invest our time each day can bring about order or disorder. <u>Note</u>: See page 44 for the complete devotional lesson on Mary and Martha for today.

IV. LESSON—Choose one or all of the topics in today's lesson based on the time allotted for class.

- If leadership team does not feel comfortable teaching this lesson, bring in an expert to share on the topic of organization. If leadership team feels comfortable, they may share their own resources and ideas on organization from their years of experience.

- Begin with the Messies Classified Sheet—Have the participants read through the list of different types of Messies to find themselves. Discuss the different types, the advantages and disadvantages of each.

- Bring organizational tools, such as stackable plastic drawers, Rubbermaid® containers, shelving, etc., to demonstrate how to make the most of your spaces.

- Discuss *clutter*, how it affects the atmosphere of your home, and ways to get a handle on it.

- **For those with children:** Give helps on how to keep play areas and children's rooms in order. Check out Pinterest for creative ways to organize children's rooms and toys.

- Consult this week's handouts on organization, or use Pinterest and Google for references and resources related to today's topic to present to the participants.

- Move to the kitchen for snack. As the participants are enjoying their snack, have the class share their own organizational ideas. Leave time for questions.

V. TIME IN THE KITCHEN

- If time allows, prepare a Time in the Kitchen recipe from pages 263-268.

VI. WEEK ONE LESSON SHEETS

- Teaching Notes on Organization
  Introduction—*Not Naturally Organized*
  Messies Classified by Sandra Felton
  A Place for Everything
  What's Needed?
  Organization Room by Room
  Devotional on Mary and Martha

VII. EQUIPMENT FOR WEEK ONE

- Have name tags and pens for each participant.

- A variety of organizational equipment for demonstrating ways to organize your home. Example: Rubbermaid® containers, baskets, vertical hangers, bins, file folders, etc.

Teaching Notes:
GETTING YOUR KITCHEN ORGANIZED

- Order means ease of living for everyone in your home. Organization happens by first cleaning out unneeded or unnecessary items.

- It also happens by keeping an area organized (to arrange or assemble in an orderly manner; to arrange by planning). Once you have organized a space or room, make every effort to not let it go back to the way it was.

- Begin with one area or room and do not move on to another area or room until you have completed the task of organizing that space.

Let's talk about some of the neglected areas of the home:

Refrigerator—Wipe up spills. Check expiration dates and discard those products that have expired. The freezer is often neglected, so clean it out regularly. Vacuum grates and under the refrigerator; it will run more efficiently and be less likely to overheat.

Kitchen Sink—The area under the sink is where we store just about everything, but mostly cleaning products. Wipe up cleaner spills. Throw out soured and overused sponges. Use caddies to hold cleaners and rags. <u>Note</u>: Leadership may want to bring a sample of a cleaning caddy.

Master Bedroom—We often neglect our bedroom typically because no guests go in there. In your workbooks you will find some great helps with keeping the master bedroom clean, the organized haven we all dream of. When you have order in your bedroom, things run smoother and you (and your spouse) rest better. Clutter makes people anxious and frustrated; with it comes a sense of chaos, but with order comes a sense of calm.

Bathrooms—Make sure you clean out all old bottles and wipe up spills in the drawers and cabinets. Throw away products you have not used in a year or two. Women tend to hold onto samples of makeup, hair products, and other "free" items. If it is not a product you use regularly, get rid of it!

Laundry Room—We neglect this area of our home because we can close it off. Begin by wiping up spilled detergent. What a mess detergent makes! To bring order to cabinets, use stackable plastic drawers to store small items such as batteries, light bulbs, etc. Once a year, clean underneath and behind the washer and dryer. A Swiffer duster is great for this project.

Children's Play Areas and Bedrooms—We often use a lot of excuses for cluttered and disorganized children's rooms. Ones like, kids will be kids or they're too young to learn to pick up their rooms or they just can't reach the drawers, or my kids are just too busy to keep their rooms straight. There are no excuses! If they learn the discipline of keeping order and cleanliness in their rooms early on, your life will be calmer, and they will have learned to be responsible for what belongs to them. Below are some of the ideas for helping regain order to your children's rooms and playroom.

- Use tubs and bins to store toys and items within their rooms and play area—tubs and bins that are easily accessible for children.

- Provide a step stool so they can reach drawers and closet poles.

- Have a small laundry basket in each bedroom or the children's bathroom and teach them to place ONLY dirty clothes in it at the end of each day.

- Children are never too young to begin to learn to clean up their messes and be responsible.

- Remember, you are the one who bears the responsibility for teaching them, not the school, the MDO (Mother's Day Out), or the church (for spiritual things).

- Realize your children may not do it as neatly or as orderly as you would, but that's not the point. You are teaching them to be responsible and that as a family unit, we all do our part.

- Have high expectations for their keeping their bedroom cleaned. Children will perform only to the level of your expectations.

Organizational Frustration—Some of you aren't naturally organized and you are constantly frustrated. Start with one area that really gets on your nerves and keep it organized for two to three months. Then move on to another area; don't expect that you can organize your entire home or life overnight.

Communicate your desire to have an orderly home with your roommate, spouse, or family, and ask for their help and cooperation. Just know you will probably have to repeat this desire many times!

Order—God did not randomly create; He did it all in order because it works better that way! Our lives run much smoother if they have order. Our homes run smoother when they are in order. Organization brings peace and order to a home and a life.

For those who are married and dealing with a messy husband—You have three choices:

1. IGNORE IT. Just leave the clothes on the floor. You decide that is the way it is and you will never change him.

2. COME ALONG BEHIND HIM for fifty years and pick it all up!

3. ON REGULAR BASIS, share with him your desire to have a home that is orderly and remind him kindly of all your responsibilities. Tell him how much it would mean to you if he could help out by taking care of his things—putting clothing in drawers, shoes in the closet, etc.

When my niece Jessica first married, we had them over for dinner. When asked, what had been the biggest adjustment they had to face, it was clothing. Apparently, when Luke undressed, he dropped his clothes, at least the ones that were not too smelly and that he hadn't worn very long (length of time is up for debate) on the floor, because he intended to wear them again. Jessica assumed that if the clothing was on the floor, they were dirty. She picked them up and threw them into the laundry basket. He would wake the next morning ready to pick up his jeans off the floor and get dressed, only to discover they were in the washing machine, all wet.

The result: Luke was continually frustrated because his pile that he had meticulously left on the floor had been messed with. When he went to dig thru the pile to find what to wear that day, he discovered she had thrown it all in the wash.

She was frustrated that there was always laundry to do because there was always a pile on the floor. As a full-time teacher and a Young Life leader, she didn't have time to be doing laundry every night and she didn't want to spend the entire day on Saturday doing laundry.

They asked us what we thought and what we would do. Our answer:

How simple if Jessica would have explained to Luke the ways in which he could help her by hanging up what he intended to wear again and then placing his dirty clothing in the dirty clothes basket—those items that were actually dirty. Both would be happy.

Now, years later with two little boys, I think Jessica has won out on the "clothing on the floor" issue. Children bring enough mess and chaos to a home setting, so it is important for the adults in the house to keep their things picked up. Luke has learned how to help Jessica with keeping his clothing either in the dirty clothes basket or in the closet. Peace reigns, and so does order!

Recommended Books:

Never Too Busy to Cure Clutter:
Simplifying Your Life One Minute at a Time
by Erin Rooney Doland

12 Steps to Becoming a More Organized Woman
by Lane P. Jordan

Unclutter Your Life in One Week
by Erin Rooney Doland

The Time of Your Life: Finding God's Rest in Your Busy Schedule
by Susie Davis

FOR FAMILIES:

The Busy Mom's Guide to a Happy, Organized Home:
Fast Solutions to Hundreds of Everyday Dilemmas
by Kathy Peel

The Family Manager Takes Charge:
Getting on the Fast Track to a Happy Organized Home
by Kathy Peel

12 Steps to Becoming a More Organized Mom:
Positive and Practical Tips for Busy Moms
by Lane P. Jordan

ORGANIZATIONAL ADVICE FROM
The Happiness Project[1]
by Gretchen Rubin

Gretchen Rubin, author of the book *The Happiness Project*, was asked, "When there's so much that needs your attention—messy kitchen, messy desk, messy kids—what's the best place to start?" She said, 'Start with the thing that's making you crazy.' Think where your biggest boost would come from. The number one resolution that people mention to me as something that has made them happier is—to my surprise—making the bed. 'Over and over people who start doing it will say, Wow! It's a concrete thing you can do first thing in the morning. Then when you come back to bed, it's so much more inviting. Making your bed does not seem to be an important thing in a happy life, and yet it can be that tiny foothold into a more orderly life that sometimes people need.'"

When asked, "Why do these small changes, like making your bed, make such a difference?" "I think that the degree to which outer order contributes to inner calm is something that people really feel. Getting control of stuff makes people feel like they have more control over their lives—maybe irrationally, but it's one of these psychological truths."

In response to the interviewer's statement, "Let's talk about closets, the bane of so many of our lives." Gretchen responded, 'I always say you can self-medicate through closet cleaning. With closets, there's a decision that has to be made, and you just put off the decision. If you have never worn it, get rid of it. If you know you should not wear it, get rid of it. If it is hanging there with tags attached and you have never worn it, do not try to keep it to justify the expense of it, get rid of it.' When asked, "What is the best advice you've ever heard, she quoted, 'Put things away where you need to use them."

---

[1] Gretchin Rubin, "Organizational Advice from *The Happiness Project* (*Good Housekeeping Magazine*, January 2011).

Introduction
NOT NATURALLY *Organized*

What makes reorganizing and cleaning out drawers and cabinets synonymous with beginning a new year? Many of us have this incredible desire to create order in our lives when a new year arrives. The stores, Pinterest, and television commercials push the sales of plastic bins and new methods for organizing. But, what about the rest of the year? Wouldn't it be nice to have order year round?

Just the idea of organizing, whether a drawer or closet, can often be frustrating and overwhelming for those who are not naturally organized. I love organization. In fact, when trying to clean the house, I am easily distracted by a closet or drawer that needs to be re-organized—which is play to me while cleaning is work! Organization is one of many gifts or abilities God gives to people. To some He gives the gift of organization, to others the gift of encouragement, and to others the gift of leadership and on and on we could go. We were all created differently and with unique skill sets.

We were given different gifts and abilities, but there is one thing that God gave to every individual and that is TIME.

> "Time is really the only capital any human being has,
> and the one thing he can't afford to waste."
>
> Thomas Edison, American Inventor

By using the word capital, Edison was saying that time is an asset or something of value. What do we do with time? We waste time, we spend time, we invest time, and we take time for granted. Being disorganized causes us to waste time. For example, time can be wasted by spending an hour looking for important papers that could have been found immediately if there had been a system in place. Before you know it, you've spent an hour looking for papers you cannot find. And that is just one hour in one day for one item—multiply that by a lifetime! How much time are you wasting each week, each month, and each year because you will not place organization as a priority? Time wasted is time lost—never to be regained!

Many people think they can succeed among the chaos of disorganization, but disorganization can cost a high price. It can cost a promotion at work, it can decrease your productivity and it can cause added stress and limit your effectiveness. Whether you have a natural gift of organization or not, you can learn to be more organized. And, when you are, your life will be much less stressful and more fulfilling. Remember, time is capital, and organization is a great way to invest in your capital!

We are so excited that you have chosen to be a part of this Secrets class! This study is designed to be fun, informative, and educational. You will be drawn to the subjects you love and for those you do not like, you will probably study anyway, out of necessity. Such is the life of a woman!

MESSIES CLASSIFIED [2]
Find yourself amidst these Messies ...

PERFECTIONIST MESSIE—Very high standards! Rest of house may be a wreck, but she decides to clean the oven and it is very, very well done; she's exhausted and can do no more!

REBELLIOUS MESSIE—Has psychological hang-ups from childhood. Mom insisted on cleanliness and order, and now that she is grown she is going to show independence by defiance!

RELAXED MESSIE—Rationalizes that the world outside is hostile and home is the place to relax. Why work at home too? So things are let go! Truth is that messiness is NOT relaxing. It causes strain, pressure, and jangled nerves!

SENTIMENTAL MESSIE—Every scrap of paper and every shell brought home by Johnny is precious! Old, undeveloped film and flash drives strewn in drawers! Stuff, stuff, stuff everywhere!

SPARTAN MESSIE—As ancient Spartans lived with only the necessities of life, this Messie believes that if there were less to care for, or if it were somehow shut up or nailed down and not used, it would be possible to handle it! Always looks for ways to eliminate "stuff."

CLEAN MESSIE—As long as things are CLEAN, they can be left out—clothes in basket not folded, dishes washed and left on counter. "But they are CLEAN, isn't that what counts?"

SAFE MESSIE—Leaves the bed unmade, "because it can air out better, and that kills more germs." Floors not waxed, "because they may be slippery and dangerous."

OLD-FASHIONED MESSIE—Loves doing things the old-fashioned way. The only good way is the old-fashioned way: clean the floor on hands and knees; bake pies and cakes from scratch; wax and buff the wooden floor with a cloth instead of a buffer; beat the rug instead of vacuuming it; use cloth instead of disposable diapers. Their motto is "Do it right, or not at all." A lot of time it turns out "not at all."

IDEALISTIC MESSIE—Head is usually in the clouds. Great thoughts and ideas are what interest this Messie. But the results are disastrous to an idealist. The beauty and charm, the satisfying family life, all melt under the heat of the messy home.

[2] Sandra Felton, *The Messies Manual* (Revell Publisher Grand Rapids, Michigan 2005).

ORGANIZATION

WHERE TO START

In Ecclesiastes 3:6b it says, "There is a time to keep and a time to throw away" (NAS). We often have good intentions of getting our homes and our lives in order, but it doesn't happen. I believe there are several reasons we never accomplish this:

- The task seems so overwhelming that we give up from the get-go
- We do not know where to start
- It is difficult to find the amount of time needed
- The task is so large that we lose motivation

Perhaps you, like so many of us, are trying to tackle too much. If you start with one drawer at a time, or one closet, and allow yourself twenty to forty minutes (more if job requires it) a week to accomplish your goal of getting that space uncluttered and organized, then maybe you wouldn't get overwhelmed or burned out and want to give up. Organization is something you learn. You learned to brush your teeth; you can learn this!

HOW TO GET STARTED

- Make a list of all the organizational projects you would like to accomplish this year; separate them by weeks and months
- Take one area or room at a time, choosing the most often *lived-in* areas first. Be reasonable and patient. Things did not get into the condition they are in overnight

If you were to decide to organize your kitchen in two hours, it would be the same as deciding to lose thirty pounds in the next four weeks. After your first week, you find that you have only lost one-half pound, so you become discouraged and give up. Make a list you can actually accomplish and learn to take advantage of small windows of time. Example: If you are on the phone catching up with a friend, clean out your jewelry case or drawer. When the children are eating lunch, choose one drawer in the kitchen to clean out. Perhaps, if you are dressed and ready early (assuming you do not have little ones to take care of), you could use the time to go through all your vitamins and medications to check for expiration dates, throwing out all the ones that have expired. Look for pockets of time and maximize them. Do not sit for hours at your computer or on your iPhone; when you do, you are wasting valuable time. Respond to your emails or Facebook messages and walk away. Choose wisely what you do with your time.

> "He (she) who tills his (her) land will have plenty of bread, but he (she) who pursues worthless things lacks wisdom." Proverbs 12:11 NKJV

> "In all labor there is profit, but mere talk leads only to poverty." Proverbs 14:23 NKJV

A PLACE
for Everything

Benjamin Franklin said, "A place for everything, everything in its place." I don't believe Mr. Franklin realized that his words were the key to organizing your home. But, if everything has a place and is kept in its place, your home will be organized.

Communication is key in any relationship, whether it be in marriage, with a roommate, friend, or family. So, as you begin your organizational projects, communicate what you desire to accomplish and enlist their help.

In the pages to come, I will help you simplify your organizational projects and provide shortcuts and systems, to save you time. Remember, time is capital!

FIVE BASIC RULES FOR BEGINNING

1. Take one room at a time. Tackling the entire house or apartment at once can be overwhelming.
2. As you approach the space, access the supplies needed to organize the room or space.
3. Purchase what is needed or find items that can be repurposed. Example: A woven basket that once held a floral arrangement can now be used to store gloves and scarves.
4. Once a room is organized, keep it that way. When that room is complete, move on.
5. If the space is really large, such as a master bedroom, children's playroom, or garage, divide the space, and take the time required to accomplish the task at hand.

An abundance of things can be one of the reasons the space you live in is unorganized. Let's start with a system to DECLUTTER…

1. Begin by preparing three bags, laundry baskets, or boxes labeled: Keep, Give-Away, and Throw Away.
   - When throwing away, a bag would make better sense.
   - When giving away, you could use a box which is easier to transport.
   - For all the items you keep, a laundry basket could be used to transport them to the location where they are normally stored.
2. Once your containers are in place and labeled, you are ready to organize your home or apartment one room at a time.
3. As you approach each item in a room, ask these questions:
   - Is this item necessary or vital to my livelihood?
   - Have I or anyone within my home used this item more than two times this year?

Example: Things such as battery cables would be an exception, as you tend not to need them regularly, but they are a necessity. Use your discretion.

- How many of these do I have? Do I need all I have? Example: Two soup ladles may be necessary, but two shrimp deveiners may not.

- Do I have sufficient room to store this item? Example: If an item cannot be conveniently stored in order to use it regularly, consider placing it in the give-away box.

Once these questions are answered, you will know what container to place the item into—the keep, throw away, or give-away.

"There is a time to keep and a time to throw away."

Ecclesiastes 3:6b NAS

ORGANIZING *Room by Room*

> "But all things must be done properly and in an orderly manner."
>
> 1 Corinthians 14:40 NAS

Even if you do not consider yourself orderly you can learn to have order beginning at the front door of your home. When others enter your home they can immediately sense if things are done in a proper and orderly manner. I am not saying that your home has to be immaculate or perfect, looking like a furniture showroom. There is nothing warm and inviting about that type of environment. But, order brings peace for those living in your home and for those visiting your home.

People "live" in homes. If you have roommates, pets, children, or a spouse, there is evidence that people "live" in your home from the front door to the back door—and that is okay. The key to restoring order is having a place for everything and everything in its place. When this is true, order can be restored quickly.

BEGIN AT THE FRONT DOOR

Typically, the front door area is where you welcome others into your home. You want to keep it as clutter-free as possible, making it easier for your guests to enter your home. When you have a closet filled with clutter at the front entrance, it can cause a major traffic jam when guests are attempting to get in the door and hang up coats. A clutter-free entryway closet and area makes it easier to welcome people into your home, and it can also help your guests to feel more at home.

ENTRYWAY

- A day or two before receiving guests, check the front closet to make sure there is no clutter.

- Clean out any excess items like seldom worn coats that can be stored in another closet or near the back door of the house where everyone exits on a daily basis.

- Keep the front closet for guests coats and items not used daily. Any items not hanging should be placed in a bin, basket, or container. Check to make sure you have plenty of extra hangers.

- To keep front door coat closets free of clutter, consider placing hooks and stackable units or baskets in the garage or in a mud room area for coats and items needed on a daily basis.

- If you do not have a front entry coat closet, direct your guests to where you would like for them to place their coats, purses, etc. Example: I direct our guests to the office where they may lay their things on one of two club chairs.

FAMILY ROOM

The family gathers in this room along with friends and guests. It is one of the most difficult rooms to keep clean and organized because it is constantly being utilized. Perhaps these tips will help you keep order in your family room.

- Look for ways to create storage space. Example: Ottoman with removable or hinged top, shelving on end tables, drawers and shelving on coffee table, bookcase, etc.

- When shopping for furniture, look for pieces that serve double-duty with more than one purpose. Example: Bench with storage underneath, sleeper sofa, etc.

- Utilizing a tray on the coffee table ensures a place for television remote controls, picture books, etc.

- Use large baskets to store magazines, throws, and books. Regularly go through these items. Discard or donate outdated magazines, toss or donate torn or used books, and give away additional throws. You can only read so many magazines and books. And, you only need one throw for each person living under your roof.

- For storing CD or DVD collections and X-Box and Wii games, purchase a decorative box. Slide a label in each window on the front of decorative box in order to find your favorite CD, DVD, or game. Stackable drawers can also be used and stored in a cabinet, bookcase, or closet.

- Products such as Bongo Straps, Flexi Tie Cables, or a D-Line Zipper Cord are excellent for getting your extra electronic cords under control. Be sure to label the cords at the plug or strip so you will always know what goes with what! For keeping track of whose charging cord is whose, use different colored or patterned washi (duck) tape around each family members set of cords.

DINING ROOM

This room may seldom get used; therefore, it seldom needs your attention. Here are a few tips for keeping it orderly.

- My dining room is casual. I have a hutch with three open shelves on the top, three small drawers across the middle and an open shelf at the bottom. I needed a way to secure and organize the stacks of bowls, salad plates, etc., that were stored on the bottom of the hutch. I purchased old wire school locker baskets of various sizes to securely store the pieces of my pottery on the open bottom shelf.

- For the dinner plates, I purchased two round low-edged wire baskets and placed the dinner plates in one and the chargers in the other one on the main shelf.

- When I need plates or other pieces of my pottery, I just pull out a basket.

- The top open shelving is used to store/display the serving pieces and a few place settings.

- The drawers hold the nicer silverware and candles, etc., used in the dining room.

- All my glassware is stored in the kitchen. If you have a hutch with a closed cabinet and shelving, your stemware/glassware can be stored there. Keeping it all in one place ensures you will always be able to find it when needed.

- A sofa table serves well as a buffet, and a low chest can be used in the dining room for storage. I have a chest with drawers in the entry hall, right outside the dining room, in which I store placemats.

MASTER BEDROOM

We are often guilty of neglecting the private spaces in our homes. We decide that no one goes into our bedroom so it doesn't really matter whether it is clean and organized. It does matter because it is the room where you unwind, relax, and sleep. Your bedroom sets the tone for your home. If it is cluttered, you will begin every day frustrated.

If you are irritated because your drawers will not close, consider cleaning them out. Take one drawer at a time, and as you remove items, ask yourself these four questions:

1. How long have I had this? Is it out of style?
2. Has it been longer than two years since I have worn it?
3. Is it a classic piece that will never go out of style and will I use it for years to come?
4. Does it still fit? If not, can I replace it for less than the cost of alterations?

Based on the answers to the above questions, determine whether you should keep each item. If not, place in give-away or throw-away bags.

- Once all your dresser and/or chest of drawers are cleaned out, wipe out the drawers and place the clothes and items you are going to keep folded neatly inside.

- Store out-of-season sweaters, skiwear, hats, gloves, etc., in plastic containers under the bed or on high shelving in the closet. Extra bedding for the master bedroom can be stored in the same manner.

- Remove coins, jewelry, and other small items from drawers. Use shoeboxes or small plastic boxes and trays to store these. Example: Cuff links, watches, pocket knives, etc.

- Discard all old or single socks.

- Throw away all stained garments.

- Cup-hooks or plastic hooks can be used to hang jewelry, such as necklaces, on a wall in the closet. A bulletin board using pushpins is also a great way to organize jewelry.

- In the dresser or nightstand, keep only the necessary items, such as the book you are currently reading and a flashlight. Place smaller items in a drawer caddy or bin. Example: Pens, highlighters, nose spray, etc. All other non-essentials need to be cleaned out.

- In a walk-in closet, use baskets, bins, and wire cubes for extra storage.

- Collect the same type of hangers. Example: The felt covered non-slip hangers. This particular type of hanger will save space in your closet.

- Use a large decorative basket beside your bed or chair to store books, writing materials, throws, etc.

- If convenient, keep a laundry hamper in your closet or under the counter in your bathroom for collecting dirty clothes.

BATHROOM

A bathroom can be difficult to keep cleaned and organized because like the family room, it is continually in use. Below are tips that will help bring order to your bathrooms.

- In cabinets and linen closet, throw away old and partially full bottles of lotion, creams, nail polish, and sundry things. If you have not used the item in a year, chances are you will not use it again.

- Only keep items you use every day. Any makeup, moisturizers, or creams older than a year old should be thrown away. Bacteria can develop in these over time.

- Place hair styling care products, like curling iron, hair dryer, etc., in a stackable metal or plastic container.

- Consider plastic trays or bamboo divided trays for things such as tooth paste, tooth brushes, make-up, nail polish, tweezers, nail clippers, brushes, etc.

- Plastic or canvas boxes are good for storing products needed in personal hygiene. Example: Bottles of hairspray, extra shampoo and cream rinse, make-up bags, extra products such as soap and Q-tips, medicine, etc.

- Check expiration date on medicines, clean out those expired.

- First aid items can be stored in a snap-lid container.

- If linen closet does not exist or is small, towels can be rolled and placed in a large wicker basket beside the tub or outside of shower.

- If space allows, place two laundry baskets, one for darks and one for whites, in the master closet or linen closet.

- If you don't have a drawer space for make up, store your make-up in a basket under the sink or in the linen closet.

- Basic cleaning products can be stored in a tub or bin under the sink.

LINEN CLOSET

Over the years, we collect linens. Some need to be kept, and others need to be cleaned out. If you have collected ten blankets thinking that one day your extended family may visit, and it has been fifteen years, and they still have not come, it may be time to give some of them away.

- Keep only the linens you can use and have room for. Place the remaining in the give-away container.

- If you have kept mis-matched sheets, that do not fit any mattress set in your home, place them in the give-away container.

- Once your final decisions are made as to what stays and what goes, wipe out the shelves and clean around the baseboards. Vacuum the carpet edges and the entire carpeted surface before returning linens.

- Fold linens neatly on the shelves, arranging sheets and blankets according to size. If floor surface is available in linen closet, store extra items in a three-drawer unit on wheels.

- Towels and washcloths can be folded and stored in the linen closet or in the cabinets below the sink in the bathroom. Keep together all bath towels, hand towels, and washcloths, and stack according to size.

CHILDREN'S ROOMS

Teaching children to keep their rooms straight can be a daunting task; often it seems easier to do it yourself. But if that becomes the pattern, your children will never learn to be responsible and will become quite dependent on you—their maid! Get them involved in the following activities for organizing their room. Once their room is organized and straight, if old enough, they should be accountable in keeping it that way.

- Consider the function of the room and organize accordingly.

- In closet and drawers: Go through all the clothing every few months and make sure pieces still fit. Clean out any clothing that the child has outgrown or is worn out. Either give the clothing items away, save them for younger siblings, or if worn out, throw away.

- In the closet: Most poles are too high for children. Replace the existing pole with one no higher than four to six inches above your child's height. Poles should not exceed thirty-two inches in height. If you choose to leave the existing high pole, you can use it to store their out-of-season clothing.

- Purchase shelving that can be used for shoes, folded clothing, etc. Place the shelving horizontally at one end of the closet; having rods and shelves at their height makes it easier for them to put away their things.

- Utilize hooks inside doors, closets, and on walls. Hooks are a wonderful invention and easy for children. Use for robes, coats, etc. Label the hooks so the child knows what goes where. If the child is too young to read, use pictures or stickers to label hooks.

- A bookcase or wall unit works well for containers of small toys, puzzles, Barbie dolls, etc.

- Place similar items in plastic bins with lids. Example: Balls in one, all the puzzles in another, etc. Bins can also be made of canvas and wood but typically will not have a lid.

- **Dirty Clothes**: Place a hamper in your child's room and ask him to be responsible for placing his dirty clothes in the hamper. **For older children** (age seven and above): Find a divided hamper with a place for white and colored clothing. Labeled laundry baskets also work well. **For younger children** (ages 6 and below): They may need an incentive to pick up their dirty clothing. Consider putting an over-the-door or suction-mounted basketball goal above the laundry basket. Then the child can "dunk" his pjs into the basket.

- For school-age children, a desk is helpful for staying organized.

- Consider a hanging shoe bag for storing small items, shoes, socks, etc.

- Different colored laundry baskets or crates are great for storing toys. Purchase colors that coordinate with their room. These can often be stacked to save space.

- A basket for books. Having a basket designated for books will make their clean-up easier.

- Store all seasonal clothes in plastic tubs under the bed or in a storage area.

- Go through their toys every few months discarding the broken ones, giving away the seldom-used toys, and organizing the ones most often used. When discarding toys, it may be best to do it while the child is napping, at school, or distracted playing.

- If space is limited, consider buying plastic tubs with lids for storage. Rotate the toys every few months. It will be like Christmas when you bring out the toys that have been stored, and they will never miss the ones you chose to put away.

LAUNDRY ROOM

Between drops of dried detergent and softener and the lint from the dryer vent, a laundry room can be challenging to keep clean and organized. Each week when you clean your house, clean your laundry room as well. These tips may help you as you strive to keep your laundry room clean and orderly.

- Begin with removing all cleaners, soaps, and items in cabinets above the washer and dryer. Wipe cabinets clean. Place back only the items you use on a regular basis.

- Keep laundry soap, softener, dryer sheets, stain remover, and bleach at eye level close to the washer and dryer. If you are limited on space, a roller caddie is a great option.

- Place products in cabinet from left to right according to usage: stain remover, detergent, bleach, fabric softener, dryer sheets, spray-on starch, and bottle of water for steam iron.

- A folding surface is a necessity; if you are short on counter space, use the top of the washer or dryer. For hang-only clothing, use a dryer rack or an over the door hanger.

- If you have a hanging pole or additional space, keep extra hangers in the laundry room.

- Hanging clothes immediately after the drying cycle will save on ironing. Avoid allowing clothes to sit in a cold dryer or into a basket for days; they will end up crumpled.

- Use a plastic container for loose socks. Never let a single sock leave the laundry room. The chances of finding a mate at that point are minimal. If mate is not found, discard lone sock.

- The ironing board should be located near the iron, starch, and water bottle, preferably in the laundry room or whatever room you determine to be convenient for ironing.

- If space allows, laundry rooms are a good place for a bulletin board to hold all the school papers, announcements, the family calendar, etc. If space allows, place hooks on the wall for backpacks and coats and have a bin for shoes and boots.

Okay, I have given you some organizational advice and systems to put in place. It's time for you to get started. Remember, time is capital, strive for a place for everything and everything in its place!

The list of supplies and organizational containers that follow will help you get started in bringing order to your home.

WHAT'S NEEDED?

SUPPLIES AND ORGANIZATIONAL CONTAINERS...

1. Permanent marker to label containers: Keep, Give-a-Way, or Throw-Away.
2. Using clear large leaf bags will enable you to see what you have placed in the bag.
3. Boxes or laundry baskets can be used for separating items when cleaning out and reorganizing, or to discard items. Laundry baskets can also be used for dirty clothes and storing toys.
4. Drawer organizers: The number and size of each organizer will depend on the project.
5. Small plastic bins: Purchase ones with snap lids if storing small items that could spill out.
6. Small plastic containers: Example: Shoe box size.
7. Canvas, wood, or plastic boxes for storage.
8. Labels: White name tags or labels run from your computer can be used to label containers.
9. Bucket, water, rags, and cleaning products to clean as you reorganize and clear out.
10. Dusting product or Swiffer products.
11. Broom, dust pan, and/or Dustbuster.
12. Zipper-lock bags: These bags are great for storing buttons, safety pins, jewelry, etc.

BABY STEPS...

- Take one step at a time, one room at a time, and one day at a time.
- Be patient with yourself. Organizing a home takes time.
- Remember to enlist the help of others living in the home. You cannot do it alone—you will wear yourself out!
- Make a list of goals or projects you would like to accomplish within your home and begin working down the list.
- Don't seek perfection for you or your home—offer yourself grace. Do the best you can in getting your place organized and keeping it that way, but realize a home is to be lived in and enjoyed.

MARY & MARTHA
Women with a Choice

Biblical Principle: As Christian women, we must choose to place God first if we desire to experience order and peace in our lives.

Many times our choices determine our ability or inability to create order in our lives. We are going to look at two women in the Bible and the choice each made. One made a wise choice that brought order and peace into her life, the other, made an unwise choice that brought stress and a lack of peace.

- Read Luke 10:38–42

- As we look at the story in this passage of Mary and Martha, we will see two very different women who made two different choices. Martha welcomes Jesus into her home and proceeds to go about preparing a meal for Him and His disciples. She is busy setting the table, preparing the food, and getting everything in place so that everyone can enjoy their meal together.

- Mary, where was she? Not in the kitchen, that was for sure! Mary was seated at Jesus' feet, attentively listening, and learning. Martha, noticing that Mary was relaxing at Jesus' feet and not rushing around helping with all the details, points this out to Jesus.

- As we read, I am sure you noticed that Jesus scolded Martha, but commended Mary for "choosing" the good thing, which would never be taken from her.

- I wonder if Martha wished she could have had an opportunity to play that scene over?

- Perhaps if given another chance, she would have chosen the "good thing," to sit at Jesus' feet.

- Mary, on the other hand, didn't have to play that scene over again. She had chosen to spend time with Jesus. It was the habit of her life, not the choice for the day!

- One translation says, "Mary has discovered it, and it will not be taken away from her." She'd made the choice to sit at Jesus' feet years before. She'd seen the value of it in her own life, and she wasn't going to be distracted from that precious time with her Savior; it was the desire of her heart to be with Him!

- The NLT Study Bible says of Martha, "She did not realize that in her desire to serve, she was actually neglecting her guest." They go on to ask, "Are you so busy doing things for Jesus that you're not spending any time with him? Jesus did not blame Martha for being concerned about the household chores. He was only asking her to set her priorities. Service to Christ can degenerate into mere busywork that is totally devoid of devotion to God."

- It was not that Mary was "good" and Martha was "bad."

- It was that Mary was "wise" and Martha was "unwise." It was Mary's choice to wait on the work and preparation in order to seek Jesus first and foremost— that was wise. Martha's choice was unwise. She could have chosen to sit at His feet and wait on the preparations. But, she busied herself therefore things were chaotic (without order) and she lacked peace.

Both sisters loved Jesus. Both had a choice, but only one chose correctly. In your life, will you be unwise and make the choice that Martha made or will you be wise and make the one Mary made? Mary was still—she sat and listened. Martha busied herself—she was distracted. What choice will you make?

Read the following verses:

> "Today I have given you the choice between life and death, between blessings and curses. Now I call on heaven and earth to witness the choice you make. Oh, that you would choose life...You can make this choice by loving the Lord your God, obeying him, and committing yourself firmly to him. This is the key to your life." Deuteronomy 30:19–20 NLT

> "Choose today whom you will serve."
> Joshua 24:15 NLT

> "A wise person chooses the right road."
> Ecclesiastes 10:2a NLT

End today's lesson with a discussion of the following questions with the class:

- How has the story of Mary and Martha's life impacted you?

- What will you do differently as a result of studying the life of Mary and Martha?

Discipling Leader: Add personal comments. If time allows, utilize the Discussion Questions.

DISCUSSION QUESTIONS

1. Martha welcomed Jesus into their home, but then "busied" herself. How did Mary respond to Jesus's visit? *Mary was relaxing at Jesus's feet, not rushing around but listening attentively.*

2. What did Jesus say to Martha after she complained about her sister, Mary, not helping her? *He gently scolded Martha for being more concerned with getting the food prepared and the table set than spending time with Him.*

3. Why was Martha's choice unwise? *Because she choose chores over time with her Savior.*

4. What was it about Mary's choice that was wise? *She knew the value of choosing to spend time with her Savior.*

5. How can making the choice to spend time with Jesus daily bring order into your life? Your home? *God promises to set our lives (days) in order if we will choose wisely and begin each day with Him.*

6. Our choices really do effect the way our lives and homes operate—the results will be either order and peace or chaos and stress. What did you learn today from Mary and Martha?

Week Two

ORGANIZING YOUR CLOSET

Week Two

LESSON PLAN

I. LEADER OPENS IN PRAYER

II. DEVOTIONAL:

- Ruth—*A Woman of Loyalty*. Read the book of Ruth in order to prepare. The emphasis today will be the love, respect, and loyalty between a daughter-in-law and her mother-in-law. For help in preparation refer to lesson outline in Devotional section of Leader Guide.

- **Biblical Principle**: When we are loyal, showing honor and respect to those older than us, we will receive God's blessings.

III. LESSON

- If there is a woman in your church or community who is qualified to speak on fashion, organizing your closet, and how to shop your closet (being creative in using the clothing/accessories you currently have in your closet to put together new outfits instead of spending money on more clothing and accessories), invite her to speak to the class. Note: The age of speaker is not necessarily relevant, the important thing is that she is current and up-to-date on fashion, style, and etiquette.

- Read the quote below from the lesson sheet titled Fashion, Frugality, and Faith and discuss the question. Use the scriptures supplied on the sheet to support the perspective of how godly women are to dress. Note: Incorporate the What to Wear along with Defining Attire lesson sheets into this portion of the lesson.

- "With today's constantly changing trends and emphasis upon expressing sexuality through clothing, many godly women find it difficult to stay current with fashion without compromising their witness. The way we dress and present ourselves to others doesn't merely reveal our sense of style or personality; it shows what's in our hearts. How can we, as women, outwardly represent Christ and still have fun with fashion without breaking the bank?"

- Help with Your Closet—Using the handout entitled Easy Steps for Cleaning Your Clothing Closet, show the different ways in which to bring order to your closet. A great way to begin is to clean it out! Discard anything you have not worn in a while or those clothing items you dream of fitting back into one day!

- In the teaching of today's lesson, refer to the lesson sheets entitled: Shop Your Closet, Easy Ways to Change Clothing Looks, Must Haves and Why, and Supplies, Fixes, and Repairs.

- Many women have to deal with small closets; show organizational utensils that help in making a small closet more effective. Example: Use plastic under-the-bed organizers to store out-of-season clothing. Use over-the-door hooks and rods for items, such as socks, jewelry, etc.—things that tend to clutter a closet. <u>Note</u>: Leadership can share closet organizing ideas they have found to be effective in their own closets.

- **Optional Lesson Activity**: We invited a lady who had previously owned a boutique and was experienced in putting outfits together. She was asked to take several pieces of clothing (two shirts, one blouse, two skirts, two jackets, two pair of shoes, one pair of boots, two different types of jeans, two belts, a scarf, and two necklaces) and put together several different outfits, showing the participants how to shop their own closet. It was amazing how many new outfits were created from these few pieces. The participants loved seeing the different ways fabrics, styles, and textures could be mixed. If you decide to do this activity, leave time at the end for questions directed to your guest.

IV. TIME IN THE KITCHEN

- Time today will probably not allow any cooking time. Serve a snack and beverages for class.

V. WEEK TWO LESSON SHEETS

- Introduction—*Taking a Closet Inventory*
  Fashion, Frugality, and Faith
  What to Wear by Linda Johnson
  Defining Attire
  Easy Steps for Cleaning Your Clothing Closet/ Shop Your Closet
  Easy Ways to Change Clothing Looks
  Must Haves/Supplies, Fixes, and Repairs
  Thrift Store Shopping
  Devotional on Ruth

VI. EQUIPMENT FOR WEEK TWO

- Samples of organizational equipment for closets

- Food and drinks for the snack time. Copies of the recipes for the snacks prepared today to hand out to participants

Introduction
TAKING A CLOSET INVENTORY

A few years ago, I was helping a widow friend change out her closet between seasons. She had not worn many of the items; they either didn't fit or were out of style. When I arrived, I jumped right in and began to carry all the clothes from her closet to the bedroom so we could lay them out on the bed in order to go through each piece, one at a time. We went through every pair of shoes, as well as all the belts and purses. I asked her the same questions I ask myself:

- How long have I had this? Is it out of style?

- Has it been longer than two years since I've worn it?

- Is it a classic piece that will never go out of style? Will I be able to wear it for years to come?

- Does it still fit? If not, can I replace it for less than the cost of alterations?

After I had been there for several hours and we were almost finished, she began to notice some of the items in the give-away bag. As she questioned me as to whether she would possibly, but not likely wear them one day, I kiddingly said, "You get away from those bags." We both laughed. She only removed one sweater; I thought that was good considering we had eight bags of clothing.

We discovered belts that belonged to outfits long gone and purses that would make a thrift store owner very happy. Did I mention the hats? We had a lot of fun trying them on. At the end of the day, we felt good about what we had accomplished.

Regularly taking inventory of our clothing and cleaning out our closet will keep clutter to a minimum. I dare say most women, myself included, could go months without buying new clothing and still have plenty to wear from their overcrowded, bursting-at-the-seams closets. God asks us to be good stewards of what He has given to us. He also instructs us as women to dress modestly. 1 Timothy 2:9 says, "Women should adorn themselves in respectable apparel, with modesty and self-control…" ESV

If we as Christian women purpose to model godly character, we are to dress modestly. In the days ahead, we will discover how to be good stewards by shopping our own closets and receive tips that will help us in dressing to honor God.

Recommended Books:

Beautiful Girlhood
by Karen Audreola

Becoming a Woman of Discretion
by Nancy DeMoss Wolgemuth

*Every Young Woman's Battle: Guarding Your Mind,
Heart, and Body in a Sex Saturated World*
by Shannon Ethridge and Stephen Arterburg

Fashioned by Faith
by Rachel Carter

Lies You Believe
by Nancy DeMoss Wolgemuth

Secret: The Delicate Power of Modesty
by Dannah Gresh

The Look: Does God Really Care What I Wear?
by Nancy DeMoss Wolgemuth

FASHION, FRUGALITY, AND FAITH [3]

"Fashion is only as good as it looks on you." Author Unknown

With today's constantly changing trends and emphasis upon expressing sexuality through clothing, many godly women find it difficult to stay current with fashion without compromising their witness. The way we dress and present ourselves to others doesn't merely reveal our sense of style or personality; it shows what's in our hearts. How can we, as women, outwardly represent Christ and still have fun with fashion without breaking the bank?

WHAT DOES SCRIPTURE SAY?

- 1 Timothy 2:9-10, "Our focus should not be merely on the outward appearance but on who we are on the inside. Our aim in our dress shouldn't be to entice or impress others." ESV

- Proverbs 31:30, "Charm is deceptive, and beauty is fleeting; but a woman who fears the LORD is to be praised." CEB

- 1 Samuel 16:7b, "…the Lord looks at the heart." NKJV

- 1 Corinthians 6:20, "Honor God with our bodies." CEB

- 2 Corinthians 5:20, "We are therefore Christ's ambassadors, as though God were making his appeal through us." NIV

- Matthew 6:21, "Where your treasure is, there your heart will be also." ESV

SPIRIT CHECK—ASK YOURSELF THE FOLLOWING QUESTIONS:

1. Does the fact that Christ lives in me make a visible difference in my appearance?
2. Am I dressing to draw attention to myself? Am I honoring Christ in the way I dress?
3. Am I spending far too much money on clothing? Does keeping up with the latest fashion trends *hold* too much importance in my life?
4. Do I spend more time focusing on my outward appearance than my inward being—my heart?

Our society has gone casual, and there is nothing wrong with casual, if the occasion calls for casual. Styles come and go, but the one thing that never goes out of style is knowing the dress code for the environment into which you are entering, i.e., workplace, church, wedding, funeral, etc. On the following pages you will find: etiquette tips and clothing guidelines related to dressing for specific occasions, help with shopping your closet, and ideas for cleaning out your clothing closet regularly.

Let's begin with etiquette tips and guidelines related to dressing for specific occasions…

[3] *Pure Fashion Guidelines,"* last modified September 7, 2012, http://mayjesuschristbepraised.com/index.cfm?load=page&page=190

WHAT TO WEAR

by Linda Johnson

There are many things to take into consideration as we stare into our closets trying to decide *what to wear*. The time of year and the weather are two factors that dictate what we put on before we go out. Another is the occasion for which we are dressing. Different types of clothing will be appropriate for different types of occasions. For a Christian young lady, there is something else she must consider: Does God care what I am wearing?

HONORING TO GOD

> "Do you not know that your body is a temple of the Holy Spirit, who is in you, whom you have received from God? You are not your own; you are bought at a price. Therefore honor God with your body." 1 Corinthians 6:19–20 NIV

This scripture can apply to many areas of life, but the context in 1 Corinthians is sexual immorality. The question must be asked:

- Will what I am wearing honor God or dishonor Him?
- Will the outfit I am wearing draw the attention to me or to Christ?

OUR OWN FREEDOM

Our society tells women (and we believe it) that we can dress any way we want because our dress is not hurting anyone else. Paul saw our freedoms (our choices) as believers in a very different light. He penned God's thoughts in 1 Corinthians: "Everything is permissible—but not everything is beneficial. Everything is permissible—but not everything is constructive. Nobody should seek his own good, but the good of others." 1 Corinthians 10:23–24 NIV

We are reminded that our freedoms (our choices) should not cause harm to another. So we must take into consideration whether or not another person will be negatively affected by how we dress. Two results are possible if we make the choice to dress inappropriately:

- Men may stumble in the area of moral purity.
- Women younger than we will be encouraged by our example to dress in the same inappropriate way.

We should set aside our freedoms for the good of others. When we take these two things into consideration and determine to be obedient to God's Word, then we will not have a difficult time making decisions about our clothing. When we are shopping, or when we are deciding what to wear to the next social outing, wedding, or shower, we will choose wisely. Keeping God's honor, others, and these guidelines in mind, consider the following rules of etiquette for what to wear on specific occasions.

WEDDINGS

The time of day will dictate the type of dress for most weddings. Attire should be dresses, skirts, or suits for a daytime wedding. If the wedding is held outdoors, you may want something a little more casual and shoes that are appropriate for lawn and garden areas. Clothing for evening weddings should be dressier, and jewelry can be more elaborate. Some invitations may tell you the appropriate dress. Casual: this is usually found on invitations to outdoor weddings. Cocktail attire: dress is usually more sophisticated and elegant. Black Tie optional: Men can wear a tuxedo and women can wear long, formal gowns if they wish, although not required. Black Tie: Men should be in a tuxedo and women in long, formal gowns.

FUNERALS

Black is always appropriate for a funeral, but other subdued colors such as gray, khaki, and navy are also acceptable. Women should wear a dress, skirt, suit, or dress pants and blouse. Shoes should be comfortable; jewelry should be understated and simple. It is interesting to note that several clothing consultants suggested that inappropriate clothing for women would be items either too tight, too short, or those showing cleavage.

OFFICE PARTIES/SUNDAY SCHOOL GATHERINGS

Most of these occasions will be casual, so wear comfortable clothes and shoes. Even a secular website recommended conservative clothing with no tight blouses or cleavage showing. Remember that you represent God to those in attendance, and your dress should honor Him.

JOB INTERVIEW

It is suggested that you find out what the office dress code is and dress with a slightly higher standard when you go for a job interview. If you cannot find out this information, then a conservative suit would be your best choice. Make sure that the skirt is long enough for you to sit comfortably. Shoes, jewelry, makeup, and hair should be conservative and professional. Do not take your cell phone, iPod, gum, soda, or coffee to an interview.

CHURCH

Remember that men and boys at church are just as vulnerable to moral temptation as those at work or on the street. As godly women, we are responsible to dress appropriately as an example to younger women and as a blessing to the men and boys we worship alongside.

DEFINING ATTIRE

You receive an invitation to an important gathering that says White Tie for the attire. What does that mean? A friend invites you to a party and says that the attire is Informal. What is Informal? One time, my husband and I were invited to a party, and the dress requirement was semi-formal. Mark and a friend of his, who was also invited, decided to wear their formal wear (tux, starched white shirt, bow-tie, cummerbund, and cuff-links) on the top half and a pair of jeans on the bottom. To them that was semi-formal. Everyone got a good laugh out of their definition of semi-formal.

White Tie: Worn on the most formal of occasions. Women wear a full length gown. Men should be dressed in black tailcoat (with vest), starched white shirt, bow tie, black slacks with satin strip and black patent shoe.

Black Tie: Women should wear a short or long evening dress or dressy separates. Men should wear a black dinner jacket, matching pants, starched white shirt, bow tie, and black patent shoes.

Formal: Same as Black Tie attire. Men can wear a nice suit and women a dressy two piece.

Informal: Can be interpreted many ways. Semi-Formal is a more modern term for what used to be called Informal. The traditional interpretation of Informal attire was one step below Black Tie, meaning women wore fancy cocktail dresses and the men wore a dark suit and tie. But, times have changed. It is best to check with the hostess to know what is expected.

Business Attire: Women should wear a dress, suit, or pantsuit. Men should wear a business suit and tie.

Business Casual: In this day and time, businesses now have a very relaxed dress code. Always check with your host, but when in doubt, dress one level above what you think will be appropriate in order to look professional.

Dressy Casual: Guidelines for Business Casual may also be used for Dressy Casual. Women can wear a skirt and jacket, dress, or pantsuit. Men can wear a sport coat or blazer with a polo or dress shirt.

Casual: Casual attire can be a minefield, everyone has a different opinion. Check with the host.

No Mention of Attire: Use your discretion but keep in mind when and where the event is held, before deciding what to wear.

EASY STEPS FOR CLEANING OUT
Your Clothing Closet

Let me ask you a question. What is most important to you when selecting clothing for your wardrobe? Trend? Fabric? Color? Style? Design? Cost? If you chose one of these, you chose incorrectly. What should be the most important thing when selecting clothing for your wardrobe is fit. Do your clothes fit?

STEP ONE: Uninterrupted time to go through your closet, trying on each piece that is in doubt.

STEP TWO: Full-length mirror to view fit from every angle.

STEP THREE: Space for placing clothes in piles. Sort by: Donate, Toss, Clean/Mend, or Keep. Begin by removing anything that is worn out, stained, out of date, doesn't feel good, or doesn't work for your lifestyle.

STEP FOUR: When trying on the clothing items in your closet ask:

- Does this item minimize or camouflage any aspects of my figure that are not my favorites?
- Does this item highlight the positives of my figure?

STEP FIVE: A kind but honest friend—sometimes it helps to recruit a friend who will be honest with us about the fit of our clothes. A friend who would not let you go out in public in something that would ultimately embarrass you. Put all the *keepers* back in your closet by color, style, length, etc.

Shop Your Closet

Many of you may be asking, how do I shop my own closet? In order to shop for clothes, don't you need to spend money? Not necessarily!

STEP ONE: Once you have taken the time to try on every piece in your closet, and have discarded everything that did not fit correctly, you are ready to shop your closet. Less is better for successfully creating new outfits.

STEP TWO: Identify the holes in your wardrobe. Are you missing some basics, like a pencil skirt or a great fitting pair of jeans? Do you need a couple of "wow" pieces to round off your wardrobe? Do you have an "orphaned" *keeper* without any other items to go with it? Discovering where your "holes" are in your wardrobe will prevent you from spending money on unnecessary clothing items.

STEP THREE: Mix and mingle the *keepers* into different outfits—be creative mixing colors and patterns. Add in the basics purchased to fill in the "holes" in your wardrobe. Doing this is called *shopping your* closet and being a good steward!

EASY WAYS TO
Change Clothing Looks

Slacks: Want a slimmer silhouette? Pants pockets tend to bunch or bow out, adding width where women least want width. Have the pockets stitched closed by a tailor, or if you are handy, do it yourself. This will give you a streamlined look.

Coats and Jackets: Give your old coat or jacket a new life—change the buttons. Any blazer, coat, or jacket can be revived just by a quick switch of the buttons. Be creative.

Lost Belt: Have you lost your belt for that skirt or pair of slacks? Purchase a coordinating colored ribbon and weave it through the belt loops and tie ends in a bow. Different colors and patterns of ribbon will add interest to the piece of clothing.

Long Lasting Shoes: Before you even wear a new pair of shoes, take them to a shoe cobbler and have rubber soles and heel tips attached. The extra layers will protect your shoes and ensure that they last longer. Just Google the closest shoe cobbler to find the one nearest to you.

Flair: To add a little flair to an older piece of clothing, throw on a colorful scarf or a fun statement necklace.

Classic Clip-ons: I know, you are thinking no one wears clip-ons anymore, right? But, if you have inherited some jewelry from your grandmother or an aunt, use them to spruce up a pair of evening heels. Clamp the costume-style sparklers onto a plain pair of pumps to make the shoes more festive. Position them slightly off-center for a contemporary look.

Ankle Boots: Don't make the mistake of thinking that because they are called a boot, they can only be worn when the temperature is below 50. Ankle boots can be a year-round accessory, worn with a short tunic dress they are adorable.

Old Jeans: Still fit at the waist but the holes almost meet one another at the thigh? Consider making shorts from your old jeans. With a sharp pair of scissors, cut jeans just at mid-knee. Either roll and iron in place at desired length or if you want a finished edge, use bias tape (fabric used to cover raw edges). You can make your own using a cute floral fabric or purchase bias tape, follow directions on package for covering the raw edges of the jeans.

Shells: An effortless shell is the ultimate layering piece. Do not throw any away. They are timeless in style. Keep a couple in solid colors in your closet year round. A cute flowy shell can change the look of a jacket or blazer.

Clothing Swap: At the end of each season, invite a group of friends over for a clothing swap. This is a great way to gain a new wardrobe without spending money.

Must Haves

Slip: This may seem like an old-fashioned clothing item, but it is a necessary one when wearing sheer fabrics.

Correct Fitting Bra: I have discovered over the years that a good bra is worth saving the money to purchase, if you can do so. Also, as embarrassing as it may seem, allowing an expert to help with the fit of a bra makes all the difference in the way your bra looks from the outward appearance.

Tanks: Flowy, loose, low-cut tops often require a tank underneath. Test each top by bending forward in front of a mirror. If you can see breast, everyone else will also. To be discreet and modest, wear a fitted tank underneath.

Correct Fitting Undergarments: If the outline of your undergarments can be seen from the outside, your clothing may be too tight, or you are wearing the wrong type of undergarment for your outfit. Check with a friend or family member before you leave the house or consult a full length mirror.

A Full-Length Mirror: Pull up a chair in front of a full-length mirror and sit down to see if what you are wearing is appropriately covering your undergarments when seated. Doing a 360 while standing in front of the full-length mirror will ensure that you have not missed anything inappropriate. I have seen women who obviously did not check the back view of an outfit. Always look to see how an outfit appears from the back since people will be behind you in line, etc.

Supplies, Fixes, and Repairs

Zippers: If you are not wearing a pair of slacks, jeans, or a jacket because the zipper is sticking, rub the trouble-spot with a dry waxy lubricant, like lip balm, a candle, or soap. Do not get it on the fabric since it may cause a stain.

Stretched Out Cuffs: Are you not wearing a sweater because the cuffs are stretched out? For a temporary fix, dampen the cuff with hot water then dry with a hair dryer. The hot water and the dryer's heat working together will cause shrinkage. Sometimes, running a hot iron across the cuff is enough to contract the fabric for a while.

Hems: A quick fix can be done with most tapes, or for a more secure fix, use stitch witchery (no-sew hemming alternative found in fabric stores or fabric departments of a store) or use a needle and thread.

Buttons: Always store extra buttons from clothing in case one comes loose or falls off. Sew in the direction of the threads of the remaining buttons on the garment.

Sewing Kit: If you don't have a regular sized sewing kit, purchase a small compact one at the dollar store, or pick up the free one in the hotel room the next time you travel. Having this handy can save frustration when your button is lose or falls off.

Stitch Witchery: This is a two-minute miracle worker sold at craft and fabric stores which makes fabric stick to itself to form a permanent bond. It does wonders for fallen hems and pocket flaps that won't stay closed.

Mini Scissors: Keep a pair of small scissors on hand to safely remove tags, washing labels, and loose threads.

THRIFT STORE SHOPPING
WHAT THRIFT STORES ARE IN YOUR CITY?

Leader: Research thrift stores in your area and prepare a list to be handed out to class participants.

Thrift Shopping in Memphis:

GOODWILL: 3830 Austin Peay Highway, Memphis, Tennessee 38128

SALVATION ARMY: 3329 Austin Peay Highway, Memphis, Tennessee 38128

GOODWILL: 1740 Whitten Road, Memphis, Tennessee 38134

SALVATION ARMY: 2649 Kirby-Whitten Road, Memphis, Tennessee 38133

DAV (Disabled American Veterans): 3440 Summer Avenue, Memphis, Tennessee 38122

MIDSOUTH OUTLET: 3432 Summer Avenue, Memphis, Tennessee 38122

JUNIOR LEAGUE REPEAT BOUTIQUE: 3586 Summer Avenue, Memphis, Tennessee 38122

SUMMER OUTLET: 3466 Summer Avenue, Memphis, Tennessee 38122

CITY THRIFT: 5124 Summer Avenue, Memphis, Tennessee 38122

THRIFT STORE SHOPPING TIPS

1. Leave your purse in the trunk, and keep your money in your pocket.

2. Set a limit as to how much you're going to spend and don't persuade yourself to go past your limit no matter how good the "deal."

3. Look through everything in the store.

4. Look at items of clothing and furniture with an eye for potential. You can turn some pretty "useless" things into treasures if you really need them.

5. Get to know the cashiers, workers, and other shoppers. You'd be surprised at the community that you get to experience with fellow bargain shoppers.

6. Keep an ongoing list of items that you want or need and look for them at the thrift store until you find them.

7. Be patient; you'll appreciate the deal a whole lot more.

8. Find unique gifts you can give for birthdays, special occasions, etc.

RUTH
A Woman of Loyalty

Biblical Principle: When we are loyal, showing honor and respect to those older than us, we will receive God's blessings.

Leader—Read the book of Ruth in order to prepare.

Biblical History for Preparation—The author of this book is thought to be Samuel. The book of Ruth begins with a woman named Naomi, her husband Elimelech, along with their two sons, Mahlon and Chilion, who lived in Bethlehem, Judah. Instead of trusting God to provide during the famine there, they fled to Moab where food was plentiful! While in Moab, Naomi suffers the loss of her husband. Her sons take for themselves Moabite women, Ruth and Orpah, to be their wives. We see Naomi suffer more losses in the deaths of her two sons. She is left in a foreign country with only the companionship of her two daughters-in-law. Hearing about the provisions of God in Bethlehem, Judah, she decides to return to her homeland. Naomi informs her daughters-in-law of her plans and tells them they are in no way obligated to go with her. Orpah turns back, but in a moving demonstration of faithfulness and loyalty to her mother-in-law, Ruth insists on going with Naomi. She is willing to sacrifice her family and the familiarity of her own homeland to stay with Naomi. This is where we pick up the story.

Women play a variety of roles; all are relational in nature. One of the most vital is the mother-in-law, daughter-in-law relationship. This relationship is quite unique! Today we will take a look at the relationship between Naomi and her daughters-in-law.

Read aloud Ruth 1:1–22

Let's first take a look at Naomi, the mother-in-law.

In reading Ruth 1:8–9, we see that Naomi uses the name Lord-Yahweh in her prayer, which was the covenant name of God with Israel. She blesses her daughters-in-law in asking the Lord-Yahweh to show His faithful, covenant-keeping love to them.

In verses 9–14, Naomi appeals to Ruth and Orpah to return to their families and tells them that even if she found a husband and birthed a son, they would be too old to marry him.

- Orpah decides to return to her family.

- But Ruth, clings to Naomi and refuses to leave her alone.

- Naomi tries one more time to talk Ruth into returning to her family, but she refuses.

"Naomi's reference to the hopelessness of her having additional sons apparently related to the custom of levirate marriage, by which the brother of the husband who died childless would marry the widow, so that the deceased would have an heir. Naomi is too old for even this."[4]

Now, let's take a look at Ruth, the daughter-in-law.

Read Ruth 1:15–18.

---

[4] Charles Ryrie. *Ryrie Study Bible*, NAS (Chicago: Moody Publishers, 2008).

- Ruth's name means "beauty of character."

- She displayed a beauty of character in the way she treated her mother-in-law.

- Ruth showed honor and respect toward Naomi.

In verses 16 and 17, we see a beautiful expression of love, loyalty, devotion, honor, and respect from Ruth to her mother-in-law.

> Exodus 20:12 says, "Honor your father and your mother, that your days may be long upon the land which the Lord your God is giving you." NKJV

God's Word is clear in commanding that children—no matter their age—should show honor to their parents and their husband's parents!

I have a friend named Cheri and she shared this story with me…

"Several years ago, I heard Dee Brestin, author and speaker to women at a conference in Atlanta. At the time I was a daughter-in-law; I was far from being a mother-in-law. That day she shared a story related to her gracious daughter-in-law. She told us that when her children were small she would drive with them, all secured in the back of her minivan; the children singing along to a Christian CD. As she drove, she remembered talking to the Lord about their future mates and wondering if her children's future mates were riding along with their mother singing to a Christian CD. Through the years, she and her husband had prayed that their children would marry strong Christians with a strong Christian heritage and family. Dee said that not long after her son married, she was with her new daughter-in-law. She asked Dee, "Am I what you prayed for, for your son?" Dee said she hesitated just a moment too long. Her daughter-in-law said, "I'm not, am I?" Dee had prayed specifically through the years for a young lady from a strong Christian family with no divorces. You see, her daughter-in-law was a brand-new believer, but from a family that had experienced four generations of divorce.

As Dee hesitated, her daughter-in-law spoke up and said, "While you were praying for a godly daughter-in-law with a godly heritage, I was praying for a godly husband with whom we could break the chain of divorce in my family." That day at the conference, those words pierced my heart. I looked around to see the women's eyes filled with tears realizing the hurt that Dee's moment of hesitation had caused her daughter-in-law and the grace her daughter-in-law extended to Dee that day. In preparing this testimony, I e-mailed Dee and asked if I had the details of the story correct; she said, I did. In fact, she said, her son and daughter-in-law now have six children and have indeed broken the chain of divorce. When I heard Dee tell the story, I was not a mother-in-law, but it made an indelible impression on me. In the last few years, our daughters and our son have married; I am now a mother-in-law. Years ago when Dee spoke, I could not fully appreciate her story, but now, as a mother-in-law, I realize the importance of my relationship to my daughter-in-law and my sons-in-law. Becoming a mother-in-law has made me more sensitive and responsive to my own mother-in-law."

Cheri's suggestions to young women:

- Remember, your mother-in-law is your husband's only mother.

- Do not speak negatively about your mother-in-law to your husband.

- Do not put your husband in the middle between you and your mother-in-law.

- If you have issues with your mother-in-law, go directly to her and have a woman-to-woman talk face to face. NO e-mails! NO texting!

- Do not speak negatively about your mother-in-law in front of your children, family members, or girlfriends.

- Love her unconditionally.

- Be willing to sacrifice for her.

- Be Christlike in your dealings with her, even if she is not!

- Be thoughtful; send a note telling her what qualities you admire in her, even if you have to look deeply for them! If she lives far away, send pictures and birthday cards.

- Give her the benefit of the doubt; do not wear your feelings on your shoulder.

- Forgive her and move on; do not hold grudges!

- You are the gatekeeper to her son's life. Keep her up to date with what is going on in your family; share your life with her.

- On Mother's Day, send her a note telling her all the characteristics you are grateful for in her son and thank her for raising such a wonderful man.

- When there is an issue around the family holiday plans, child rearing, etc., let your husband be the one to deal with those issues with his family. They will receive it from him better than from you; they will always love him, just as your family would receive better from you than your husband.

- Adopt the philosophy of: NOT OFFENDED! NOT OFFENDED!

- Love her unconditionally!

Cheri ends with this: "I recently sent my mother-in-law a Mother's Day card and I thanked her for the strong role model she has been for me as I have taken on the new role of mother-in-law. She has set the example for me in accepting me into her family and loving me unconditionally. She is the only mother-in-law I will ever have and I want her to know that I am grateful for her."

Ruth *sacrificed* a great deal in order to take care of her mother-in-law. She willingly *sacrificed* her family, her homeland, her comfort, and her heritage, all for Naomi. In her sacrifice, she showed honor, respect, and loyalty toward her mother-in-law. Because of this—God blessed her.

In God's Word, we see a principle that is repeated over and over again—the principle of obedience equals blessings!

We see this principle lived out in the life of Abraham, Isaac, Jacob, Joseph, Moses, Rahab, and now, Ruth. She was obedient to care for Naomi and to God's calling in her life; therefore, God blessed her.

If you read the *rest of the story*, you will see God's blessings in Ruth's life.

- He sends her a Kinsman Redeemer—Boaz.

- He blesses her with a son, and Naomi with a grandson, Obed.

- Her marriage to Boaz placed Ruth in the lineage of Christ.

In Ruth 4:17 and 22 it says, "So they named him Obed. He is the father of Jesse, the father of David ... and to Obed was born Jesse, and to Jesse, David."

Donna Gaines, noted speaker and author says of Ruth, "Ruth placed her faith in God, she followed and obeyed Him, she loved well, and these became her reputation." [5]

Discipling Leader: End today's lesson with discussing the following questions with the class:

- How has the story of Ruth's life impacted you?

- What will you do differently as a result of studying the life of Ruth?

If time allows, utilize the Discussion Questions and the Examining the Heart Questions.

Book Recommendation: *A Woman's Journey through Ruth* by Dee Brestin

---

[5] Donna Gaines. *"Ruth."* (Chronological Bible Study, Memphis, September 10, 2010).

DISCUSSION QUESTIONS

1. What do we know about Naomi based on her apparent willingness to leave her family and homeland to go with her husband, Elimelech? *She understood that Elimelech was the head of their home and trusted his leadership.*

2. What is the blessing Naomi pronounces on her daughters-in-law? *That the Lord would bless them as they had blessed her.*

3. What does this tell you about Naomi's walk with the Lord? *She obviously knew Him as her Lord and Savior; she knew Him to be a covenant-keeping God. She obviously had experienced His blessings and care in her own life.*

4. What do the scriptures today tell you about Ruth's feelings toward her mother-in-law? *She loved her, respected her, trusted her, and was loyal to her.*

5. What have you learned about Ruth? *She was loyal to her mother-in-law and felt a sense of responsibility in caring for her.*

6. What has Cheri's story and the story of Naomi and Ruth taught you about showing honor, respect, loyalty toward parents and in-laws? About obeying God's Word? *God blesses obedience; we see this in the way He blessed and provided for Ruth and Naomi through Boaz. We also see the Father's blessings in placing Ruth in the lineage of Christ.*

Examining the Heart

1. Could the term *beauty of character* be used to define you, especially when it comes to the way you treat your mother-in-law?

2. Does your mother-in-law know that you love and respect her? Do you show her honor?

3. Do you have a spirit of sacrifice when it comes to your mother-in-law? Are you loyal to your mother-in-law?

4. What is your reputation as a daughter-in-law and a daughter of the King?

5. Do you have a relationship with your mother-in-law that would be a reflection of Ruth's relationship with Naomi, if your answer is no, why not? What do you need to do to make the relationship right in the Father's eyes?

Week Three

TIPS ON LAUNDRY, IRONING, AND SEWING

Week Three

LESSON PLAN

I. LEADER OPENS IN PRAYER

II. DEVOTIONAL:

- Jezebel—*A Woman with a Wicked Disposition*. Read 1 Kings 16:29–31 thru Chapter 21, 2 Kings 9:29–37. Extra resource verses: Revelation 2:18–28. For help in preparation refer to lesson outline in Devotional section of Leader Guide.

- **Biblical Principle**: A woman with a Jezebel spirit seeks to destroy true worship, the family, morality, and the God-ordained role of male authority. God will not bless such a wicked spirit.

III. LESSON

- Today's lesson should be practical in nature, giving helps for doing laundry, ironing, and teaching simple sewing skills. The discipling leadership should refer to the lesson sheet entitled Teaching Notes on Laundry or Google today's topic for preparation of this lesson.

- Give the participants tips for simplifying laundry. Example: Tip #1: Place two small laundry baskets labeled colored and white in master bedroom closet to simplify washing. Baskets can also be placed in children's rooms and labeled colored and white. If child is too young to read, tape pictures of colored and white clothing on each basket. The children should be responsible for placing their dirty clothes in the appropriate basket each day. If the child is old enough to carry the basket, they should deliver their baskets to the laundry room on laundry day. Children are never too young to help out around the house. Tip #2: Tear fabric softener sheets in half before placing in dryer; it makes the softener sheets last twice as long and it works just as well as using a full sheet.

- The leadership can share their laundry secrets of what has worked for them throughout the years. Ask the participants for any tips on laundry they want to share with the class.

- Ironing—Have an ironing demonstration. Many young women today have never been taught how to iron a man's shirt, a pair of khakis, a woman's white blouse, or little girl's dress. I recommend Rowenta® irons; they are heavy enough to handle cotton pants and shirts giving neatly pressed results without paying dry-cleaning costs.

- Sewing—Give each participant a small plastic sandwich size bag with a swatch of fabric, needle inserted into the fabric, and a button along with thread. Demonstrate how to thread a needle and then how to sew the button onto the swatch of fabric. You may also want to show them some simple sewing skills such as hemming or mending a hole or tear. <u>Note</u>: If leadership is not skilled in this area, you may want to bring in a guest who is.

- Folding Demonstrations—Many women do not know how to fold sheets (especially a fitted sheet) in such a way that they lay flat on the shelf in a linen closet. Demonstrate how to fold a set of sheets, especially fitted sheets. If you Google folding sheets, you will have lots of help in preparing for this demonstration. Consider doing a demonstration on folding t-shirts and other challenging garments.

- Leave time for questions.

IV. TIME IN THE KITCHEN

- Today the young women will make their own detergent. I recommend making the powdered detergent; it's less mess and easier to store. The liquid recipe is included for those who prefer liquid over powder.

- Follow the recipe in lesson.

- You may either provide the ingredients for the detergent or divide the class participants into groups and have them purchase the ingredients needed. Leadership will need to provide the plastic storage bags or containers for transporting the detergent.

V. WEEK THREE LESSON SHEETS

- Recipes for Laundry Detergent
  Teaching Notes on Laundry
  Introduction—*To Sew or Not to Sew*
  Laundry Tips
  Care Label Chart
  Know Your Fabrics
  Laundry Techniques
  Three Types of Stains
  Treating Special Stains/Baking Soda in Clothing Care
  Mending Tips
  Devotional on Jezebel

VI. EQUIPMENT FOR WEEK THREE

- All the ingredients necessary for making one batch of powdered laundry detergent, food processor, and a box of plastic sandwich-size storage bags for transporting detergent. Ironing board, starch, iron, and clothing in need of ironing. Mini sewing kits: Made from sandwich-size plastic zipper bags containing a button, swatch of fabric, needle, and thread.

Powdered Laundry Detergent

3 bars of soap—Fels Naptha®, Zote®, or Ivory® (these are marketed for laundry)

3 cups Borax®

3 cups washing soda/baking soda or Oxi-clean®

Place chopped soap in a food processor and process until fine. Pour into a large bowl. Mix with Borax® and washing soda; stir until combined. Use ¼ cup (same as four tablespoons) in HE front loader, use ½ cup in top loading machines.

FOR YOUR INFORMATION:

Use a mild soap, one with little to no additives. Castile soap is another good choice; it's made with 100 percent pure olive oil. Dr. Bonner's All-One Hemp Unscented Baby-Mild Pure Castile Soap® is a good choice if there is a child with sensitive skin, such as eczema.

Washing soda is not the same as baking soda. Washing soda is an environmentally safe product that helps remove laundry stains. Borax® is a natural deodorizer, stain remover, and laundry booster.

Liquid Laundry Detergent

1 (5.5 ounce) Fels Naptha®

4 cups water

⅓ cup Oxi-clean®

Large pot

New 5-gallon paint bucket (purchase at any paint store, Lowe's® or Home Depot®)

Place grated soap in water and bring to a boil over medium heat. Then turn heat to simmer and simmer until soap is melted. Keeping on low heat, add the other ingredients and stir. Continue to stir until thickened and once thickened, remove from heat. Pour 4 cups of hot tap water into the paint bucket and follow with soap mixture; stir and allow settling overnight. Use ¼ cup per wash load. Use distilled white vinegar in order to keep soap residue from collecting on your clothes, washing machine, and pipes. Vinegar is an acid and helps restore the pH balance of your wash load. It also works great as fabric softener. Use ½ cup added before the last rinse of the cycle. Do not use the vinegar with chlorine bleach.

Teaching Notes:
ON LAUNDRY

<u>Note</u>: Discipling leadership will find that much of the information in today's teaching notes can be found in this week's lesson sheets.

- Blue Dawn® gets spots out, especially grease and butter. Rub it into the stain and spray with Shout-it-Out® or other stain remover then wash. Hang to dry in order not to set the stain in case you have to repeat the process.

- Make use of a mesh laundry bag—Use the bag for placing socks, bra inserts, etc., in order not to misplace them. This way they do not get lost.

- Turn your large size container of liquid detergent upside down in cabinet or place a small saucer under spout in order to avoid leaks and mess.

- Remember most detergents are concentrated, so little is much.

- Wash all whites together, colors together and towels together—this avoids the bleaching of dark clothes, getting fuzz from towels onto dark clothes, and sanitizes underwear and dishrags—use bleach only in the white load.

- Have a trash can in the laundry area for emptying the dryer lint trap. If you will empty the trap after each load it will help the dryer to run more efficiently. By doing this you will avoid the possibility of fires due to an overloaded lint trap.

- Be sure to have some type of hanging device for the clothing that cannot go in the dryer. Example: Over the door hanger, etc.

- Fold clothes as soon as they come out of the dryer. Your clothing and towels will be less wrinkled. If you are not home upon completion of dryer load, turn the dryer back on for 5 to 10 minutes to remove wrinkles. Then fold.

- Put away laundry immediately after folding. Piles of clean wrinkled clothes in laundry baskets can be overwhelming. What is the point of washing and drying if the clothes remain wadded up in a basket for days.

- Have a laundry routine. Set two days a week for laundry and stick with your schedule (or whatever is needed to meet your need).

- Take advantage of pockets of time. After dinner or after putting children to bed, place a load in the washer and then first thing in the morning put it in the dryer—at least you will have one load going as you get ready for your day. Or begin a load upon waking in the morning and as soon as you can move it to the dryer.

- If it isn't dirty—like after one wearing—hang it back up or fold it and put it back in the drawer.

WHAT YOU SHOULD KNOW:

- Dryers collect lint down under the lint trap. You can unscrew and temporarily remove the trap casing to vacuum lint that has fallen down around the tub of the dryer. You can also purchase a wire cleaning rod at any hardware store to get down in the lint trap compartment and clean out excess lint.

- Every year or so, clean out vent hose on the back of the dryer that exits from the house.

- Every year or so, vacuum or Swiffer® under your dryer and washing machine.

IRONING:

- DO IT! This is often hard to accomplish if you are working full time or caring for small children, but with pressed clothing, you, your family, and your husband will look much better. Who wants to look like they slept in their clothing for days!

- If you cannot iron as you would like, remove shirts and pants and all cotton items from the dryer right away and hang on hangers.

- If you just don't like to iron, buy no-iron pants and shirts. Be sure to remove them from the dryer upon completion of drying time and hang on hangers.

- Watch local magazines and coupon flyers for deals at your local dry cleaners. Never take clothing to the dry cleaners without a coupon. Dry cleaning is expensive and can wreck your budget.

That's it! Happy Laundry!

Introduction
TO SEW OR NOT TO SEW

As I mentioned before, each of us four kids had responsibilities around the house. My brother did the yard with the help of my older sister. I enjoyed the indoor work. I can remember setting up the ironing board in the basement and ironing my dad's shirts for ten cents. My mom would starch dad's shirts with real liquid starch that she mixed herself. The shirts would soak in the starch, and then she rolled them up and placed them in the refrigerator overnight. The next morning she hung them to dry before ironing. I loved ironing, and to this day, I take pleasure in the finished product: a clean, fresh, crisp pair of khakis or a nicely pressed shirt. Ironing was my thing. I was good at it—but not sewing!

My mother-in-law, on the other hand, loved to sew. Over the years, she gave me two sewing machines. She hoped that I would love sewing as much as she did. But, I did not love sewing for several reasons. First, as a child all my clothing was either hand-me-downs or made by my grandmother. The second reason is the homemade dress I wore on the first day of fifth grade. My mother made it. The dress was olive green, covered with red fuzzy dots, and it had bell sleeves! Oh, it gets better! At that time, there was a fringe that was used mostly on kitchen curtains; it was a fringe with little fuzzy balls hanging from it. My mom decided to purchase the fringe in red and attach it to the edge of my bell sleeves. Did I mention that my mom wasn't a seamstress? It was quite a unique dress!

Another reason I didn't love sewing was a small part of the sewing machine called the "bobbin." You could lose your patience in a hurry with that little gadget—at least, I could!

The last reason was my attempt at sewing in my ninth-grade Home Economics class. Our teacher sent us to the store for a Simplicity pattern. Assuming the name meant simple, I got to work on my sleeveless sundress. I chose it because I didn't want to set in sleeves; I wasn't concerned with the fact that it was the middle of winter! Did you know that just because the pattern says Simplicity doesn't mean that it will be simple to make? Putting in darts was a real challenge for me, but eventually my sundress was complete. For our final grade, we had to model our creations while our teacher critiqued them in front of the entire class. I walked in the classroom door and turned to face the teacher. When I did, she pointed out that the darts were not even, and then she had me to stand in front of a mirror. Darts are to be right at the bust line, coming out from the side seam. Well, I got the dart on the right side pretty close, but the one on the left was about waist high—not good! I decided right then that sewing was not my gift! Even though machine sewing was not my gift, I made sure over the years that I learned how to hem, mend a seam, and attach a loose button to shirts and pants.

All I keep on hand now is my little sewing kit; that's all I need. No sewing machines for me!

LAUNDRY TIPS

A few years ago, I was keeping the grandchildren while our youngest daughter and her husband were out of town. I began to notice that every morning the kids would put their pajamas in the dirty clothes basket. Now, knowing they had taken a bath before bed and then put on clean pajamas, I wondered why they threw their pajamas into the dirty clothes basket the next morning? I put a stop to that after the second day! Mimi was not washing clean pajamas just because it was easier for them to throw them in the basket than to fold and place them back in the drawer.

Many times we make more work for ourselves, or others make more work for us because of laziness. It is easier to throw what we have had on in the basket than to put it away. If you are clean when you put on the new clean item, chances are it is still clean after being worn once (except for summertime wear). Don't make more work for yourself—don't throw it in the dirty clothes basket just because of laziness. Train those under your roof to hang or put away clothing that can be worn again.

Laundry, as well as house work, can be daunting or just downright overwhelming! The bane of my youngest daughter's life is laundry. She loathes laundry. Yet, with a family of five and two boys playing baseball, she always has laundry!

Mounds of dirty clothes can seem like mountains you have to climb. If you don't keep up with the laundry, it can become a daunting task, one you loathe. Becoming knowledgeable about fabrics, ways to handle specific stains, and having a system in place will help as you tackle the task.

Perhaps with the following tips you will be able to climb the mountain of laundry, make the job less painful, and speed up the process.

UNDERSTANDING YOUR CARE LABELS

One of the first steps toward doing laundry quickly and efficiently is to know what each item is made of and the best way to care for it.

- Most garments have permanently attached labels. They can be a great help in determining exactly how you should remove stains and clean an item.

- Certain information is not required on care labels. Neither the manufacturer nor the retailer is required to inform a consumer that a certain fabric will shrink. The label assumes that the purchaser knows that an item labeled hand wash should be washed in lukewarm water by hand and that all non-white articles should not be treated with chlorine bleach.

- Another important piece of information contained on fabric care labels is the fiber content of the material. This is especially important with blends. These fabrics are combinations or blends of fibers, such as cotton and wool, cotton and polyester, or wool and acrylic. Blends should be cared for in the same way as the fiber with the highest percentage in the blend. Example: A blend of 60 percent cotton and 40 percent polyester should be cleaned as though it were 100 percent cotton. However, when you remove spots and stains you should follow procedures recommended for the most delicate fiber in the blend. Example: To remove a stain from a blend of cotton and silk, use the procedure recommended for silk. If after such treatment the stain is still apparent, follow the procedure for cotton, the most durable fiber in the blend.

CARE LABEL CHART

CARE LABELS

Machine wash	Wash, bleach, dry, and press by any customary method, including commercial laundering and dry-cleaning.
No chlorine bleach	Do not use chlorine bleach.
No bleach	Do not use any type of bleach.
Cold wash/cold rinse	Use cold water or cold washing machine setting.
Warm wash/warm rinse	Use warm water or warm water machine setting.
Hot wash	Use hot water or hot washing machine setting.
No spin	Remove wash load before final spin cycle.
Delicate cycle/gentle cycle	Use appropriate machine setting; otherwise hand wash.
Durable press cycle/ permanent press cycle	Use appropriate machine setting; otherwise, use warm wash, cold rinse, and short spin cycle.
Wash separately	Wash alone or with like colors.

NON-MACHINE WASHABLE

Hand wash	Launder only by hand in lukewarm (hand-comfortable) water. May be dry-cleaned.
Hand wash separately	Hand wash alone or with like colors.
No bleach	Do not use bleach.

DRYING

Tumble-dry	Dry in tumble dryer at specified setting: high, medium, low, or no heat.
Drip-dry	Hang wet and allow drying with hand shaping only.
Line-dry	Hang damp and allow drying.
No wring	Hang to dry or drip-dry.
No twist	Handle to prevent wrinkles.
Dry flat	Lay garment on flat surface.

IRONING

Cool iron	Set iron at lowest setting.
Warm iron	Set iron at medium setting.
Hot iron	Set iron at hot setting.
Do not iron	Do not iron or press with heat.
Steam iron	Iron or press with steam.
Iron damp	Dampen garment before ironing.
Dry-clean only	Garment should be dry-cleaned only.
No dry-cleaning	Garment cannot be dry cleaned.

Know Your Fabrics

NATURAL FABRICS

COTTON: Strong, long wearing, and absorbent. Will shrink and wrinkle unless given special treatment. Machine wash and tumble dry, using a water temperature ranging from cold to hot, depending on manufacturer care instructions. Chlorine bleach can be used on white or colorfast cotton unless a fabric finish has been applied. It is recommended that you use fabric softener to reduce wrinkling. The softener makes cotton less absorbent, so do not use on towels, washcloths, or diapers.

LINEN: Pure linen wrinkles easily; therefore, many manufacturers make linen blends or add wrinkle resistant finishes to overcome this problem. Machine wash and tumble dry linen; all-purpose detergent is the best cleaning agent. Chlorine bleach can be used on white linen, following the manufacturer's recommended amount so as not to damage the fabric. Linen can also be dry-cleaned.

SILK: Silk feels good to wear but requires special care. Most silk garments are marked dry-clean only. However, some silks can be washed by hand. It is suggested that you test a corner of the fabric for colorfastness before washing an entire garment; some dyed silk will bleed. Never twist or wring washable silks. Hang silks to dry. Press silk with a damp cloth and a warm iron, below 275°F, or use a steam iron. To remove stains from a washable silk, use only oxygen bleach or a mix of 1 part hydrogen peroxide to 8 parts water.

WOOL: Highly resilient, absorbent, and sheds wrinkles well, but wool will shrink and mat if it's exposed to heat and rubbing. It is recommended to treat stains on wool with solvent based spot removers. Wool should always be dry-cleaned unless it is specifically marked washable.

SYNTHETIC FABRICS

ACETATE: Closely related to rayon, has body, and drapes well. Taffeta, satin, crepe, and double knits often contain acetate. They should be hand washed using a light-duty detergent, if the care label specifies that the article is washable; otherwise, have it dry-cleaned. Use a press cloth when pressing the right side of the fabric.

ACRYLIC: Many acrylic weaves resemble wool's softness, weight, and fluffiness. Acrylics are usually wrinkle-resistant and are usually machine washable. They are often blended with wool and polyester fibers. Dry-clean acrylic garments or wash them by hand. If fabric is marked *colorfast*, it can be bleached with either chlorine bleach or oxygen bleach. Press at a moderate temperature setting.

NYLON: Is extremely strong, lightweight, smooth, wrinkle resistant, and nonabsorbent. Often combined with spandex, nylon knits are very stretchy but hold to their original shape. Always follow the manufacturer's cleaning instructions. Use chlorine bleach only when nylon article is colorfast, and use fabric softener to reduce static electricity. Tumble dry your nylon at low temperature setting and press at cool temperature setting.

POLYESTER: These garments are usually strong, resilient, wrinkle-resistant, colorfast, and crisp. They hold pleats and creases well, but are nonabsorbent. Polyester is used for clothing and filling; bed linens and towels are also made of polyester blends. It can be safely dry-cleaned or machine washed. Do not over dry polyester; this will cause gradual shrinking. Press all polyester fabrics on a moderate temperature setting or use steam iron.

RAYON: Is a strong, absorbent fabric, but it tends to lose its strength when wet. Used for draperies, upholstery, and clothing. Dry-clean rayon or hand-wash unless the label specifies to machine wash. Drip-dry and press rayon on the wrong side with an iron at the medium temperature setting while fabric is damp.

SPANDEX: Is a lightweight fiber that resembles rubber in durability. It has good stretch and recovery. Spandex blended with other fabrics provides the stretch in waistbands, foundation garments, swimwear, and dancewear. Hand or machine wash spandex-blend garments in warm water using all-purpose detergent. Line-dry or tumble-dry garments made with spandex at a low temperature setting. When removing from dryer, press clothing that contains spandex quickly at a low temperature setting.

LAUNDRY TECHNIQUES

Sorting your laundry is important and recommended for the safety of your garments and to shorten the time spent doing laundry.

COLORS: Sort laundry by color. Put all the whites or predominantly white articles together in one pile, light colors and pastels in another, and dark and bright colored clothes in another. Separate the dark pile into two piles: one for colorfast items (dyed in colors that will not fade or be washed out) and one for non-colorfast items (having a color that tends to fade when washed or worn).

DEGREE OF SOIL: Separate each pile into two smaller piles: lightly soiled and heavily soiled.

COMPATIBLE LOADS: Now you have up to twelve various-sized piles of laundry. Combine or divide the piles to come up with compatible, washer-sized loads.

The following five hints will help you with your final sorting:

1. Combine white and light-colored items that have similar degrees of soil into the same pile.
2. Combine the non-colorfast items with similarly colored colorfast items with the same degree of soil.
3. Create a separate pile for delicate items that must be hand washed.
4. Separate white synthetics, blends, and permanent-press fabrics from natural-fiber fabrics without special finishes.

Separate items made from fabrics that produce lint, such as chenille robes and terry cloth and bath towels, from fabrics that attract lint, such as corduroy, knits, synthetics, and permanent press.

PREPARING THE WASH

Follow these helpful hints to minimize damage to the articles and to clean thoroughly.

- Know fabric content so you can select proper water temperature and cleaning products.
- Save care information so you can follow the recommended cleaning procedures.
- Close all zippers, hook all hooks, button all buttons, and tie or buckle all belts and sashes.
- Mend seams, tears, holes, or loose hems to prevent future damage during wash cycle.
- Turn sweaters and corduroy garments inside out to prevent lint from attaching itself to the garment.
- Pre-treat spots, stains, and heavily soiled items with pre-wash spot-and-stain remover.

WATER TEMPERATURES

Sorting the clothing to be washed and understanding what temperature is best for each load will keep you from turning your undergarments pink or shrinking your favorite t-shirt!

THE TYPE OF LOAD	WASH TEMPERATURE	RINSE TEMPERATURE
White and light-colored cottons and linens	130–150°F	Warm or Cold
Diapers	Hot	
Heavily soiled permanent press		
Wash-and-wear fabrics		
All other greasy or heavily soiled clothes		
Dark colors	100–110°F	Cold
Light or moderately soiled permanent press	Warm	
Wash-and-wear fabrics		
Some woven or knit		
Synthetic fibers (see care label)		
Some washable woolens (see care label)		
Any other moderately soiled clothes		
Non-Colorfast Fabrics	80–100°F	Cold
Some washable woolens (see care label)		
Some woven or knit synthetic fabrics (see care label)		
Fragile items		
Bright colors		
Any lightly soiled clothes		

WASHING MACHINE: Clean the detergent depositing area of your washer. **For Dryers:** Clean out lint trap regularly. Two to four inches of lint is too much; you have waited too long! The lint trap is a fire hazard; it is very important for safety and the efficiency of the dryer to keep it cleaned out.

THREE TYPES OF STAINS

GREASY STAINS

- You can sometimes remove grease spots from washable fabrics by laundering; pre-treat by rubbing detergent directly into the spot or use dry-cleaning solution on the stain.

- If you are treating an old stain or one that has been dried and ironed, a yellow stain may remain after treatment with a solvent. Bleach can sometimes remove this yellow residue.

- To remove grease spots from non-washable fabrics, sponge the stain with dry-cleaning solution. Elimination of the stain may require several applications. Allow the spot to dry completely between sponging.

- Greasy stains may also be removed from non-washable fabrics by using an absorbent, such as cornmeal, cornstarch, French chalk, or Fuller's Earth® (mineral clay found in a local drug store). Dust the absorbent on the greasy spot. When it begins to look caked, it should be shaken or brushed off. Before using any of these products, carefully read the care label on the stained item and the label on the product container.

- If you do not have either one of these labels, it is recommended that you test the cleaning product on the fabric in an inconspicuous area. Note: As mentioned previously, Blue Dawn® dish washing soap worked into the greasy stain on clothing and then laundered works wonders!

NON-GREASY STAINS

- Non-greasy stains are easily acquired but not impossible to remove.

- If you are treating a non-greasy stain on a washable fabric, it is recommended that you sponge the stain with cold water as soon as possible.

- In the case of stains where the above process does not remove your stain try soaking the fabric in cool water. The stain may soak out within an hour, or you may need to leave the item in overnight.

- If some of the stain still remains after this treatment, try gently rubbing laundry detergent into it, and then rinse with cool water. The last resort is to use bleach, but always read the fabric care label before you use bleach.

COMBINATION STAINS

Some stains can be double trouble. For instance, coffee with cream or Thousand Island dressing and lipstick are a combination of both greasy and non-greasy substances. Getting rid of these stains is a two-part process. Get rid of the non-greasy stain and then attack the greasy residue. On most fabrics, you will need to sponge the stain with cool water, then work liquid detergent into the stain and rinse thoroughly.

- After the fabric has dried, apply dry-cleaning solution to the greasy part of the stain.

- Allow fabric to dry.

ADDITIONAL STAIN REMOVAL TIPS

- The quicker you treat a stain the better.
- The longer it sets, the more likely it is to become permanent.
- Know what you are cleaning, both the stain and the fabric.
- Remove as much of the stain as possible before cleaning the entire fabric to avoid setting the stain.
- Be gentle. Rubbing, folding, squeezing, twisting, and ringing can cause the stain to penetrate more deeply.
- Keep it cool. Avoid using hot water; heat makes some stains impossible to remove.
- Pre-test stain removers.
- Follow directions. Read manufacturers care labels and directions on products.
- Work from edges into the center to prevent spreading the stain or leaving a ring.

ADDITIONAL TIPS

- **Have a system**. If you have a large family, you may want to do laundry on M, W, and F. If you are single or newly married Saturday might be the best day for doing laundry. No matter the days you choose, set a system in place that works for you and stick with it. Systems relieve stress and frustration!
- **When using fabric softener sheets**, tear them in half to make them last longer and to help on your budget. It will not be less effective in keeping static from the load or making your clothes smell fresher.
- **No time to iron** when removing clothes from the dryer, hang them on hangers to keep the wrinkles to a minimum until ironing can be done.
- **When you can, set aside time to iron** those items coming out of the dryer. If you drop them into a basket until they can be ironed a week or two later, you will never know they have been cleaned. When you have freshly pressed clothing in the closet, getting ready will be much less stressful.
- **Sorting will save you time** and a lot of headaches. If you don't, you will end up with the fuzz from the throw rug all over your husband's black socks.
- **Ironing your husband's shirts** (especially the casual shirts) will save on the dry-cleaning bill. Using spray starch will improve their appearance.
- **For slips and nylon undergarments**, attach a small safety pin to the seam and you won't have a slip with static.
- **Purchase a mesh laundry bag** for washing small items such as bras, socks, etc.

Treating Special Stains

TO ELIMINATE ALCOHOL STAINS DUE TO PERFUME:

- Use a paste of baking soda and ammonia; test for colorfastness first
- Wear rubber gloves, and use this mixture in a well-ventilated area
- Dry the fabric in the sun
- Then wash it as usual

TO REMOVE BLOOD STAINS:

- Dampen the area with cold water
- Rub it with baking soda; test for colorfastness first
- Follow by dabbing with hydrogen peroxide until the stain is gone

POOL CHLORINE:

- Can be rinsed out of bathing suits in a sink full of water with 1 tablespoon baking soda added

CHEMICAL FINISHES in new clothes can bother sensitive skin. To remove the finish:

- Soak the new clothes in water and ½ cup to 2 cups vinegar
- Rinse them
- Add ½ cup baking soda to the wash load

SHOES:

- To remove black scuff marks from shoes: Rub on baking soda paste (part water and part baking soda)
- Wipe it off
- Apply polish
- Clean the rubber on athletic shoes with baking soda sprinkled on a damp sponge or washcloth
- Keep smelly feet at bay by sprinkling baking soda into athletic shoes and street shoes to control odor and moisture

DRY-CLEANABLE CLOTHES:

- Some dry-clean only items can be cleaned with a solution of 4 tablespoons baking soda in cold water. Test for colorfastness first

Baking Soda in Clothing Care

HOW TO USE BAKING SODA PASTE IN DOING LAUNDRY:

- Add ¼ cup baking soda with your detergent to freshen your laundry and help liquid detergents work harder
- Use baking soda in place of fabric softener, add ½ cup at the rinse cycle
- Add ½ cup baking soda (¼ cup for front load washers) with the usual amount of bleach to increase whitening power

PERSPIRATION STAINS:

- Scrub in paste of baking soda and water
- Let it sit for one hour
- Launder as usual

To treat stubborn perspiration stains around the collar:

- Mix a paste of 4 tablespoons of baking soda and ¼ cup water
- Rub it in
- Add a little white vinegar to the collar
- Wash the clothes

LAUNDRY OOPS!

Crayon in with a load of clothes:

- Rewash the load with the hottest possible water
- Add ½ to full cup baking soda
- Repeat if necessary

Stained your white clothes by washing them with colored ones, to undo the damage:

- Add baking soda, salt, and detergent to warm water
- Soak the clothing
- Rewash

Mending Tips

SUPPLIES TO KEEP ON HAND...

- **Scissors**—A small pair of sharp-pointed scissors will be useful for removing broken buttons, cutting thread, and trimming frayed edges. Keep your sewing scissors in a place where little or big hands cannot use them to cut paper or cardboard.

- **Seam Ripper**—A seam ripper can also be used to help remove broken buttons as well as removing stitching in order to make a repair.

- **Needles**—You can get by with two types of needles for basic mending. The #7 sharp needles have a round eye and are great to use with buttonhole thread. A #8 embroidery needle can be used for replacing invisible hems or other applications where all-purpose sewing thread is used. Both of these needles can be used for general sewing.

- **Thread**—All-purpose sewing thread in several basic colors should be a part of your repair kit. This thread will be 100 percent polyester. Machine embroidery thread is not suitable for basic sewing due to its lack of strength. A specialty thread known as buttonhole twist can be used to reattach buttons. It is very strong and only one strand of it needs to be used. This thread is available in a limited number of colors.

- **Fusible Interfacing**—Fusible interfacing is a product that is primarily used in the garment construction process, and it comes in several weights. A light-to-medium weight fusible interfacing can be used in mending tears in a garment by ironing it on the wrong side of the article to cover the tear.

- **Scraps of Fabric**—Small amounts of denim and soft woven fabrics from discarded clothing can be used to make repairs in blue jeans and other garments.

- **Iron-on-Patches**—Patches can be purchased from the fabric store to iron on to clothing to cover holes and tears. Patches are usually fairly stiff and are most often used on pants or jeans.

- **Stitch Witchery**®—A double-sided fusible material used to adhere two layers of fabric together. This product is sold in packages of narrow tape that can be used to repair hems. The glue is heat activated with an iron and care must be taken to avoid getting the adhesive on your iron or ironing-board cover.

JEZEBEL
A Woman with a Wicked Disposition

Biblical Principle: A woman with a wicked disposition seeks to destroy true worship, the family, morality, and the God-ordained role of male authority. God will not bless such a wicked spirit.

Read 1 Kings 16:29–31 thru Chapter 21, 2 Kings 9: 29–37 and Revelation 2:18–28 in order to prepare. This lesson will require more reading for preparation of the lesson. The following pages are provided to give background into Jezebel, her marriage to Ahab, and her hatred for Elijah and all of God's prophets.

Biblical History for Lesson—The story of Jezebel actually begins in 1 Kings 16:29, with the story of Ahab. He was the son of Omri, king of Israel. When Ahab came into office, Asa was the king of Judah. 1Kings 16:30 says of Ahab, "Ahab the son of Omri did evil in the sight of the Lord more than all who were before him." The NAS Ryrie Study Bible tells us about Ahab, "Ahab is remembered for two things: his wickedness and his marriage to Jezebel, who advanced Baal worship in Israel."

In 1 Kings 16:31–33, it says concerning his marriage to Jezebel, that he began to worship her idols, her gods, and even constructed an altar for Baal, in the house of Baal, which he also built. In verse 33b it says, "Thus Ahab did more to provoke the Lord God of Israel than all the kings of Israel who were before him." This gives us great insight into the man, Ahab. As you continue reading, you are introduced to God's chosen man, Elijah, the Tishbite. Elijah means "Yahweh is God." His name was a very significant name in a time when the worship of Baal threatened to eliminate the worship of Yahweh in Israel. We discover several things about Elijah:

- God provided for Elijah at the brook of Cherith.
- Elijah was obedient in doing what God asked of him.
- God told him to go to Zarephath, the town that was located between Tyre and Sidon, the home of Jezebel, the very heart of Baal worship.
- God told Elijah to go to a widow and He, through her, would provide for Elijah.
- The widow and her son were suffering from the famine.
- When Elijah asked for food, she must have thought he was blind not to see she was a widow—with a son—poor and without food.
- But God provided in abundance, she had more oil than she could have ever imagined. The sale of the oil provided food for her, her son, and Elijah.
- The widow's son dies.
- Elijah cries out to God to heal the boy, and "the Lord heard him."

Now God sends Elijah to Ahab. You can see that the brook, the trip to Zarapheth, the provisions from the widow, and the healing of her son were all God's way of strengthening Elijah's faith.

- By the time God asked Elijah to go to Ahab and challenge the priests of Baal, he was ready, fitted with a suit of great faith!

- Jezebel had destroyed the prophets of the Lord, but within Ahab's household God had His own man, Obadiah.

- Obadiah had hidden, fed, and cared for a hundred prophets of God, in order that they would not be killed.

- We see Elijah meeting up with Obadiah—he falls on his face before Elijah—recognizing him as God's anointed.

- Elijah gives Obadiah an assignment, to go and announce to Ahab that Elijah wanted to meet with him.

- Reluctantly, Obadiah did just that. So they met face to face. Ahab had the nerve to say to Elijah, "Is this you, you troubler of Israel?" Elijah came back with a scorching reply, "I have not troubled Israel, but you and your father's house have, because you have forsaken the commandments of the Lord and you have followed the Baals."

- He tells Ahab to gather all the people of Israel, the 450 prophets of Baal, and the 400 prophets of Asherah and meet him at Mt. Carmel.

- They gather there and Elijah addresses the people: "How long will you hesitate between two opinions? If the Lord is God, follow Him; but if Baal, follow him."

- The people had not totally abandoned Yahweh, but they sought to combine worshipping God with Baal worship.

If you go on reading, you will see where Elijah tells the prophets of Baal and Asherah to place animals on top of a pile of wood, and then he would place his animals on a pile of wood. They were not allowed to light a fire under their animals—and Elijah would not light a fire under his. He further tells them to call upon their gods for fire and sacrifice, and he would call upon his God. Elijah tells them that the god who answers by fire—He is the one true God! So they did as he said.

They called, begged, and pleaded with their gods for three hours! Guess what? No fire! So, Elijah places twelve stones on the ground. He prepares his animals atop his wood, digs a trench around it, and tells the people to cover his sacrifice with pitchers of water, not just once, but a second time and a third time—now that was wet wood! He prays, "Answer me, O Lord, that this people may know that You, O Lord, are God, and that You have turned their heart back again."

The power of God came and consumed the burnt offering, the wood, the stones, the dust, and licked up all the water that was in the trench. It says, "When all the people saw it, they fell on their faces and they said, 'The Lord, He is God; the Lord, He is God.'" I would imagine they did! Elijah seized all the false prophets and they were slain.

In Chapter 19, Ahab tells Jezebel what happened at Mt. Carmel. She is not happy and sends a threatening message to Elijah. Amazingly, after all Elijah had witnessed of God's provisions and power, HE RUNS! "And he was afraid and arose and ran for his life." What! Seriously, all because a woman threatened him! Elijah comes to rest under a juniper tree and tells God, that he had had enough. "I cannot take it; let me die!" What? Seriously, all because of a woman!

Moving on to Chapter 21, we read about Ahab's desire to have the vineyard of Naboth. Once again, Jezebel is busy controlling and manipulating—working evil. Ahab wants Naboth's vineyard because it is close to his house and because he is coveting the good land. But Naboth refuses to sell him the land because it was his God-given inheritance. Pouting, Ahab enters his home and refuses to eat. Jezebel asks him, "What's wrong with you, that you will not eat?" Oh, the whining that followed! "Because I spoke to Naboth, the Jezreelite and said to him, 'Give me your vineyard for money; or else, if it pleases you, I will give you a vineyard in its place.' But he said, 'I will not give you my vineyard.'" In other words, I didn't get my way!

Now, Jezebel kicks into gear. She basically says, "Why are you acting like a two year old, when you are the king? I'll get the vineyard for you."

- She plotted and planned, manipulated, committed murder, and got the vineyard.

- God saw all that was going on because He sees all! The Lord sent Elijah with a word to Ahab: "Thus says the Lord, 'Have you murdered and also taken possession?' And you shall speak to him saying, 'Thus says the Lord, "In the place where the dogs licked up the blood of Naboth the dogs shall lick your blood, even yours."'"

- Elijah goes on to tell Ahab all God had planned for him and then addressed what God was going to do with Jezebel…"of Jezebel also has the Lord spoken saying, 'the dogs shall eat Jezebel in the district of Jezreel.'" And verse 25 says of them both, "Surely there was no one like Ahab who sold himself to do evil in the sight of the Lord, because Jezebel his wife incited him."

God keeps His word. As to Ahab, we read in Chapter 22:37, "So the king died and was brought to Samaria, and the dogs licked up his blood, according to the word of the Lord, which He spoke." As to Jezebel's end, see 2 Kings Chapter 9:29–37. In these verses, we see Jehu (King of the Northern Kingdom of Israel) giving orders to kill Jezebel, "Throw her down (out of a window)." So they threw her down and some of her blood was sprinkled on the wall and on the horses, and he (Jehu) trampled her under foot." Jehu gave orders to his attendants to see to the "cursed woman" and told them to bury her. When they went to bury her they found only her skull, her feet, and the palms of her hands. "Therefore they returned and told him. And he said, 'This is the word of the Lord, which He spoke by his servant Elijah the Tishbite, saying, 'In the property of Jezrell the dogs shall eat the flesh of Jezebel.'" God is serious about His Word!

As we look at Jezebel, we can see that her spirit—the Jezebel spirit—can be found within several vital entities, the first being the church.

In her book *Prayer Portions*, Sylvia Gunter[6] says, "To understand the nature of the spiritual battle, we must see the behavior of the biblical Jezebel against the prophet Elijah. Elijah had a word for idolatrous Israel in that day. Elijah challenged the people, 'Why hesitate between two opinions? If God is God, serve Him only.' Elijah was attacked by Jezebel. The spirit of Jezebel attempts to neutralize the purposes of God's kingdom, but ultimately God cannot be kept from watching over His purposes to accomplish them in His strategic time."

- Pastors and leaders ignore the spirit of Jezebel at their own peril. Women with a Jezebel spirit have picked off and neutralized unsuspecting leaders and ministries through sexual immorality, physical sickness, debilitating fear, failure, discouragement, and depression

---

[6] Sylvia Gunter. *Prayer Portions*. (The Father's Business Publishers, 2005).

(which we call burn- out), the stress disease—all have taken their toll on Christian leaders.

- In this present conflict between Jezebel and Elijah, the church in these last days can expect increasing assault by this spirit.

- One of Satan's end time strategies is to stir up the spirit of Jezebel, Elijah's archenemy and the church's.

The other entity, in which the Jezebel spirit can be found, is within the family.

In *Prayer Portions*, Sylvia says, "The spirit of Jezebel is one of the dominant evil authorities over our nation. It is in the church and in your family. Our society, the church, families and individuals personally have been attacked, infiltrated, sabotaged, and robbed by Jezebel. She is no respecter of persons. This spirit is genderless but seems to work more effectively in women. There are only two classes of people—Jezebels and those who have been Jezebelled.

In the nation, the Jezebel factor is the spiritual driving force behind the high divorce rate, the feminist movement, sexual permissiveness, abortion on demand, and the prominent place of women in the New Age and the occult. The Jezebel spirit exercises a major role in the power of evil over our nation today. The spirit of Jezebel seeks to destroy true worship, the family, morality, and the God-ordained role of male authority"

Discipling Leader: Tell the story of Jezebel to the class, referring to the verses referenced in the beginning of this lesson. Included in the participant's workbook on page 221, there is a list of the Ten Characteristics of a Jezebel Spirit, use this as a reference for this lesson. A Jezebel spirt is totally contrary to the true nature of God. It should not and cannot live within the heart of a born-again believer.

End today's lesson with discussing the following questions with the class:

- How has the story of Jezebel's life impacted you?

- What will you do differently as a result of studying the life of Jezebel?

If time allows, utilize the Discussion Questions and the Examining the Heart Questions.

DISCUSSION QUESTIONS

1. What type of King was Ahab? *He did evil in the Lord's sight; he was worse than any king before him. He relinquished his authority and leadership to his wife, Jezebel. He broke God's law in marrying Jezebel. (See Deuteronomy 7:1–5).*

2. Describe Jezebel. *She was the daughter of a religious man, her religion was idolatry, she was a murderer, she hated God's servants and God's Word, she was a controller, and usurped her husband's authority.*

3. What did Jezebel lead her husband to do? *She led him to worship other gods; she set out to convert him to her religion of idolatry.*

4. Who was Jezebel set on destroying? *She was set on destroying the prophets of God. She had many of them killed.*

5. Describe the culture at the time. *It was an idolatrous culture; the people wanted to hold on to God as well as all their other gods. There was a spiritual battle going on.*

6. What prophet did God raise up in order to bring His message to the people? *Elijah*

7. In what ways does a Jezebel spirit manifest itself in the church? *Through manipulation, control, negative attitude, critical spirit, attempts to usurp authority, personal attacks on the pastor, staff, and leadership.*

8. In what ways does a Jezebel spirit manifest itself within a family/marriage? *Through control, attacks, manipulation, a burning desire to have your own way, undermining your husband's authority, having flattering lips and a "religious" spirit. It's all about "you."*

9. How does a church stand against a Jezebel spirit? *The church must be a discerning body, one of prayer, and the church leadership must be willing to confront the guilty party. Sylvia says, through "rug-biting" repentance, the pastor, staff, leadership, and church must be sure that they are in a right relationship with the Father—broken, repentant, and seeking after Him.*

Examining the Heart

Ask some or all of the questions below according to time allotted. Give the class time to prayerfully consider each one, asking the Lord to point out any that applies to them as you read through the list:

1. Do you seek within your marriage relationship to take control of the home and family from your husband?

2. Are you determined to have your own way?

3. Are you submitted to your husband as the God ordained authority in your home?

4. Do you try to manipulate by nagging, emotional outbursts, endless demands, complaining, and sarcasm, by using a sharp tongue or public humiliation of others or your spouse?

5. Are you outwardly gracious in front of others, yet at home you are brash, overt, aggressive, and bossy?

6. Are you, through your actions and attitude, cutting off the life of your husband? Your pastor and staff?

7. Are you self-promoting?

8. Do you threaten to leave your husband in the middle of a disagreement or when you do not get your way?

9. Do you operate on a performance-based acceptance level?

10. Do you have bitterness and unforgiveness in your heart toward someone who has wounded you in the past?

11. Do you dominate, control, and manipulate in order to accomplish your own agenda?

12. Do you have a prideful spirit, an independent spirit, or a rebellious spirit?

13. Even if your husband does not show strong leadership skills, are you willing to submit to his leadership and not usurp his God-given role as head of your home?

14. Are you bearing fruit in your life? Do you have an intimate relationship with God or are you just religious—going through the motions, talking the talk?

We all need to examine our hearts and make sure we are free of the Jezebel spirit. When she rears her head and threatens to take dominance in our lives, we need to ask God to work in us to change our spirit from a Jezebel spirit to a Christlike spirit. Jezebel caused Ahab to fall into idolatry. She cost him his respect as king, the loss of his friends, his relationship with God, and ultimately his life. What a weight to carry and what a sin she had to answer for!

Closing: As Leader prays, proclaim these three realities in the lives of the class participants. The fulfillment of these will diminish the effect of a Jezebel spirit:

1. Personal submission to God and for Him to develop godly character rooted in humility, equipped by the Holy Spirit, and enlightened by the Word of God to know what is true.

2. God-directed submission to your God-given family covering—husband or father.

3. Submission to the order of spiritual authority in the church where God has placed you.

Week Four

ETIQUETTE

Week Four

LESSON PLAN

I. LEADER OPENS IN PRAYER

II. DEVOTIONAL

- Tamar—*A Woman of Great Suffering.* For a background reference into David, Tamar's father, read 2 Samuel 11:1–27. Continue by reading about Tamar in 2 Samuel 13 in order to prepare. For help in preparation refer to lesson outline in Devotional section of Leader Guide.

- **Biblical Principle**: Women do not have to live under the burden of shame, Christ came to set us free.

III. LESSON

- Have participants turn to the Etiquette Quiz. Give the young women a few minutes to answer questions. Once quiz is completed, talk over the answers. Tally up the correct answers given by each participant. If desired, give a prize related to today's topic to the top winner. Example: Note cards, pens, book on manners/etiquette.

- The responsibility of teaching today's topics may be distributed among the leadership, giving each an opportunity to instruct. Topics to consider for today: General rules of etiquette, cell phone etiquette, etiquette for social settings, thank-you and condolence notes, dressing for a job interview, etc.

- **Activity**: Hand out a blank note card and pen to each participant. Without any instructions, allow them to write either a thank you note or a condolence note. As the topic of note writing is being taught, have participants compare what they wrote to what is correct.

- A qualified guest may be invited to address today's topics.

- **Role Playing**—For the topic of cell phone etiquette. Choose two class participants or use leadership to role play a scene where two women are having lunch, one's cell phone rings, she picks it up, and goes on talking as if she were all alone, ignoring her friend. Then change scenes and have them eating lunch together, the one friend's phone rings, she looks at it, explains that it is a very important call and that she must take it, but explains that she will not be long and asks to be excused in order to take the call. Have the participants choose which response was the socially acceptable response. Be creative and have several role playing scenes in order to teach the participants the different topics of Etiquette covered in today's lesson.

- **If offering Book Two starting in January:** Leadership may want to prepare a couple of the Valentine recipes supplied in today's lesson and bring them to share with class. <u>Note</u>: If time allows, cut out and bake pre-made sugar cookie dough and ice or dip in chocolate.

IV. TIME IN THE KITCHEN

- While enjoying the Valentine recipes, give the participants time to talk about the topic discussed today and answer any questions they may have. Recipes included in today's lesson: Heart-Shaped Cookies, Red Velvet Cupcakes, Cream Cheese Icing, Linda's Old Fashioned Sugar Cookies, Peppermint Ice Cream, Chocolate Truffles, Strawberry Cupcakes, and Lover's Midnight Spiced Hot Chocolate.

V. WEEK FOUR LESSON SHEETS

- Introduction—*Dos and Don'ts*
  The Etiquette Quiz
  General Rules of Etiquette
  Cell Phone Etiquette
  Proper Etiquette in a Social Setting
  Creative Conversation
  Fun Ice Breakers
  Etiquette for Notes and Invitations
  Week Four Valentines Recipes
  Devotional on Tamar

VI. EQUIPMENT FOR WEEK FOUR

- Provide prepared and chilled sugar cookie dough, rolling pins, flour, heart-shaped cookie cutters, cookie baking sheets, parchment paper, 1 (12 ounce) bag semi-sweet chocolate chips, oil, measuring spoons, sauce pan, 2 (10 ounce) bags Ghiradelli® Melting Chocolate Chips and/or icing

- Prepared/baked heart-shaped sugar cookies to dip and chocolate dipping ingredients

- Plastic zipper bags for cookie transport, should the participants want to take some home

- Prizes for Etiquette Quiz winners

Introduction
DOS AND DON'TS

I was so excited. It was our first company function and in St. Thomas, of all places! Growing up, taking a family vacation to an exotic place was never an option. Now, I was going to St. Thomas, wow! I spent weeks purchasing just the right outfits and all on a young married couple's budget—so you can just imagine. Our last night in St. Thomas was to be a formal dinner. The dress I purchased was an empire-waist, scooped neck, taupe colored dress with the little white linen jacket. It was a knockout. Well, I thought so, anyway! I was so excited to get to wear it alongside this young, up-and-coming life insurance salesman, all decked out in his white tux. Yes, I said white!

That formal evening arrived, and we proudly went to the dinner all dressed up in our new attire, only to arrive to discover that Mark was the only man in a white tux. He was humiliated. My dress was great in my eyes but a little on the casual side compared to what the older women were wearing who were wealthier and more informed on dressing for formal dinners. We did notice one man in a formal black tux without any socks, but that didn't make Mark feel any better. Somehow, his sockless feet seemed a lot cooler and more socially acceptable than Mark's white tux!

Once we swallowed our pride, we entered the banquet hall and found our table. I looked down at the table setting to see four forks, three knives, several spoons of every size, and numerous glasses. My stomach was in a knot! What were all these utensils? I had never seen so many at one place setting. As I sat down, the waiter approached on my left and placed my dinner napkin in my lap. I gave Mark a look that said, *Help, what am I to do?* He smiled back at me as if to say, *It will be all right, follow me.* I was not sure I had a lot of confidence in the young man seated beside me in the only white tux in the banquet hall!

---

*T*he servers began to serve the first of many courses. I thought to myself, *I really don't have to eat. I could just sit here and be quiet, hoping no one would notice. I'm not really hungry anyway.* But I knew that would never work and might be more embarrassing than using the wrong utensil. I decided to watch Mark, and he decided to watch the others at our table. What they did, we did, hoping they knew what they were doing. They all seemed more seasoned than we were at this; they were very kind to us and tolerant of our minuscule knowledge of proper etiquette.

When I think back on our once-in-a-lifetime trip to St. Thomas, years ago when we were young, I get quite a chuckle. It is always easier to look back. I should have researched the proper attire for such a company function and studied up on proper table etiquette. But we live and learn, don't we? It is good to be informed.

You will always feel more comfortable in any setting if you are educated—thus the necessity of learning proper etiquette!

THE ETIQUETTE QUIZ

Before you take the etiquette quiz below, we need to talk about what etiquette is!

Etiquette is polite and proper behavior, using good manners, and being courteous. When I think of etiquette, I think of the word, R.E.S.P.E.C.T. A few synonyms for respect are words such as: considerate, thoughtful, showing esteem and regard for another.

Practicing proper etiquette is thinking of others first, being polite, using good manners, being courteous, being considerate, thoughtful, and showing regard or esteem for others.

Let's see where you rate when it comes to appropriate etiquette and showing respect toward others...

#1

WHEN SOMEONE SNEEZES YOU ...

A. Say, "God bless you"

B. Offer the person a tissue

C. Do nothing to acknowledge the sneeze

D. Ask if he or she is okay

#2

YOU RAN INTO A REALLY GOOD, OLD FRIEND YOU HAVE NOT SEEN IN FOREVER. YOU ...

A. Shake his or her hand

B. Give the person a hug or kiss

C. Wave and keep moving on

D. Pretend you do not know them

E. Offer a quick hello but do not make small talk

#3

WHILE DRIVING SOMEONE CUTS YOU OFF. YOU ...

A. Wave as a gesture that it is okay

B. Lay on your horn

C. Return the favor by speeding up and cutting the person off

D. Count to ten and try not to lose your cool

#4

WHEN YOU ARE IN A RESTAURANT OR A PUBLIC PLACE WITH OTHER PEOPLE AND YOUR CELL PHONE RINGS, YOU …

A. Excuse yourself and step outside to not bother anyone with your conversation

B. Take the call and make an effort to keep it down/quiet

C. Wait until you get home to call the person back

D. Carry on as if you were in the comfort of your home

#5

YOU ARE BEHIND TWO PEOPLE IN THE GROCERY STORE CHECKOUT WHEN ANOTHER LINE OPENS UP. YOU …

A. Let the people standing in front of you go

B. Race to the next line before anyone gets there

C. Wait a few seconds and give the people in front of you the opportunity to move before go yourself

D. Stay where you are

#6

WHEN SOMEONE GIVES YOU A PRESENT, YOU RESPOND BY …

A. Sending a thank-you note

B. Saying, "Thank you" in person (this does not take the place of a note)

C. Not saying anything

D. Refusing the gift

#7

YOUR DOG DOES HIS BUSINESS IN THE NEIGHBOR'S YARD. YOU …

A. Only pick it up if someone is looking

B. Act like you do not notice

C. Pick it up with a plastic bag

D. Return to the scene of the crime after the fact

#8

WHICH OF THE FOLLOWING ARE YOU MOST LIKELY TO WEAR TO A WEDDING?

A. A black dress

B. A white dress

**C. Any color but black or white
(black is fine for evening wedding)**

D. Who cares about color

#9

HOW MUCH SHOULD YOU USUALLY TIP YOUR SERVER?

A. I don't

B. 5%

C. 15% to 20%

D. About 30%

E. Depends on the service

#10

HOW OFTEN SHOULD YOU USE PLEASE AND THANK YOU WHEN ASKING FOR SOMETHING?

A. Always

B. Never

D. Most of the time

E. When I remember

#11

WHAT DO YOU DO WHEN YOU HEAR A JUICY TIDBIT OF GOSSIP ABOUT A FRIEND OR CO-WORKER?

A. Spread it around as quickly as possible

B. Only discuss it with close friends

C. Forget about it immediately

D. Ask the person concerned if it is true

E. Acknowledge the gossiper but don't contribute to the conversation

#12

IF SOMEONE SAYS SOMETHING YOU DO NOT HEAR, YOUR RESPONSE SHOULD BE ...

A. What?

B. Huh?

C. I'm sorry, could you please say that again?

D. "Excuse me!"

E. Nothing

#13

FOR WHOM DO YOU HOLD OPEN DOORS?

A. Anyone who follows close behind

B. Only women who follow close behind

C. Let the door close behind me without holding it open

D. Only for older people and those who cannot open doors themselves

E. People do not need any help opening doors; it is insulting to do so

#14

HOW MUCH TIME DO YOU ALLOW BEFORE YOU SEND A THANK-YOU NOTE FOR A GIFT OR KINDNESS YOU RECEIVED?

A. I never send thank-you notes

B. You should write and send thank-you notes immediately

C. Whenever I get around to it.

D. Within a week of receiving the gift.

E. Within a month of receiving the gift (with wedding gifts, within six months of receiving the gift)

GENERAL RULES *of Etiquette*

HOSTESS GIFT: When you are either invited for dinner or for an extended stay in someone's home, it is proper to bring the hostess a gift. It should be a gift your hostess is not obligated to use that night, gifts such as candy, a candle, note cards, or a framed piece. A thank-you note can be left with the gift or written in the days to follow. This applies to occasions, such as showers and parties, given in your honor—take a gift and thank-you note for each hostess.

NAME GAME: In remembering names use the Rule of Three suggested by Nancy R. Mitchell in her book, *Etiquette Rules!*[7]

1. When you shake hands or in your first sentence of conversation repeat the name. "Hi, Jane."

2. Say the name again during conversation.

3. Say the name again as you say goodbye. If you didn't retain the name from the introduction, you may say as you are parting, "It was great talking with you about the organization. Thanks so much for the tip/information/sharing your thoughts. And, please tell me your name once more. I am sorry; it's been one of those days."

DON'T INTERRUPT: When people are talking: LISTEN. Don't interrupt. Effective listening takes work. To listen you must give your undivided attention to the person speaking. Being a good listener makes the person you are listening to feel cared about and special.

BODY LANGUAGE: Your body language can speak louder than words. It can convey a variety of emotions from anger, annoyance, comfort, insecurity, mistrust, stress, dominance, readiness, etc. Your posture, eye contact, gestures, facial expressions, placements of arms and feet, all deliver a message to others.

RESPONDING TO NEGATIVE COMMENTS: It is important to keep your emotions in check. Do not become defensive or allow yourself to be drug into a discussion with no possible resolution. It is important to remember that negative comments or remarks are usually not directed at you, but at circumstances. Apologize, ask what the person would like to see happen or how the issue can be resolved, and clearly state what you plan to do. Do not take it personally!

RETAIL RUDENESS: Treat all sales staff with respect. Be courteous! Don't monopolize their time. When you have ten items and someone behind you has two, allow them go ahead of you. When a new register opens, allow the person in front of you to go first.

HANDICAP HELPS: Be courteous, not condescending. Offer a handshake. Offer help in general terms as you greet or escort them. "Please let me know if I can help. Look them in the eye, directing conversation to them. Use a normal tone of voice, they are handicapped—not deaf!

[7] Mitchell, Nancy R. "Etiquette Rules!." 2017. New York, New York: (Well Fleet Press.)

CELL PHONE ETIQUETTE

Cell phones play a leading role in our world and in our personal lives, from being a helpful tool to being a bad influence.

Turn off your cell phone, switch it to vibrate before sitting down to eat, or leave it in your purse. It is impolite to answer your phone during dinner, and even more impolite to text! If you must take a call, excuse yourself and step away from the table, or when eating out, go outside the restaurant.

Do not text in theaters, concerts, church, restaurants, meetings, public restrooms, or when you should be paying attention.

Do not text when engaged in face-to-face conversations, unless it is an emergency and you explain what and why you have to respond.

A text is not a proper way to communicate serious concerns, condolences, personal announcements, or gratitude.

Return a text message with a text message, not a call, because it is the initiators preferred method of communication. Always think R.E.S.P.E.C.T.

When texting for the first time, identify yourself. Be careful when group texting. Not everyone wants to receive every single response text. If you are engaging in an on-going conversation with one member of the group, switch to their private number.

Don't expect immediate responses and don't feel you have to respond in a nanosecond to every text. We are all busy and responses can wait! Sending follow-up texts to receive a quicker response is annoying. Don't do it!

DON'T say anything on social media that you would not say in person in a face-to-face conversation. The obscurity of the virtual world has brought out the dark side of many people.

Do not "overshare." Do not make every post about you. Do not share intimate details.

Tagging: Ask permission before tagging people in photos. If you are tagged and wished you were not, you can unlink a photo of yourself and then ask the poster to remove it.

Remember that technology is a means of communication—a tool—not a part of your body. Your iPhone, iPad, and laptop can be turned off, put away, silenced, and even left at home! Be respectful of those around you, those you love, and those you do life with!

PROPER ETIQUETTE in a Social Setting

TABLE ETIQUETTE [8]

- Always pass food counter clockwise.

- When serving plates, serve to the left and remove the plates from the right.

- Napkins are placed in the center of the plate for formal dinners. The server will place it in your lap.

- Napkins may be placed to the left of the forks with the fold facing away from the plate if a course is already on the table or for informal dinners. Unfold and place napkin in your lap. If you excuse yourself from the table, loosely fold your napkin and lay it to the left or right of your plate. Once you return, place it back in your lap. When the meal is finished, leave the napkin semi-folded at the left of the place setting.

- General rule for using the utensils is to start from the outside of your place setting and work your way toward the main plate.

- Foods you can eat by hand are bread, rolls, and muffins; slice or tear into small pieces before buttering.

- Foods that are meant to be eaten by hand are corn on the cob, lobster, sandwiches, certain fruits, olives, celery, cookies, and some cakes, spareribs, clams, and oysters on the half shell.

- When in a restaurant do not start eating until everyone is served. At a private dinner party, wait until the host or hostess picks up his/her fork to eat, then you may eat.

- Remember this rule: eat to your left, drink to your right. Any plate to your left is yours and any drink to your right belongs to you.

- Knives go to the right of the plate, blade inward with spoons to the right of the knives. Forks go to the left of the plate.

- Once utensils are used, they must not touch the table; forks, knives, and spoons should be placed on the edge of your plate.

- When dining out, signal that you are done by resting your fork, tines up, and knife blade in, with the handles at five o'clock and tips pointing to ten o'clock on your plate.

- Glasses go above the knife on the right. Bread-and-butter plates go above the forks on the left.

- Filled salad plates go in the center of the plate, if served before the entrée; to the left if served with meal.

[8] The Taste of Home Cookbook (Reiman Media Group, Inc. 2009).

ADDITIONAL RULES OF ETIQUETTE

- Never excuse yourself from a dinner table and announce you are going to the bathroom; it is sufficient to say *Excuse me*, or *I'll be right back*.

- Keep elbows off the table. If right-handed, keep your left hand in your lap unless you are using it.

- Do not talk with your mouth full! This is rude and very distasteful for others to watch. Wait until you have swallowed to speak.

- Always say *please* when asking for something and *thank you* after receiving it.

- Whenever a woman leaves the table or returns, all the men seated should stand up.

- Always allow for the unexpected when determining your arrival time for a dinner party or event; it is rude to be early, so plan to arrive on time or no more than five to ten minutes late. Any later requires a call to the hostess informing her of your late arrival. Try to be punctual!

ETIQUETTE GOOFS [9]

1. Chewing or talking with food in your mouth.
2. Slurping, smacking, or making any unpleasant noise while eating.
3. Holding your utensil like a shovel.
4. Picking your teeth at the table.
5. Not using a napkin or failing to place it in your lap.
6. Drinking while chewing (unless you are choking).
7. Cutting up all the food on your plate at once.
8. Slouching over your plate or placing your elbows on the table while eating.
9. Using the *boarding house reach* instead of asking someone to please pass the food.
10. Leaving the table without saying *Excuse me*.
11. Applying makeup, except for a quick dab of lipstick done discreetly.

[9] The Taste of Home Cookbook (Reiman Media Group Inc. 2009).

CREATIVE CONVERSATION

Do you know how to word a question in order to have good conversations when out with friends or family?

These seven suggestions may help you in structuring questions when in a social setting...

1. Use questions that are easy to answer. Example: How long have you lived in the area?

2. Use questions that are not offensive. Example: Have you adjusted to the area?

3. Use questions that include everyone present—a question anyone could answer. Example: As a child, what was your most embarrassing moment?

4. Use questions in which the people answering will not be judged by their response; people are reluctant if they feel their answer will be judged. Example: Stay away from political hot topics, such as who your guests voted for in the last election.

5. Use questions that leave the person being questioned with a warm feeling—where they feel good about their answer. Example: Questions dealing with family, trips/vacations, accomplishments, etc.

6. Use questions that create greater conversation among the group. Example: Utilize the Fun Ice Breakers sheet.

7. Ask creative questions. Example: Whom do you go to for advice?

    - Creative and fun questions promote conversation and keep the energy going.

    - Be sensitive to those who may be in a difficult place in life.

    - Great questions are good for starting conversation, for helping to keep the conversation flowing, and are a way to get to know others better.

    - Be well versed on a few topics; this will make it easier for you to enter into conversations.

FUN ICE BREAKERS

Choose any of the following to use in social gatherings to generate appropriate conversation.

1. Name one thing you miss about being a kid?
2. What did you enjoy most about school?
3. Who was your favorite music group in middle school? In high school?
4. When you were a kid, what did you want to be when you grew up?
5. What injuries did you have as a kid?
6. What was your worst dating experience?
7. As a kid, what was your most embarrassing moment?
8. Do you have any hidden talents?
9. Name one thing people do not know about you.
10. Tell about a funny family story from your childhood.
11. Was there ever a time you were frightened for your life?
12. What outdoor activity do you like to do?
13. Did you ever fight with your siblings? Who won?
14. What is your favorite place on earth?
15. What do you like about living in this area?
16. What do you consider the most important event of your life so far?
17. What do you consider your greatest achievement?
18. What is the one thing you would most like to be remembered for after your death?
19. Do you feel you have a calling or purpose in life?
20. Name three exotic countries you'd like to visit.
21. If your house was on fire and you could only grab three things, what would they be?
22. What do you value most in life?
23. What do you feel has been the greatest invention of all time?
24. What would be your dream job?
25. If you could live anywhere in the world, where would it be?

26. If you knew you were going to die in twenty-four hours, name three things you would do in the time you had left.
27. If you could go on a road trip with any person (dead or alive), who would you choose and where would you go?
28. What is your favorite verse in the Bible?
29. What is the most amazing thing you've discovered about God?
30. If you could be any one person from the Bible, who would it be? Why?
31. What has been your favorite book that you've read?
32. If you could take the place of a person in history, who would it be?
33. What is your favorite outdoor activity to do with your friends/spouse?
34. What is your greatest fear and what is one activity you would do if not for fear?
35. What was your favorite childhood Christmas memory?
36. What is the one toy you desired to receive as a child for Christmas, but never got?
37. What is your favorite restaurant? Your favorite ethnic food?
38. When you think of your childhood, what food comes to mind first?
39. Do you have a favorite memory of your grandparents?
40. If you were given $100,000, what would you do with it?
41. What is the greatest answer to prayer you have ever experienced?
42. When you get to heaven, what would you like to ask God?
43. If you could design and build your own home, what would it look like?
44. What is the single most important event you have attended?

ETIQUETTE FOR
Notes and Invitations

THANK-YOU NOTES

- It is NEVER wrong to send a *thank-you* note!

- An e-mail or a phone call is acceptable for a close friend or relative, but a handwritten note is always the best form for showing appreciation.

- You should be prompt in your response to a gift.

- Always make the thank-you note personal, mentioning the gift by name and thanking the giver for his/her thoughtfulness.

WEDDING GIFT: A wedding gift must be acknowledged with a written note within three to six months of receiving it. Shower gifts also require a written thank-you note, even if you thanked the giver in person.

GET-WELL GIFT: Should be acknowledged as soon as the patient is well enough to respond.

CONDOLENCE GIFT: When receiving condolence gifts, (such as flowers or food) a personal handwritten thank-you note should be sent to the one who gave the gift. It is not necessary to send a note for a sympathy card if it is merely signed with the sender's name and brief words of sympathy.

CONGRATULATIONS GIFT: When you receive a congratulations gift (graduation from high school or college), you should send a personal handwritten thank-you note.

HOSTESS GIFT: A handwritten note must be sent after staying with someone as their houseguest. Taking or leaving a hostess gift during your stay is an especially nice way to say thank you.

REMEMBER: The giver has taken his/her time and effort, not to mention having spent their money in selecting a thoughtful gift for you. You should show proper gratitude and appreciation by sending a handwritten note.

In writing thank-you notes, follow this six-point formula:

Greet the giver—"Dear Aunt Sally,"

Express your gratitude—"Thank you for the gift card."

Discuss use—"I am going to use it to purchase bedding for my dorm room."

Mention the past, allude to future—"It was great to see you at my graduation and I hope to see you again soon."

Grace—"Thank you again, for the generous gift." (It is not overkill to say thank you again)

Regards—"Love, Mandy"

RESPONDING TO INVITATIONS

RSVP (repondez, sil vous plait) means **RESPOND PLEASE!**

- Upon receiving an invitation, you must respond within a day or two: do not wait more than a week.

- You may decline an invitation, but never accept and then forget about it.

- If you accept, there are few excuses for not attending, barring illness, a death, or other major disaster.

- Keep your word; if you say you are going, Go!

Be sure to respond to wedding reception invitations since the host/hostess must plan on food for the proper number of guests. Be sensitive to those holding the event, if you commit to be there follow through on your commitment.

WRITING CONDOLENCES [11]

Often when tragedy and loss occur we do not know exactly what to say. But whether friend, family, co-worker, or acquaintance, you should always offer sympathy. Do not worry about saying the wrong thing. Just giving your condolences is the kindest thing you can do, as you acknowledge their loss and show that you care.

Think of writing a condolence note as a part of basic etiquette. Just as you would say please and thank you, you should express your sympathy in the form of a written note or letter to the bereaved. You may use a note card, a sympathy card, or a blank card for your condolences; remember, it is the thought that you put into words that counts.

Always give a lot of thought to your words expressed on paper or in a card. It does not have to be long. Your words should be simple and sincere. Below you will find a format to follow:

- Give a tribute to the deceased: pay your respects and provide a tribute to the dead.

- Offer the grieving your condolences: say to the bereaved how sorry you are for their loss. Be yourself and write as if you were speaking the condolences to them.

- Acknowledge their grief: you can acknowledge the grief has happened by offering whatever support you can and personally expressing your own deepest sympathy.

- If you knew the person who has passed away, write about a memory you have of them, or an act of kindness that they did for you.

- If you have some photos, you could include those in the note.

---

[11] Deborah R. Chappa, *Words for When There Are no Words: Writing a Memorable Condolence Note* (Haverford, Infinity Publishing, 1999).

THE RIGHT WORDS FOR CONDOLENCES:

- "We were sorry to hear about your great loss."
- "My thoughts and prayers are with you at this time of sorrow."
- "God bless you and your family during this painful and difficult time."
- "May God give you the strength you need to get through this difficult time."
- "May God bless you in this time of need."
- "During this time of sorrow, you are in our thoughts and prayers."
- "Our hearts go out to you."
- "May time heal your sorrow and memories sustain you."
- "In friendship and sympathy . . ."
- "We are remembering you and your family in our thoughts and prayers."
- "May the God of all comfort bring great comfort and peace to your hearts."
- Offer scripture verses that have ministered to you and your family in times of loss.

Remember that no words or gift will eliminate the pain of bereavement, but you can offer comfort, which is the precise reason we give them.

- Do not shy away from ministering to those who are hurting or determine you have nothing to offer.
- In times of pain and loss, we all need to be comforted.
- You can offer yourself, your words, your prayers, and your encouragement.

A Word from Dianne: I can personally testify that notes and cards sent following the death of a loved one, mean a great deal to those who have suffered the loss. For three to four months after Mark passed away, I received cards and notes. Not one word of encouragement and show of love was wasted. Each one along with the promise and assurance that they were praying for me brought comfort.

Notes and condolence cards are just a small way we can encourage and express love to others!

VALENTINE RECIPES

Red Velvet Cupcakes

2¼ cups all-purpose flour

1 teaspoon salt

2 tablespoons red food color

3 tablespoons unsweetened cocoa

1 cup buttermilk

1 teaspoon vanilla

1½ cups sugar

1 stick butter, softened

2 eggs, room temperature

1 teaspoon baking soda

1 teaspoon white vinegar

Preheat oven to 350°F. Line standard muffin tin with paper baking cups. In mixing bowl, combine flour and salt. Gradually add food coloring into the cocoa in separate bowl until well blended. Set aside. Combine buttermilk and vanilla together in a small bowl. Beat sugar and butter with mixer until light and fluffy. Add eggs, one at a time, until creamy. Add cocoa mixture; beat well. Add flour mixture alternately with buttermilk mixture; beat until well blended. Combine baking soda and vinegar in small bowl and gently fold into batter with a spatula. Spoon batter into prepared muffin cups, fill two-thirds full. Bake 15 to 18 minutes or until toothpick inserted comes out clean. Cool on wire racks 10 minutes and remove from pan. Frost cupcakes with cream cheese icing; top with red sprinkles.

Cream Cheese Icing

1 stick butter (½ cup), room temperature

1 (8-ounce) package cream cheese, softened

1 tablespoon vanilla

6 to 8 cups powdered sugar

Cream butter and cream cheese until light and smooth. Add vanilla; mix well. Add powdered sugar one cup at a time until you reach the desired consistency. Pipe onto cupcakes and top with red sprinkles.

Heart-Shaped Cookies

5 cups all-purpose flour

2 cups sugar

1 teaspoon baking powder

¼ teaspoon baking soda

1 teaspoon salt

1 cup butter (2 sticks)

4 large eggs, room temperature

¼ cup milk

2 teaspoons vanilla

Preheat oven to 350°F. In large bowl, mix together flour, sugar, baking powder, baking soda, and salt. Cut in butter until mixture resembles coarse crumbs. Add eggs and mix well. Beat in milk and vanilla. Cover and chill at least 2 hours. Work with one-third of dough at a time on well-floured surface; roll dough to ¼-inch thick. Cut into heart shapes and place on lightly greased cookie sheet. Bake for 8 to 10 minutes, only until edges are the slightest brown. Cool 5 minutes; loosen cookies from cookie sheet. Ice cookies or dip in chocolate.

ICING:

2 cups powdered sugar, sifted

2 tablespoons butter, room temperature

¼ teaspoon almond extract (optional)

4 to 5 teaspoons milk

In a small bowl, beat together powdered sugar, butter, and almond extract with electric mixer. Beat in milk until icing is of piping consistency. For spreadable icing, add more milk. Red food coloring can be added if desired for heart shaped cookies.

DIPPING CHOCOLATE:

1 (12 ounce) package semisweet or milk chocolate chips

4 to 6 tablespoons oil

Pour chocolate chips in saucepan over low heat, or use a double boiler. Add oil and stir continually as chocolate melts. When melted, remove from heat and dip one side of each heart cookie; place on parchment or wax paper atop cookie sheet. Chill to set. Note: Ghirardelli® melting chocolates can be used in place of above recipe.

Lovers' Midnight Spiced Hot Chocolate

2 cups milk

1 ounce semi-sweet chocolate

4 tablespoons cocoa powder

2 tablespoons warm water, approximately

¼ cup sugar

1 teaspoon ground cinnamon

½ teaspoon finely pulverized coffee granules

1 teaspoon cornstarch

½ teaspoon pure vanilla

2 pinches crushed red pepper flakes

In a 2-quart saucepan, heat milk over low heat. Melt chocolate in a small glass bowl in a microwave. Whisk cocoa, warm water, sugar, cinnamon, coffee granules, vanilla, and cornstarch into warm milk. Stir chocolate mixture into warmed milk. Stir in red pepper flakes. Heat until frothy. Pour into warmed-up glass mugs. Add marshmallows or top with fresh whipped cream.

Linda's Old Fashioned Sugar Cookie

1½ cups all-purpose flour, sifted

½ teaspoon baking powder

½ teaspoon salt

½ teaspoon baking soda

¾ cup sugar

½ cup shortening (if using butter, increase flour slightly)

1 egg, room temperature

2 heaping teaspoons milk

1 teaspoon vanilla

Preheat oven to 375°F. Sift together flour, baking powder, salt, soda, and sugar. Cut in shortening until mixture resembles coarse meal. Blend in egg, milk, and vanilla. Roll out on floured (use plenty!) board. Cut with cookie cutter; place on ungreased cookie sheets. Bake for about 6 to 8 minutes. <u>Note</u>: Ice if desired.

Peppermint Ice Cream

4 (7½ ounce) bags striped, round, hard peppermint candies

2 cups heavy cream

2 cups light cream, divided

In a blender or food processor bowl, place unwrapped candies and 1 cup light cream. Cover and blend or process until candies are crushed. Pour peppermint mixture into freezer can of an ice cream freezer. Stir in the remaining 1 cup light cream and heavy cream. Freeze according to manufacturer's directions. Makes 1½ quarts.

Strawberry Filled Cupcakes

- 2 cups all-purpose flour
- 2 ½ teaspoons baking powder
- 1 teaspoon salt
- 1 cup milk
- 2 teaspoons vanilla
- 1½ cups plus 3 tablespoons sugar, divided
- ½ cup butter, softened
- 3 eggs, room temperature
- 1½ cups whipping cream, cold
- 2 quarts fresh strawberries

Preheat oven to 350°F. Spray 18 standard muffin cups with nonstick spray. Combine flour, baking powder, and salt in medium bowl. Combine milk and vanilla in a small bowl. Beat 1½ cups sugar and butter in large bowl with mixer at medium speed until creamy. Add eggs one at a time. Add flour mixture alternately with milk mixture, beating until well blended. Spoon batter into greased muffin pan, ¾ full. Bake 15 to 18 minutes or until toothpick inserted comes out clean. Cool cupcakes on cooling rack 10 minutes. Remove from pans; cool completely on wire racks. Beat whipping cream in large bowl with electric mixer at high speed until soft peaks form. Gradually add remaining 3 tablespoons sugar; beat until stiff peaks form. Cut cupcakes in half crosswise. Place 2 tablespoons whipped cream and strawberries in the middle. Top with additional whipped cream and strawberries.

Lemon Bars

If your family or friends like lemon, give them a special lemon treat for Valentine's Day.

- 2½ cups all-purpose flour, divided
- ½ cup confectioners' sugar
- ¾ cup butter
- ½ teaspoon baking powder
- 4 large eggs, lightly beaten
- 2 cups sugar
- 1 teaspoon lemon rind, optional
- ⅓ cup lemon juice
- Confectioners' sugar

Preheat oven to 350°F. In mixing bowl, combine 1½ cup flour and ½ cup confectioners' sugar; cut in the butter with fork or pastry blender until crumbly. Spoon mixture into a greased 9x13-inch pan; press firmly and evenly into bottom of pan. Bake for 20 minutes until lightly browned. Combine remaining 1 cup flour and baking powder. In separate bowl, combine eggs, 2 cups sugar, lemon rind, and lemon juice. Stir in flour mixture. Pour over prepared crust. Bake for 25 minutes until lightly brown and set. Cool and dust with confectioners' sugar.

TAMAR
A Woman of Great Suffering

Biblical Principle: Women do not have to live under the burden of shame, Christ came to set us free.

Read 2 Samuel 11:1–27 and 2 Samuel Chapter 13 in order to prepare.

We live in a sinful world where pain is inflicted by evil people, upon many innocent women. They are physically violated, often by incest, and left to bear their hurt, pain, suffering, and shame alone. Where can they turn for help? Tamar turned to her brother Absalom.

Today, we will read about her life and about the life of a modern day woman, who was physically violated. She took her pain, suffering, and shame to the only One who could bear them—Jesus Christ. The One who restored, healed, and gave her hope.

Statistics for reference in preparing for today's lesson: [12]

- 1 out of 6 women in the U.S. has experienced an attempted rape or completed rape.

- In 2005, there were overall 191,670 victims of rape.

- According to the Bureau of Justice Statistics, 38% of victims were raped by a friend or acquaintance, 28% by "an intimate," 7% by another relative, and 26% committed by a stranger to the victim.

- About four out of ten sexual assaults take place at the victim's own home.

- In 47% of rapes, both the victim and the perpetrator had been drinking.

- A survey of more than 23,000 college students across nine higher education institutions found that 1 in 5 students in their fourth year of college had experienced attempted or completed sexual assault while in college.

- About 65% of the surveyed college rape victims reported the incident to a friend, family member, or roommate. Less than 10% reported it to police or school officials.

- According to statistical average over the past five years, about 60% of all rapes or sexual assaults in the United States are never reported to the authorities.

- These statistics are of women ages twelve and above.

Biblical History for Lesson—First Samuel ends with the death of Israel's first king, Saul. Second Samuel records the history of King David's reign. The book covers many events of David's reign and personal life, including his making Jerusalem the political and religious center of the nation, the establishing the Davidic dynasty, David's great military victories, his shameful sin with Bathsheba, and his mistake in numbering the people. Tucked within the pages of this book is one of the most tragic stories in all God's Word—the story of David's daughter, Tamar, and her brother, Amnon.[13] For a clearer picture of the events that led up to this story, read 2 Samuel 11:1–27.

[12] "Statistics." http:/rain.org/statistics.
[13] "A marriage relationship with one's half-sister was forbidden by Mosaic Law" (Ryrie, 2008).

Now that we have some history on David, Tamar's father, let's pick up the story of Tamar.

In verse 2, it states that Amnon was *frustrated* because of his sister.

- He obviously had feelings for her that went beyond the natural brother-sister relationship.
- He was consumed with lust toward his half-sister.

It says in 2 Samuel 13:2b, "And it was improper for Amnon to do anything to her." NKJV

Throughout the Bible, we see one example after another of those who followed bad advice: there was Eve who listened to the serpent, then Adam who listened to Eve, and Sarah who listened to Abraham and lied about who she was in order that he might not be killed, on and on we could go. We see that Amnon proves to be no different than these.

"But Amnon had a friend whose name was Jonadab, the son of Shimeah, David's brother; and Jonadab was a very shrewd man." (Jonadab was actually Amnon's cousin) 2 Samuel 13:3 NAS

- Additional words for shrewd are: "crafty" or "streetwise." You get the feeling Jonadab was not a man to be trusted; you certainly would not want to take his advice.
- Jonadab devised a deceptive plan and Amnon did as he suggested.

"So Amnon lay down and pretended to be ill; when the king came to him, Amnon said to the king, 'Please let my sister Tamar come and make me a couple of cakes in my sight, that I may eat from her hand.'" 2 Samuel 13:6 NAS

Now, this is the amazing part; David does as Amnon requested.

"Then David sent to the house for Tamar, saying, 'Go now to your brother Amnon's house, and prepare food for him' You have to wonder how David missed what was about to happen." 2 Samuel 13:7 NAS

I am wondering, at this point, did Tamar realize what was happening? I truly believe she had no idea, but she soon would.

"Then Amnon said to Tamar, 'Bring the food into the bedroom that I may eat from your hand.' So, Tamar took the cakes which she had made and brought them into the bedroom to her brother." 2 Samuel 13:10 NAS

We see in Tamar a spirit of obedience and trust. She obeyed her father; she trusted both her father and her brother. But, we see within Absalom, her half-brother, a spirit of deceit and lust.

"When she brought them to him to eat, he took hold of her and said to her, 'Come, lie with me, my sister.'" 2 Samuel 13:11 NAS

Charles Stanley says, "With his many wives and concubines and his illicit affair with Bathsheba, David had not modeled for his sons a godly love life. Children learn better by example than by words."[14]

The NAS Ryrie Study Bible says of 2 Samuel 13:14–15, "Amnon's love was really lust, which when gratified turned to hatred."

---

[14] Charles Stanley, Charles Stanley's Life Principles Bible, NKJV (Thomas Nelson Inc., 2005).

Charles Stanley goes on to say, "Lust relieved frequently gives way to hatred expressed. Lust often masquerades as love, but the two result in profoundly different outcomes."

- Afterwards, she pleaded with him to do the right thing and not to send her away, for she would bear public shame the rest of her life.

- "But she said to him, 'No, because this wrong in sending me away is greater than the other that you have done to me! Yet he would not listen to her. Then he called his young man who attended him and said, 'Now throw this woman out of my presence and lock the door behind her.'" 2 Samuel 13:16–17 NAS

Often, those who have been physically violated have been betrayed by those closest to them—the person who was supposed to protect them. David failed as a parent. He failed to protect his daughter, to console her, and he failed to punish his son appropriately.

"Then Tamar put ashes on her head, and tore her robe of many colors that was on her, and laid her hand on her head and went away crying bitterly." 2 Samuel 13:19 NKJV

"She was wearing a long sleeved gown (That's how virgin princesses used to dress from early adolescence on.) Tamar poured ashes on her head, then she ripped the long sleeved gown, held her head in her hands, and walked away, sobbing as she went." 2 Samuel 13:18–19 The Message Bible

- Her brother, Absalom, takes her into his home.

- He is filled with anger toward, Amnon, for violating his sister, Tamar.

- He orders his men to kill Amnon, and they do.

- This act of violent revenge does not remove Tamar's pain, suffering, or her shame.

Joni Eareckson Tada says about suffering, "Suffering is when God uses what He hates to accomplish the good He loves."[15]

Iva May in W3 says, "We live in a world where fallen people do fallen things. Bitterness settles in and poisons the soul when the shame is not released to the Lord Jesus. He knows and He understands. God, too, has suffered at the hands of evil doers."[16]

IF TIME ALLOWS—Assign the following verses to be read aloud: Isaiah 53:4–5; 10–12 NIV; Deuteronomy 32:35 NIV; Isaiah 61:1–3; Psalms 94:1, and discuss.

Iva May in her W3 study said, "It is only in Christ that shame can be replaced with dignity of redemption."

Discipling Leader—Read the following modern-day story about a woman who was raped and took her pain, suffering, and shame to the only One who could help her—Jesus Christ our Redeemer, our Shame Bearer.

> My name is Angel and this is my story. I was raised in a home where the name of Jesus was never spoken of, just blasphemy of His holy name. My father was raised in a Christian home, which caused him to despise the church his entire adult life. (The reason why, I never knew.) My mother was a devout feminist and taught me to never depend on any man to do anything for me. So, I took my mother's advice and

[15] Joni Eareckson-Tada. *The God I Love*. (Grand Rapids: Zondervan, 2003).
[16] Iva May. *W3: Women, Worldview, and the Word*. (Chronological Bible Discipleship, 2007). Revised 2010.

began to live my life entirely about me; I had goals for myself from a very early age. After graduating from high school, I immediately left the small town in which I grew up and headed to the big city. I had my life all figured out and planned down to what I was doing next. But my life changed for the worst (or so I thought) at 3:45 a.m. one night when a man broke into my apartment and raped me with a gun to my head and a knife to my throat. All I could think about at that moment was that I just knew I was going to die and if I did, I would spend eternity in hell. I was asking out loud for God not to let me die. Even though, I didn't know Him as my Savior and Lord at the time, He allowed me to live and make it through that horrible night and ultimately every day thereafter. I was distraught for about five years after the rape. I was trying to forget it ever happened; I used every means from prescription pills to psychiatry—nothing worked. The Holy Spirit began drawing me at age twenty-three, and I finally repented of my sins and asked Jesus to forgive me and to save me and He did. The bondage that comes from a life of sin doesn't change just because you get saved. For me to be free in Christ, I had to give God thanks for EVERYTHING—for this is God's will for me in Christ Jesus—and that included allowing me to be raped. His Word tells me this in I Thessalonians 5:3. God also says in Isaiah 55:8 that His thoughts are not my thoughts and His ways are not my ways, so I don't understand why I was raped. I just know if it hadn't happened to me, I possibly would have never come to the place in my life of knowing Jesus Christ as Lord. It was the greatest night in my life, not the worst. My Savior is one who loves me and comforts me in ways that I cannot describe. In 2 Samuel 13:30, Absalom told his sister Tamar, after his brother Amnon raped her, "Be quiet now, my sister, he is your brother. Don't take this thing to heart." Tamar lived in Absalom's house, a desolate woman. I am so grateful that I didn't stay quiet and become a desolate woman, as Tamar did. If you remain silent and try to forget anything that God has allowed you to go through without giving Him thanks and praise for it, you will become desolate, as Tamar did. Satan means everything for evil and destruction but God means it for good.[17]

Discipling Leader: Be especially attentive to the Spirit's leading following this lesson before moving on to the discussion questions. Today's topic is a very sensitive one and may require individual ministry and prayer for some of the young women participating in the class.

Discuss the following question with the class:

1. How has the story of Tamar's life impacted you?

2. What will you do differently as a result of studying the life of Tamar?

If time allows, utilize the Discussion Questions and the Examining the Heart Questions.

DISCUSSION QUESTIONS

1. Who was Tamar and how was she described? *She was King David's daughter by Maacah of Geshur. Tamar was a beautiful young woman.*

2. How was Amnon described? *He was Tamar's half-brother.*

[17] Shared with permission by Angel Osborne.

3. What advice does Jonadab give Amnon? "O son of the king, why are you so depressed morning after morning? Will you not tell me?" Then Amnon said to him, "I am in love with Tamar, the sister of my brother Absalom." Jonadab then said to him, "Lie down on your bed and pretend to be ill; when your father comes to see you, say to him, 'Please let my sister Tamar come and give me some food to eat, and let her prepare the food in my sight, that I may see it and eat from her hand.'"

4. What was Tamar's response to her father's request? "So Tamar went to her brother Amnon's house, and he was lying down. And she took dough, kneaded it, made cakes in his sight, and baked the cakes. She took the pan and dished them out before him, but he refused to eat. And Amnon said, 'Have everyone go out from me.' So everyone went out from him."

5. How does Amnon take advantage of Tamar's trust? *He tricks her into coming close to his bed, she thinks it is in order to feed him, because he is ill, but he has something else in mind.*

6. What is Tamar's response to Amnon? "But she answered him,' No, my brother, do not violate me, for such a thing is not done in Israel; do not do this disgraceful thing! As for me, where could I get rid of my reproach? And as for you, you will be like one of the fools in Israel. Now therefore, please speak to the king, for he will not withhold me from you.'"

7. Did Amnon honor his sister's request? *No, he did not.* "However, he would not listen to her, since he was stronger than she; he violated her and lay with her."

8. Amnon gave way to his flesh; how did he feel afterwards toward Tamar? *He hated her.* "Then Amnon hated her with a very great hatred; for the hatred with which he hated her was greater than the love with which he had loved her. And Amnon said to her, "Get up and go away."

9. What was the outcome of Amnon's lust for Tamar? *She paid the price for his lust and violation of her; she lived as an unmarried woman in the house of her brother Absalom with life-long shame.*

10. What was the outcome for Amnon? *He was hated by his brother; he never saw his sister again and eventually he was killed by order of Absalom, his brother.*

11. What was David's response to what his son Amnon did to Tamar? *He was angry, but did not inflict upon Amnon the punishment due him by law—death. You do not see him going and comforting his daughter or apologizing for not protecting her as a father should.*

Examining the Heart

Discipling Leader: After reading Angel's personal testimony and discussing the above questions, close in prayer; be especially sensitive to those who might have suffered as Tamar and Angel have. Acknowledge that shame can follow such an offense. Shame is not from God. God sent His Son to remove all our shame, he carried it to the cross. We can live free from shame in Christ Jesus!

Week Five

ETIQUETTE FOR CHILDREN

Week Five

LESSON PLAN

I. LEADER OPENS IN PRAYER

II. DEVOTIONAL

- Hannah—*A Woman of Sacrifice*. Read 1 Samuel 1:1–28, 2:1–11, and 2:18–21 in order to prepare. For help in preparation, refer to the Devotional section in today's lesson.

- **Biblical Principle**: When we choose to give God everything, it will cost us something—it will require a sacrifice.

III. LESSON—For high school/college, single, and newly married young women consider replacing this week's lesson with the optional week titled Shower and Party Etiquette.

- If the leadership is uncomfortable teaching today's topic and knows of a qualified guest for teaching on children's etiquette, consider inviting the guest to address today's topic.

- If the leadership chooses to teach today's topic, as you begin, distribute the following verses and have the participants read aloud. Discuss the verses and the application of training up children: Proverbs 22:6, Proverbs 23:13, and Ephesians 6:1 and 4. These verses should open the way for the leadership to cover the topics below related to children's etiquette.

- Using the *What In the World Am I to Do?* Activity sheet in this week's lesson, read aloud a few of the behavioral situations and ask the participants the proper way to handle the child in each of the situations. Discuss the correct response of the parent and the etiquette lesson they would desire to teach the child. <u>Note</u>: Refer to the answer sheet at the end of the lesson.

- Consider using resources such as today's lesson sheets, web-sites, and written material to cover a few or all of the following topics:

    Children's Table Manners
    Dining In/Dining Out for Children
    Please, Thank You, and Excuse Me
    Introductions and Greetings for Children
    Playing Well with Others
    Children's Etiquette for Social Media
    Etiquette for Children's Devices
    Party Manners
    Travel Manners
    Shopping, Offices, and Waiting Room Manners
    R.E.S.P.E.C.T

- **Optional**: Have samples of books, games, and resources related to Children's Etiquette available for the participants to view.

- **Optional Activity**: If time allows, consider this activity for teaching on children's etiquette. Divide the class into groups of four and take fifteen minutes, letting them play an etiquette game geared for children, such as BLUNDERS or *365 Manners Kids Should Know*, just to give them a sense of the benefit these resources are in teaching children manners.[18]

IV. TIME IN THE KITCHEN

- **Optional Activity**: If time allows, choose a Time in the Kitchen recipe to prepare from page 263.

V. WEEK FIVE LESSON SHEETS

- Introduction—*Thank You*
  What in the World am I to Do?
  Children's Etiquette
  Children's Etiquette for Social Media
  Etiquette for Children's Devices
  Parent Pointers
  Resources and Books on Children's Etiquette
  Devotional on Hannah
  Answer Sheet: What in the World am I to Do?

VI. VI. EQUIPMENT FOR WEEK FIVE

- Books, children's etiquette games, and materials related to teaching etiquette for children.

- If Time in the Kitchen recipe is chosen for today, you will need all the ingredients called for in the recipe.

- Plates and forks for enjoying the recipe prepared.

---

[18] Games may be checked out from the library, purchased online, or in an educational resource store.

Introduction

THANK YOU!

When I was a little girl, it was *expected* of each of the four children in my family to set the table in the evenings before dinner. We ate together every night as a family. My mother taught us where to place the plate, glass, napkin, and utensils. Once we were shown, it was our responsibility to remember and to place each piece correctly. I grew up knowing how to set a table because it was *expected* of me.

We didn't eat at a restaurant as a family until I was a young teen. We didn't have the financial means to do so. But knowing my dad, I can tell you if we had been able to eat out, we would not have been running around the restaurant. We would not have been allowed to throw food or leave a mess for the bus boy to clean up. I know this because we were not allowed to act that way at home, so in public, we would have been *expected* to show the same respect for others that was shown at home.

Recently, I was visiting my niece, Jessica, her husband, Luke, and their two little boys, Micah, age 4 and Levi, age 2. I told them that if they wanted to eat out, I would treat. I have never known a young couple who could turn down an offer like that! Luke chose the restaurant. Once seated, I anticipated that Jessica would pull out her iPhone for the boys, after all that is what young couples with kids (and without kids) do these days. But, she did not. In fact, she didn't even have toys or any objects to entertain them. The waiter brought a coloring sheet and crayons, they did busy themselves with that for a few minutes. The service was slow that day, but at no point did Jessica or Luke resort to their iPhones to occupy the boys—instead they were *expected* to sit nicely until each one had finished their meal. I was very proud of them for teaching their boys how to act in a restaurant—for *expecting* good behavior and getting it!

Other *expectations* my parents had:

- Address adults by Mr. and Mrs. or Miss. We were not allowed to call an adult by their first name unless given permission by the individual.

- To say please, thank you, yes ma'am and yes sir, no ma'am and no sir, when answering our parents or another adult, and to write thank-you notes for a kindness shown us.

- Respect of other people and their property. We were not allowed to walk through a neighbor's yard and certainly not allowed to ride our bikes through their yard.

These things my parents taught and demonstrated before me are called *Rules of Etiquette* or *Manners*. Manners are a person's way of behaving toward others, their way of speaking to and treating others. Perhaps your parents never taught or demonstrated these Rules of Etiquette, but you do not have to make that same mistake. Just Google the words *Children's Etiquette* and you can educate yourself and your children. You will reap the benefit and the blessings of having children who are well mannered—so will all those who come in contact with your children—as I did that day with Micah and Levi. You will only get the type of behavior from your children that is *expected* of them and that is modeled for them—who knows—one day they may thank you!

WHAT AM I TO DO?

Read each of the following scenarios. What should the parent's response be and what rule of etiquette should be taught?

SITUATION #1

You are in the play area at the mall with your children for two hours. Upon packing up to leave, you decide to have lunch in the food court on the level below. As you approach the escalator, your five-year-old son jumps in front of an elderly woman and almost sends her flying forward down the escalator. What in the world are you to do?

SITUATION #2

You and your family are in a restaurant with some friends and their children. It has been a long evening and the service is slow. The other children have been instructed to stay in their seats, but your children are getting fussy and want down. You finally give in so you can finish your conversation with your friends. Your children are running through the restaurant and almost knock over a waiter with a tray full of food. What in the world are you to do?

SITUATION #3

The phone rings and you have gone upstairs, so your eight-year-old son answers it. As you descend the stairs, you hear him say, "Yeah sure, hold on a minute." Then he slams the phone down on the counter and yells up to you to come get the phone. What in the world are you to do?

SITUATION #4

Your three-year-old daughter sees a candy bar she wants as you are checking out at the grocery store. You tell her you are not going to buy the candy today and she proceeds to throw herself down on the floor. The man behind you sees what is taking place and offers her a piece of candy from his pocket. She slaps it out of his hand. What in the world are you to do?

SITUATION #5

You and your two sons, ages four and six, are at the park playing on the swings when a little boy, age five, comes up and asks if he can please use the swing. Your four-year-old says no and refuses to get off. What in the world are you to do?

SITUATION #6

Your husband's parents have asked your children over for dinner. They have prepared all kinds of fun food and even planned ice cream sundaes for dessert. As you arrive to pick up the children, you hear your youngest complaining because they did not have the flavor of ice cream she likes. What in the world are you to do?

SITUATION #7

You are in the waiting room at the doctor's office and the children are playing. All is going well until you hear another child tell your son to shut up, and horror of all horrors, you hear your son tell the other child to shut up. What in the world are you to do?

SITUATION #8

Your family has been out to eat. As you are exiting the restaurant, your two oldest children decide to race out the door and run to the car. As they burst through the door, they almost knock over a young pregnant woman. What in the world are you to do?

SITUATION #9

You and your family are at a friend's home for dinner. After the prayer, your five-year-old reaches across the table and grabs a chicken breast off the meat platter and begins to dig in. What in the world are you to do?

SITUATION #10

You are at church and an elderly man comes up to your nine-year-old son and puts his hand out in order to shake hands and introduce himself. Your son refuses to shake his hand and hangs his head. What in the world are you to do?

SITUATION #11

It is bedtime and your four-year-old has just been handed a snack before bed, but refuses to say thank you for it. What in the world are you to do?

SITUATION #12

Your six-year-old daughter is having her birthday party. She opens a present given from a friend and begins to complain that it's not what she wanted. What in the world are you to do?

Answers: The proper responses to the above situations are found on page 142.

CHILDREN'S ETIQUETTE [19]

You know you are raising a gentleman and a lady if they know how to ...

1. Say please, thank you, and excuse me on a consistent basis.
2. Do not point out other children's lack of manners.
3. Always knock on a closed door, particularly one that leads to a bathroom or bedroom.
4. Remove cap or hat when sitting down to eat at a table in a home or restaurant.

Introductions and Greetings

1. Refer to an adult as Mr. or Mrs. until asked to do otherwise.
2. Greet and converse with adult friends and acquaintances in a friendly and courteous manner.
3. Shows respect by standing when introduced.
4. Performs introductions, using first and last names among peers and Mr. and Mrs. when referring to adults.
5. When introducing family members to others, explains the relationship. *"This is my mother, Mrs. Chadwick, and my sister, Lilly."*

Shopping, Offices, and Waiting Rooms

1. Stays close to parents when shopping or in other public places.
2. Not greedy with samples in a grocery store.
3. Does not badger parent or other adult to buy things.
4. Does not rummage around, exploring desks or closets, in offices, or peeking under doors in dressing rooms.
5. Gives seat to an adult in a crowded waiting room.
6. Uses trash receptacles in public places.
7. When entering buildings, open door for adults, elderly, and handicapped persons.

Plays Well with Others

1. Does not shove or hit.
2. Does not throw objects at another child.
3. Shares toys with other children.
4. Does not spit on other children.

---

[19] This section extracted from Kay West, *How to Raise a Gentleman—A Civilized Guide to helping Your Son Through His Uncivilized Childhood*, Revised and Expanded (Nashville, Rutledge Hill Press- Division of Thomas Nelson Publishers, Inc., 2001, Update 2012).

5. Waits patiently in line for turn at an activity.

6. Does not push or crowd other children in line.

7. Does not hog the swings, but takes turns.

8. Does not knock down another child's sand castle or mud fort.

Party Manners

1. Considerate of other children who weren't invited or just didn't attend a party by not talking about the party.

2. Greets and bids farewell to the guest of honor, and thanks parents for the invitation.

3. Makes an effort to include everyone in the fun and thanks every guest for coming.

4. Never tries to steal the spotlight at another person's party.

5. Participates in all the party activities if possible. Realizes that by accepting the invitation he or she should be a cheerful guest.

6. Does not ask for more of anything—drinks, pizza, popcorn, candy, cake, pony rides, laser tag games, or arcade tokens—unless offered.

7. Never says, I already have this, when opening a present.

8. Sends invitations through the mail, rather than backpack.

Dining In and Out

1. Washes hands and removes hat before coming to table.

2. Keeps all four legs of chair on the floor.

3. Keeps elbows off the table, does not chew with mouth open, or talk with mouth full.

4. Does not play with one's hair at the table.

5. Asks for salt or pepper to be passed, rather than reaching across the table.

6. Does not take the last helping without offering it to someone else.

7. When being served, does not refuse a dish unless allergic to it. Instead, asks for a very small amount.

8. Does not eat before others begin, before host is seated, or before the blessing.

9. Asks to be excused from table when finished.

10. Does not talk about dessert while everyone is still eating the salad.

11. When dining in a restaurant does not get up from the table and wander about.

12. Does not waste or play with condiments on the table.

13. Treats the server cordially and with respect, saying thank you when meal is delivered and when plate is taken away.

Traveling Manners

1. Shows respect and courtesy toward the parent driving carpool and does not engage in back seat verbal or physical jousting.

2. Removes all belongings from the carpool car.

3. Does not leave trash in another's car.

4. Does not try repeatedly to open a bathroom door that is clearly occupied in an attempt to hurry the occupant.

5. Leaves lavatory in better condition than found it.

6. Keeps volume of music at level not disruptive to others.

7. If someone holds the door open for him, he is to say "thank you."

Temper, Temper

1. Does not express anger, disappointment, or frustration by using bad language or insulting someone.

2. Does not express anger, disappointment, or frustration by throwing, kicking, hitting, biting, or breaking something.

3. If loses temper and does any of the above, needs to apologize as soon as he/she has calmed down.

4. Does not shout to get someone's attention, or pout, sulk, or cry to get what they want.

5. Never uses words like fatso, stupid, idiot, retard, ugly, when addressing another person.

CHILDREN'S ETIQUETTE
for Social Media

At the rate we are going, communication skills will be non-existent among young people due to the constant usage of iPhones. Sociability is now seen as a text, twitter, and snap-chat instead of face to face communication. Families are drifting further and further apart due to the influence of "outsiders" in their children's lives via social media.

Phones have become a part of a child's body, person, and identity. Many find it hard, and even impossible, to function emotionally or socially apart from their phone. Parents are ignorant of the new technology leaving them in the dark as to how to control this out-of-control iPhone usage. But, the good news is that you as the parent, ignorant or not, pay the bill and **you can set the boundaries**.

The price of your child's heart, soul, mind, and emotional well-being is too high for you not to set boundaries on their social media. A boundary is something that indicates or fixes a limit or extent. Even if your child doesn't understand that you are setting boundaries for his good, the ultimate responsibility for protecting their physical and emotional well-being, and controlling their behavior is the parent's job.

WHAT CAN PARENTS DO?

- PARENTS need to set the example. If the perception your child has is that your phone is more important than he is—his phone will become more important than you!

- Limit time on the devices (screen time) the child has access to in your home. You bought it, you make monthly payments on it—you control when it will be used. Define what is a screen.

- Make a list of rules and expect that they will be followed or the technology will be taken away. Example: No cell phone out at school unless required by a teacher, no cell phone at the dinner table, no cell phone will be allowed to be taken into their bedroom, no texting past 8 p.m., no texting unless their homework is completed, etc. When your rules are broken—take the device away for long enough to make an impression!

- There are many tracking and monitoring systems that can be placed on all your devices. This will help you keep strict tabs on all the text, emails, tweets, and snap-chats your child receives. Example: Integrity Online, Accountable2You, Covenant Eyes, etc.

- No device should be allowed at social gatherings: church, party for friend or family, dinner, or eating out, etc.

ETIQUETTE FOR
Children's Devices

WITH FAMILY AND FRIENDS

1. **Ask permission**: An elementary-age child should ask the adult for permission to use the phone. This reinforces the idea that phone usage is a privilege.

2. **Be courteous** to those you are with; turn off your phone if it will be interrupting a conversation or activity.

3. **Private/Personal information** can be forwarded, so don't text it, especially in a group text. Example: Saying that their dad is on a business trip, or telling about a fight between them and a sibling, etc.

4. **Texting doesn't replace talking**. Children/Tweens should understand that texting should not take the place of one-on-one interaction with their friends/family. If your child is going to bond with his or her friends, you need to encourage their spending time together.

5. **Don't text in front of others**. Explain to your children/tweens that they should never, ever text another person while they're spending time with a friend. It's extremely rude at any age and can hurt feelings. **Only exception** would be the need to text either parent as to a ride or other important information.

6. **Text messaging** and phone etiquette requires children/tweens to think about how their actions make other people feel. Talk to your children/tweens about thinking their text through before typing it and pushing "send."

7. **Be kind**. Children/Tweens need to understand that they are responsible for what they text to other people. Teach your children/tweens to refrain from gossiping about others, trashing others, and being unkind in general.

8. **It's all about context**. Explain to your children/tweens that sometimes text messages are misunderstood because of a lack of context. The person receiving the text message can't see the sender's facial expressions or hear their tone of voice. Jokes and sarcastic comments may cause hurt feelings if they're passed along in a text message.

9. **Text at the right time**. Your child should refrain from texting during class, at church, dinner, the movies, a friend's birthday party, a funeral, or in other public settings. The same applies if your family is going out for a meal or enjoying an activity together. Also, no texting early in the morning or late at night. If you, the parent, control the phone during those hours of the day, it should not be a problem.

10. **Think before you text**. Teach your child/tween to refrain from texting a friend if they're in a fight or are angry with one another. Ask your child/tween to wait until they have calmed down. Encourage them to work things out in person or over the phone.

11. **Making a call**. Teach children/tweens to introduce themselves to whoever answers the phone

before asking to speak to their friends. Example, "Hello, this is Will. May I speak to Drew?"

12. **Answering a call**: The child/tween should use a polite tone when answering the phone. Once the person identifies him or herself, the child should ask, "Who would you like to speak with?" If the person is not there, particularly if it's a parent, the child should say that the person is not able to come to the phone at that time. As many parents know, children should never tell callers that mom or dad are not home.

13. **Upon answering**, the child should never give his or her first name or the family's surname. A proper greeting would be, "Hello, may I ask who's calling?" This immediately puts your child at an advantage and immediately puts an adult off guard.

14. **Ending a call**: Teach your child/tween how to end a conversation politely, with good manners. He or she should say, "My dad is calling me to dinner, so I have to go. But it was very nice speaking with you, Libby."

IN PUBLIC

1. **Control your phone**, don't let it control you!

2. **Watch your words**, especially when others can overhear you.

3. **Speak softly**. No one wants to overhear a private conversation.

4. **Keep it short and sweet**. Children/Tweens should keep text messages short and to-the-point. If a "conversation" goes on for more than a few minutes, encourage your child to pick up the phone and continue the conversation by talking with their friend.

5. **Don't make calls** in a library, theater, church, grocery or store check-out line, or from your table in a restaurant.

6. **Don't text during class/school**.

7. **When in public** and the phone must remain on and could bother those around them, instruct them to use the silent ring mode. If it does ring in public, move away to talk.

8. **Keep content in mind**. Teach your child/tween that they should never deliver bad news in a text message. Example: "I heard your soccer coach quit!" or "I heard you and Sarah had a fight."

9. **Texting is a privilege, not a right**. Texting should be regarded as a privilege, and your child/tween should know that bad behavior will result in the loss of that privilege. Remind your tween that part of the responsibility of using a cell phone is following the family cell phone etiquette rules. That's a responsibility of growing up.

10. **No annoying ring tones** will be allowed.

11. **When with a group** and expecting a phone call, teach them to warn the people they are with that they are expecting a call and, therefore, they will need to step away to receive it.

12. **Nothing takes precedence over** (is more important than) **people**—especially an iPhone!

PARENT POINTERS

TEMPER TANTRUMS AND OTHER BEHAVIOR...

- Do not respond to a temper tantrum by giving a child what he/she wants or promising to give a treat if he/she stops.

- Do not respond to a temper tantrum with a blast of your own. Remember, you as the parent are to set the example!

- If child is having a temper tantrum in a public place, remove him/her from other people's presence.

- Do not react to your child's bad behavior with similar bad behavior. If you have a child who bites, do not bite back so your child can see how it feels, or hit a child to stop the child from hitting. You as the parent are to set the example!

- Do your best NOT to raise your voice in anger to a child. You need to set a good example!

- Do not fight with your spouse in front of your children. You need to set a good example!

- If you lose your temper in front of your child, apologize; if you lose your temper with your child, apologize. You as the parent are to set the example!

- Accept apologies quickly and graciously when they are made to you.

- Get your children to school on time, properly dressed, and prepared with what they need for the day. Remember, you as the parent are to set the example!

- Let your children know that within the school the faculty and administration are in charge.

- Communicate frequently with your child's teachers about your child's behavior in class, regarding play and work. Discipline may need to be administered at home.

- During church do not whisper with your spouse, friends, or children. As the parent, you set the example!

- Pay attention to the service, including the sermon, and do not use the time as an opportunity to pay bills or catch up on correspondence, or text! As the parent, you set the example!

- Address the clergy with their proper titles. As the parent, you set the example!

- Get your children in the habit of writing thank-you notes as young as possible.

- In sports, teach your children that games are meant to be fun, and if his conduct is making it less so, he cannot play.

- Teach children to include everyone who wants to play in the game, even if abilities are not as good as others.

- Yield to the authority of coaches and referees. If they need parents' advice, opinion, or help, they will ask. As the parent, you set the example!

- Do not do anything to embarrass your child ... yelling at umpires or calling the child by a private family nickname when he/she comes to bat.
- Resist urge to run onto the field to check a child's injury, or to usurp the coach's game plan or question his decisions. Remember, you as the parent set the example!

RESOURCES FOR CHILDREN'S ETIQUETTE

365 Manners Kids Should Know: Games, activities, other fun ways to help children learn proper etiquette by Sheryl Eberly

BOOKS FOR CHILDREN'S ETIQUETTE

A Kids Guide to Manners: 50 Fun Etiquette Lessons by Katherine Flannery

A Little Book of Manners: Courtesy and Kindnesss for Young Ladies by Emily Barnes

Don't Behave Like You Live in a Cave by Elizabeth Verdick

Dude That's Rude by Pamela Espeland

Emily's Everyday Manners by Cindy P. Senning

Emily Post's Table Manners for Kids by Cindy P. Senning

How to Raise a Gentleman—A Civilized Guide to Helping Your Son Through His Uncivilized Childhood by Kay West

How to Raise a Lady—A Civilized Guide to Helping Your Daughter Through Her Uncivilized Childhood by Kay West

My Manners Matter by Pat Thomas and Lesley Harker

Teeth Are Not for Biting by Elizabeth Verdick

The Giggly Guide of How to Behave at School by Phlippe Jalbert

The New Christian Charm Course: Today's Social Graces for Every Girl by Emily Hunter, Jody Capehart, and Angela Carnathan

You've Got Manners: Table Tips from A to Z for Kids of All Ages by Louise Eldering

DVD FOR CHILDREN'S ETIQUETTE

What Every Kid Should Know About Manners and Etiquette by Joel Swenson

HANNAH
A Woman of Sacrifice

Biblical Principle: When we choose to give God everything, it will cost us something—it will require a sacrifice.

Read 1 Samuel 1:1–28, 2:1–11, and 2:18–21 in order to prepare.

Biblical History for Lesson—Samuel emerged as the last judge. The book of 1 Samuel describes the transition of leadership in Israel from judges to kings. The book covers a period of about ninety-four years, beginning at the time of Samuel, Israel's final judge, moving through the ascension of Saul as the first king of Israel; continuing through David's anointing as king and the persecution of Saul that followed; and ending with the final years of Saul's reign. As the book opens, we are introduced to Elkannah, a man from the mountains of Ephraim. He was a Levite by birth and an Ephraimite by residence. Elkannah had two wives, Hannah and Peninnah. Note: Polygamy was allowed when there was a case of a childless marriage, although the practice caused great misery. Hannah was barren, while Peninnah had born several children to Elkannah. "Peninnah had children, but Hannah had no children." We see that it was Elkannah's habit to go yearly to worship. "And whenever the day came for Elkannah to make an offering, he would give portions to Peninniah his wife, and to all her sons and daughters. But to Hannah he would give a double portion, for he loved Hannah, although the Lord had closed her womb." (Ryrie, 2008)

Let's pick up the story in 1 Samuel 1:1–18. Elkannah had two wives that are mentioned in these verses. It stated that of the two, Elkannah loved Hannah.

> In 1 Samuel 1:6 it says of Hannah, "And her rival (Peninnah) also provoked her severely, to make her miserable, because the Lord had closed her womb. So it was year by year, she went up to the house of the Lord, that she (Peninnah) provoked her; therefore she wept and did not eat."

We see from this verse that Peninnah obviously taunted Hannah because she had born Elkannah several children, while Hannah had not.

Don't you just love Elkannah's response to Hannah's deep need to bear a child? Then Elkannah her husband said to her, "Hannah, why do you weep and why do you not eat and why is your heart sad? Am I not better to you than ten sons?" He basically says, "I am better than ten sons! Why do you desire a child when you have me?" He just does not get it! Her heart and her womb were empty; she desired a child more than anything.

Dianne's Personal Testimony: Note: The leader may want to share her testimony of a time in her life when she experienced great and bitter anguish. *I have been in a place of great and bitter anguish. I have laid myself out before the Lord and wept, petitioning Him for an answer to my prayers. Before my husband's diagnosis of Multiple Systems Atrophy, I had never experienced such fervency in my prayer life. Many times over the eleven year journey of Mark's suffering with Multiple Systems Atrophy, God had me in a place, where if He did not answer my prayers, I would have had no hope.*

Charles Stanley says of Hannah, "Hannah faced a battle she could not win on her own. When she finally fought that battle on her knees, she won a great victory. So can we." [20]

Hannah took her pain and her anguish to the only One who could answer the deepest desires of her heart—her heavenly Father.

Hannah's fervent prayer is found in 1 Samuel 1:10-18. Following her passionate prayer, Eli, the priest responds. He says, "How long will you make yourself drunk? Put away your wine from you."

There is a state of desperation in the heart of Hannah's fervent prayer. This was a place that without God's intervention, without His answering her prayer, her condition would not change.

The definition of fervent prayer is "pouring out one's soul before God."

Dianne's Personal Testimony: Note: The leader may want to share her testimony of a time in her life when she connected with God on a level she had never known before experiencing hardship. *For so long I have wondered why God allows hardship in the lives of His children. Hannah knew, and now I know—in order that His children connect with Him on a level they never knew before. I can honestly say, over these few years, I have connected with my heavenly Father on a level I had never known before.*

Eli tells Hannah to go in peace and, "May God grant your petition that you have asked of Him."

"Hannah vowed that if she were given a son, he would be dedicated to lifelong Levitical service and become a lifelong Nazirite"

Hannah so desired to bear a son, that she was willing to give him up if God would grant her request. What a sacrifice!

"And Elkannah had relations with his wife, and the Lord remembered her."

I love the word **remember**. As you daily read your Bible, highlight each time you read the word **remember**, and **remember** that God loves you, He hears your cries, your petitions, and your prayers. He **REMEMBERS** you!

"Hannah left behind her grief, not when her circumstances changed—they hadn't—but after she poured out her soul to the Lord. Because of her grief, she connected with the Lord on a level she had never known." NAS Ryrie Study Bible

- Psalm 66:17–20 says, "Come and hear, all who fear God, and I will tell you of what He has done for my soul. I cried to him with my mouth, and He was extolled with my tongue. If I regard wickedness in my heart, the Lord will not hear; but certainly God has heard; He has given heed to the voice of my prayer. Blessed be God, who has not turned away my prayer nor His loving-kindness from me." NAS

- Psalm 99:6b says, "They called upon the Lord and he answered them." NAS

We don't know how long Hannah waited for God to answer her prayers. What we do know is that she went time after time to the temple with her husband, Elkannah, to fervently petition God for an answer to her prayers.

---

[20] Charles Stanley. *The Charles F. Stanley Life Principles Bible: New King James Version.* (Nashville: Thomas Nelson Publishing, 2005).

When we are fervently petitioning the Lord to answer a specific request, we must **remember**, He hears, He answers, but it is according to **His timing**, **His plan**, and **His will**.

- Read 1 Samuel 1:19–28. "It came about in due time, (God's time) after Hannah conceived, that she gave birth to a son; and she named him Samuel, saying, "Because I have asked him of the Lord."

- The name Samuel means "heard by God" and serves as a continual reminder of God's mercy toward those who call upon His name. (Ryrie, 2008).

Charles Stanley from the Life Principles Bible says, "Would Samuel have been born if Hannah had not asked God to give her a son? The Bible seems to answer, 'No.' Samuel appeared on the scene in direct response to Hannah's heartfelt prayers" (Stanley, 2005).

After Samuel is born, we see Elkannah once again return to the temple to offer the yearly sacrifice and make his vow, which was the habit of his life. Hannah informs him that she will not be going with him.

- 1 Samuel 1:24, says, "Now when she had weaned him, she took him up with her, with three bulls, one ephah of flour and a skin of wine, and brought him to the house of the Lord in Shiloh. And the child was young." NAS

Children were typically weaned between the ages of two and three. Samuel was thought to be about three years of age when Hannah took him to the temple.

- "Then they slaughtered a bull, and brought the child to Eli. And she said, 'O my Lord! As your soul lives, my Lord, I am the woman who stood by you here, praying to the Lord. For this child I prayed, and the Lord has granted me my petition which I asked of Him. Therefore I have also lent him to the Lord; as long as he lives he shall be lent to the Lord.' So they worshiped the Lord there." 1 Samuel 1:25–28 NKJV

Hannah had obviously told Samuel that he was dedicated—set apart—to the Lord. She saw keeping her vow, relinquishing Samuel to the Lord, as an act of worship. She was willing to sacrifice her son in worship, praise, and thanksgiving for God's answering her petitions. She was a woman who kept her word.

In 1 Samuel 2:1–11, we see Hannah's Song of Worship. "Then Hannah prayed and said, 'My heart exults in the Lord; my horn is exalted in the Lord . . .'" NAS

The word horn is an image of invisible strength. Hannah acknowledges God as her strength and her deliverer. How else, could she have sacrificed what her heart so longed for—her son?

"Hannah's praise is in response to God's answer to her prayer and was probably delivered before the congregation of worshipers. The theme of Hannah's praise is her confidence in God's sovereignty. Hannah praises God for His holiness, His knowledge, His power, and judgment. Hannah was delivered from disgrace to strength and honor."

In other words, she testified before all the people of God's faithfulness in her life. He answered her prayers, gave her a son, and she fulfilled her vow in giving Samuel back to the Lord. Hannah had the privilege of seeing God fulfill His purpose for Samuel in being a prophet of God. "Samuel ministered to the Lord before Eli the priest."

> "The Lord visited Hannah; and she conceived and gave birth to three sons and two daughters. And the boy Samuel grew before the Lord." 1 Samuel 2:21 NAS

As we study the life of Hannah, there are several things we learn about her:

- She was a woman of fervent prayer—willing to pour out her soul before her God—despite what others may have thought.

- She was a woman who believed God to be a BIG God; there was nothing He could not do.

- She was a woman who would not give up—persistent in prayer. Her motto: Never give up!

- She was faithful.

- She was willing to sacrifice her son in order that God would answer her prayer and fulfill His plan for her and for Samuel.

- She was a woman who knew how to worship and taught Samuel, her son, how to worship (1 Samuel 2:28), "'So I have also dedicated him to the Lord; as long as he lives he is dedicated to the Lord.' And he (Samuel at the age of three) worshiped the Lord there."

- She was a woman who shared with others, all that God had done for her; she willing shared her testimony of God's faithfulness.

- She is another example to me of the principle I see over and over again in the Bible—obedience equals blessings. "She conceived and gave birth to three sons and two daughters. And the boy Samuel grew before the Lord."

Discipling Leader: Discuss the following questions with the class:

- How has the story of Hannah's life impacted you?

- What will you do differently as a result of studying the life of Hannah?

If time allows, utilize the Discussion Questions and the Examining the Heart Questions.

DISCUSSION QUESTIONS

1. What other women in the Bible were barren? *Sarah, Rachel, and Rebekah*

2. Who was responsible for Hannah's barrenness? The Lord had closed her womb. The Ryrie Study Bible NAS says, "The Lord closed Hannah's womb, not Satan, not an accident, not nature. He is sovereign and He does according to His will."

3. The scriptures tell us that Elkannah loved Hannah more, how do you think this made Peninnah feel? *She must have felt jealousy toward Hannah.* What other woman in the Bible competed with the other wife for her husband's love? *Leah competed with Rachel, because Jacob loved Rachel more.*

4. What do the verses we've read reveal about female relationships? *Women can be vicious, cruel, and mean; they often compete with one another.*

5. According to 1 Samuel 1:10, what was the condition of Hannah's soul? *Her soul was in anguish, in great pain. She wept aloud. One version says, "She wept bitterly."*

6. What does Eli, the priest, assume about Hannah? *That she is drunk.* "As for Hannah, she was speaking in her heart, only her lips were moving, but her voice was not heard. So, Eli thought she was drunk."

7. What is Hannah's response to Eli? "No, my Lord, I am a woman oppressed in spirit; I have drunk neither wine nor strong drink, but I have poured out my soul before the Lord."

8. In Hannah's prayer, what does she tell the Lord she will do if He chooses to grant to her a son? *She will give him back to the Lord all the days of his life.*

9. What does this tell you about Hannah's relationship with the Lord? *She fully expected God to answer her request and grant her a son; she trusted her God. Hannah had a BIG view of God!*

10. Did the Lord answer Hannah's prayers? *Yes.*

11. After Samuel was born, why didn't Hannah go with Elkannah to the temple? *She was staying behind to care for her baby; she would go after she had weaned Samuel and when it was time to fulfill the vow she had made to the Lord.*

12. Iva May in her W3 study asked the question, "What did it cost Hannah to keep her promise (vow) to God? What does she receive in return? *It cost her her son and the privilege of raising him. She gained a prophet of God—a man greatly called and used of God.*

Examining the Heart

1. Are you facing a battle you cannot win on your own? Are you fighting it on your knees, fervently asking God to answer, to intervene?

2. Can you imagine praying with such a deep passion and fervency that others who are watching think you are intoxicated?

3. Is there something you are petitioning God for that has brought you to a place of *pouring out your soul before the Lord*? A request, that if God doesn't answer, you have no other hope? Will you continue to petition even if you don't get an immediate answer? Will you keep on believing?

Using the What I Learned Today sheet in the lesson, have the participants write out a prayer of supplication, a "pouring out of your soul" prayer, and believe as Hannah believed that God hears and answers our prayers.

ANSWERS TO—WHAT AM I TO DO?

SOLUTION TO SITUATION #1

You apologize to the woman and ask her to wait at the bottom of the escalator so you can have your son apologize. When you get to the bottom of the escalator, you take him aside to explain. "First of all, as a young man and gentleman, *women always* go before men, and secondly, *older* people *always* go before younger people." You tell him he will have to go to the lady and apologize for jumping in front of her and almost causing her to fall. Walk him over to her and listen as he apologizes and then you apologize as well. Once he gets home, any further punishment is left up to you!

SOLUTION TO SITUATION #2

You and your husband should decide before taking your children out to eat what the rules are going to be. If your children are old enough to understand, explain the rules for eating out at a restaurant. You must train them to sit still and wait. Realize their limits—do not push them beyond their limits—especially if they are very young. Children should not be allowed to run around a restaurant. If the wait has been long and they are tired, maybe it is time to leave. If your children run into a waiter or waitress causing them to almost spill an entire tray of food, have the children apologize and then you need to apologize as well because you are the one who is really responsible.

SOLUTION TO SITUATION #3

Immediately apologize to the person on the phone. After finishing your conversation give your son a lesson in answering the phone correctly: "Yes ma'am, my mom is here. Just one minute please." You instruct him to lay the phone down gently and go to where you are to tell you that the phone call is for you.

SOLUTION TO SITUATION #4

You apologize to the gentleman and ask him to wait a moment after he pays for his purchase, so your daughter can say, "I am sorry." You take her aside and explain what she did wrong and that her behavior is unacceptable. Tell her, "We do not treat others that way and especially when they are offering us a gift. We are to thank them for the gift." Tell her she is to apologize for hitting him and thank him for the candy. When in the car, do what you deem best!

SOLUTION TO SITUATION #5

You go over and remove your three-year-old from the swing, explaining that when someone asks us politely to share with them, we are to share. After he has calmed down, have him apologize for saying no and for not being willing to share the swing.

SOLUTION TO SITUATION #6

You ask to be excused to another room along with your youngest and explain to her all the grandparents had done for her and her siblings that evening. Tell her that she is to be grateful and never complain about what others have freely and lovingly done for her; she is to always have an attitude of gratitude. Have her return to the room where the rest of the family is and apologize to her grandparents.

SOLUTION TO SITUATION #7

You approach both boys and explain that in your family you do not allow anyone to say shut up. Have your son apologize for his part. Once out of the waiting room, explain to him the level of disrespect that comes with telling someone else to shut up and that you will not allow him to do so, even when someone has said it to him.

SOLUTION TO SITUATION #8

You apologize to the young woman and ask if she will wait just a moment, while you get your children, in order for them to apologize. Call the children back, without screaming, if possible! Explain what they did wrong and ask them to apologize to the young woman. "I am sorry for almost knocking you down because we were racing to the car." After she has gone, explain to them that they could have really hurt her and the baby. Make it clear, you will not allow them to run out the doors ahead of you and race across the parking lot, and any time they run into someone they must apologize.

SOLUTION TO SITUATION #9

You apologize for him and ask if the two of you may be excused. Take him into another room and explain that he is to ask for the food he wants and wait for it to be passed to him. "May I have the chicken, please." Reintroduce him to silverware and its usage. Return to the table and have him apologize to the hostess.

SOLUTION TO SITUATION #10

Apologize and ask the man to wait a minute. Take your son aside and explain that what he just did was rude. Tell him the proper way in which he should respond in this situation. Return and have him reach out to shake hands with the man and introduce himself. Work on this at home so that if it were to happen again, he will know what to do.

SOLUTION TO SITUATION #11

You are to explain: No "thank you," No snack! Tell her, she is to always say *please* when asking for something and *thank you* when she receives it. If she does not say *please*, she will not receive it. If she does not say *thank you*, it will be taken away from her. If she refuses to say thank you, you must take it away!

SOLUTION TO SITUATION #12

Before your guests arrive, have an etiquette lesson on receiving gifts. First, always say thank you. Second, never complain about any gift. Third, be grateful!

Optional Week Five

SHOWER AND PARTY ETIQUETTE

Optional Week Five

LESSON PLAN

I. LEADER OPENS IN PRAYER

II. DEVOTIONAL—Lesson on Hannah is located at the end of the Week Five Children's Etiquette lesson.

- Hannah—*A Woman of Sacrifice*. Read 1 Samuel 1:1–28, 2:1–11, and 2:18–21 in order to prepare. For help in preparation, refer to the Devotional section in today's lesson.

- **Biblical Principle**: When we choose to give God everything, it will cost us something—it will require a sacrifice.

III. LESSON

- If the leadership is uncomfortable teaching today's topic and knows of a qualified guest for teaching on shower and party etiquette, consider inviting the guest to address today's topic.

- If the leadership chooses to teach today's topic, utilize the lesson sheets available, plus your own experiences, as a resource for covering shower and party etiquette.

- Invite a florist or creative guest to demonstrate cost-friendly table décor ideas for wedding and baby showers, and parties.

- The leadership may prepare a few of the recipes given in this week's lesson or some of your favorite shower and party recipes for the participants to taste.

- Leave an appropriate amount of time for questions and discussion.

IV. WEEK FIVE LESSON SHEETS

- Introduction—*You're Invited*
  Wedding Shower Etiquette and Shower Recipes
  Baby Shower Etiquette and Shower Recipes
  Party Etiquette and Party Recipes
  Devotional on Hannah (Located at the end of Week Five: Children's Etiquette)

V. EQUIPMENT FOR WEEK FIVE

- Prepared dishes for participants to taste. Plates and silverware for serving food.

- Table décor to demonstrate creative ideas for decorating a table for showers and parties.

Introduction

YOU'RE INVITED!

*T*here is nothing more rewarding than giving a party or shower in a friend's honor. When your closest friend announces her engagement or another friend and her husband announce that they are expecting their first child, immediately all your female friends begin to plan ways to celebrate. Most people love a party and a reason to gather.

Recently, I was asked to be a hostess for a "Sprinkle." My first thought was, "What is a Sprinkle?" I had never heard of such a party. I have heard of baby showers, wedding showers, engagement parties, birthday parties, and even spiritual birthday parties, but I had never heard of a Sprinkle!

A couple of years ago, I was told that a young woman I knew (who was expecting) and her husband, were going on a Babymoon. "A what,?" I asked. My friend explained that many young couples these days take a sort of second honeymoon before the baby arrives—I guess because life is over when you have a baby, and you will never travel again. I am just kidding. But, when we were expecting our first child, we were just wondering how we were going to pay for the delivery; the last thing on our minds or that we could afford was to take a Babymoon!

Things have changed and so have parties and showers. A "Sprinkle" I was told is a lower-key gathering that allows friends and family to "shower" or "sprinkle" a pregnant woman with love and a couple of gifts (like diapers) without all the bells and whistles of a big shower. Now, in the South we do things fancy and big. Nothing I have ever been a part of has been low-key or without all the bells and whistles! Our daughter lives in Texas. I am sure those of us in Tennessee don't do it up as big as Texans, because everything is big in Texas—but we come close. So, we will see if the Sprinkle is just that—a sprinkle of gifts and love!

---

*W*e can find a variety of ways and reasons to celebrate. I have over the years, attended or been a hostess for a *New Home* party, a *Blessing Party*, *Graduation* parties, *Tea* parties, *Garden* parties, *Christmas* parties, *New Year's Eve* parties, *Gotcha Day* (adoption) parties, and a *New Job/Promotion* party. People like to throw parties; they are fun. Throwing a party implies physical effort, and parties, as any good hostess worth her hummus knows, can be exhausting. But, you don't have to go through the event running on empty. In the pages to follow, I will explain the proper etiquette for giving a party and shower, as well as provide you with a list of necessities, table decoration ideas, and recipes.

I am hopeful that the information in the pages to come will assist you in not only hosting a shower or party—but help you enjoy it as well!

You're Invited to join me. Get ready, this is going to be a fun lesson!

WEDDING SHOWER ETIQUETTE

Who may Host a Shower? Anyone can host a shower. Years ago, it was thought unacceptable for a family member to host a shower for the engaged couple. But, times have changed, and it is appropriate under certain circumstances. Example: The bride is visiting her future in-laws and the groom's mother and sister want to invite the hometown friends and family to meet her. Let individual circumstances be your guide.

Must bridesmaids host a shower? Contrary to what you have heard, bridesmaids and the maid/matron of honor are not required to host a shower as a part of their "official" responsibilities. They certainly can if they want to.

When should a shower be held? The perfect timing is three months to two weeks prior to the wedding—after the couples plans are firmly in place.

How many showers can be given? Multiple showers are okay, but make sure you invite different guests to each party. Only close family and members of the wedding party can be invited to more than one shower.

Is a couples' shower acceptable? Showers for both the bride and groom, called Jack and Jill showers, are acceptable. Also, showers just for the groom are a recent phenomenon. Couples or groom showers can be themed. Examples: Room of the Day, Hour of the Day, the Great Outdoor Shower, His needs—Her needs, etc.

Are shower guests wedding guests? Yes, typically anyone invited to a shower would be invited to the wedding. There are only two exceptions, one would be if a group of co-workers wanted to give an office shower for the bride even though they are not being invited to the wedding and the other is a destination wedding. When a destination wedding is chosen, a shower may be given for the bride and groom by a group of individuals not attending the wedding due to distance or the size of the venue.

If invited to more than one shower, is a gift expected for each shower? If you are invited to more than one shower, you are only expected to bring a gift to the first one—that goes for members of the wedding party, too.

What should be printed on the invitation?

- Name of Bride-to-Be and Hostess
- Location
- Date and Time
- Directions
- Phone number of main hostess
- R.S.V.P. (include information about how to R.S.V.P.) or Regrets Only
- Theme of the Shower (if applicable)
- Dress Code (if desired)
- When addressing, use formal name. Example: Dr. and Mrs. William S. Brown

Who should be invited? The guest list should be made up of the couple's close friends, family, and attendants. The host should consult the bride to make sure that shower guests are wedding guests.

How many should be invited? It is up to the hostess to determine the number of guests. A shower is to be an intimate gathering. It is not to rival the wedding.

When should the invitations be mailed? Four to six weeks prior to the date of the shower.

Which response is better, R.S.V.P. or Regrets Only? The phrase R.S.V.P. means Respond Please and Regrets Only means that if you do not reply, it will be taken as an acceptance—you will attend. The guests should respond when either of these responses is requested on an invitation.

Can registry information be placed in the shower invitation? Yes, it is fine for the hostess to include registry information with, but not on, the invitation. A registry list is a suggestion; but remember the choice of gift is always up to the giver.

How much should be spent on a gift? As with any gift, how much you choose to spend should have more to do with your relationship with the recipient and what you feel comfortable spending than with an arbitrary dollar amount. If you are not a family member of the honoree, a basic rule of thumb is to spend no less than $30 and no more than $50 on a wedding gift.

Can an encore bride have a wedding shower? If a bride has been married before, she may be given a shower. Other than her close friends and family, the guests list should not include anyone who came to a shower for her first wedding.

WEDDING SHOWER RECIPES

Menu Selection: The menu chosen will depend on the time of day that the shower is given. Example: If the shower is from 11:00 a.m. to 2:00 p.m., a lunch menu would be appropriate. Below are a few good recipes for a lunch menu:

Hope's Coffee Slush

- 3 cups brewed coffee, cooled
- 3 pints half and half
- 2 tablespoons pure vanilla
- 2 cups granulated sugar

Mix thoroughly the ingredients above. Place in two large plastic zipper-lock bags. Press out the air, seal securely, and lay flat on shelf in freezer. A half hour before serving (may require 45 minutes in the wintertime) remove from freezer. As ingredients soften begin to break into pieces, creating slush. Serve in slushy consistency. <u>Note</u>: Replace one pint half and half with heavy cream for richer slush.

Refreshing Punch

- 2 lemons, sliced
- 3 large oranges, sliced
- 1 (6 ounce) frozen lemonade concentrate, thawed
- 2 (25.4 ounce) bottles sparkling apple cider
- 1 liter club soda
- 1 tablespoon granulated sugar
- 24-30 ice cubes

Thinly slice lemons and oranges. Place in large serving bowl. Pour in the thawed lemonade. Mix thoroughly. Gently stir in apple cider and club soda. Add sugar to taste and stir until dissolved. Add ice and serve.

Baby Carrots with Herb Dressing

- 1 (8 ounce) cream cheese, softened
- 1 cup sour cream
- 4 green onions, (white and green parts), chopped
- 2 tablespoons dill
- ¼ cup parsley, chopped
- 2 teaspoons sea salt
- 1 teaspoon black pepper, ground
- 40 petite rainbow carrots

Using a food processor, place cream cheese, sour cream, green onion, dill, parsley, salt and pepper in the work bowl. Process until smooth. Refrigerate until ready to serve. Using six 8 ounce clear plastic or glass serving cups, spoon ¼ cup dip into individual serving cup. Stand four to five carrots in the dip around the outer edge of the cup. Serve immediately.

Pesto and Turkey Pinwheels

½ cup mayonnaise

4 tablespoons pesto

1 tablespoon Dijon mustard

5 large flour tortillas

2 cups Arugula, chopped

10 pieces Provolone cheese, thinly sliced

½ pound deli smoked turkey breast, thinly sliced

In small mixing bowl, combine mayonnaise, pesto, and mustard. Evenly spread 2 tablespoons mayonnaise mixture onto each tortilla. Sprinkle each with arugula. Top each with 2 slices of provolone and 3 slices of turkey. Roll up tortillas tightly, and wrap in plastic wrap. Refrigerate for 2 to 4 hours. Remove and cut tortilla rolls into one inch thick slices making colorful pinwheels. Can be refrigerated in an air-tight container up to 2 days.

Bacon and Cheese Dip

5 slices of bacon, cooked and crumbled

1 (8 ounce) cream cheese, softened

1 cup mayonnaise

1 (8 ounce) Swiss cheese, shredded

2 green onions, finely chopped

1 tablespoon garlic powder

4 buttery crackers, finely crushed

Preheat oven to 350°F. Cook bacon over medium-high heat until evenly brown. Drain, crumble, and set aside. In a small mixing bowl, mix cream cheese with mayonnaise until creamy. Stir in swiss cheese, onions, and bacon. Place dip into a small oven-proof baking dish. Bake for 20-30 minutes until bubbly and lightly brown around the edges. Sprinkle top with crushed crackers. Serve warm with crackers.

Chocolate Hazelnut Dipped Strawberries

Fresh Strawberries

1 cup heavy whipping cream

1 (12 ounce) can evaporated milk

4 (3.5 ounce) bars dark chocolate, chopped (Ghiradelli®)

½ cup hazelnut chocolate spread

In a medium saucepan, heat cream and evaporated milk over low-medium heat, stirring continually until bubbles form around the edges of pan. Do not boil. Remove from heat; add chocolate and hazelnut chocolate spread. Whisk until smooth. Serve immediately with strawberries. Note: Can also be served with Biscotti.

Mini Almond Cupcakes

2 Duncan Hines® white cake mixes

6 egg whites, room temperature

1 cup oil

1¼ cups water

2 tablespoons almond extract

1 (4 ounce) sour cream

Preheat oven to 350°F. Line two 24-cup mini muffin tins with paper liners. Sift the cake mixes in the bowl of an electric mixer on low speed until lumps are removed. Add all the wet ingredients. Mix on medium speed until batter is smooth, scraping regularly to remove dry mix from sides and bottom of bowl. Pour batter evenly into prepared muffin pans. Bake for 15 to 20 minutes, until a cake tester comes out clean. Cool on rack.

ICING:

1 cup butter, softened

1 cup shortening

2 teaspoons pure vanilla

1 teaspoon almond extract

¼ teaspoon salt

8 cups confectioners' sugar

6 tablespoons milk (use more if needed)

In large mixing bowl, beat together butter and shortening until smooth. Add vanilla, almond extract, and salt. Gradually add confectioners' sugar and milk, beat until blended and smooth. Using piping bag, ice mini cupcakes and top with two sliced almonds.

Mini Lime Tarts

6 tablespoons sugar, additional 2 tablespoons

2 egg yolks, room temperature and slightly whipped

1 medium lime, grated

⅓ cup lime juice

3 egg whites, room temperature

1 cup heavy whipping cream

2 tablespoons confectioners' sugar

2 (8 each) packages of mini pastry shells, freezer section of grocery

In double boiler over medium heat, mix 6 tablespoons sugar, egg yolks, grated rind, and lime juice. Whisk over heat until custard-like texture is formed. Remove from stove. Cool. In bowl, beat egg whites and gradually add in 2 tablespoons of sugar until stiff. Fold egg whites into custard until smooth. Whip heavy cream with 2 tablespoons of confectioners' sugar. Fold into custard until light and creamy. Cook pastry tarts according to package directions, let cool. Fill with lime custard filling and top with fresh whipped cream.

WEDDING SHOWER GAMES AND CREATIVE IDEAS

WHO SAID IT?

This is a fun interactive bridal shower game. This game will test your guests as to how well they know the bride and/or groom It is a perfect choice for throwing a couple's shower. **How to Play**: Prior to the shower, have the couple answer a series of questions. At some point during the shower, plan a time to read their answers aloud. The guests will attempt to guess whose response they think has been read by holding up a hand when the hostess says "Bride" or "Groom." The participant with the greatest number of answers correct wins!

T.P. WEDDING ATTIRE:

Utilize your guests' creativity with this fun and interactive bridal shower game. All you will need is a package of toilet paper rolls—a fashion expert might come in handy as well! **How to Play**: Divide everyone into teams and give them two to four rolls of toilet paper in order to create a wedding gown. Each team will need a model on which to create their luxurious gown. Give them fifteen to twenty minutes. As you play the traditional wedding march, have each team's bride model their gown. The winner will be selected by the bride-to-be. If you are having a couples party, divide the men and the women. Give the women several rolls of toilet paper and the men duct tape along with broken down cardboard boxes. Each team will have 15-20 minutes to dress the bride and groom in appropriate wedding attire. It is a fun way for your guests to interact.

BRIDAL PICTIONARY:

The Bridal Pictionary game is a fun way to test your guests' artistic skills! Divide the guests into two or three different teams and let the games begin! **How to Play**: You will need a large wipe-off board or pad of paper and some markers for each team. Cut about ten slips of paper and write a wedding-related term on each. Place the slips of paper into a basket or jar. Each team will take turns pulling from the container, giving each one a try at guessing the wedding term/word their teammate is trying to draw. The team with the most correct guesses wins!

BLESSING CARD:

Have each guest write a special blessing or a favorite scripture verse that would be an encouragement to the Bride-to-be.

"WHAT I WISH" CARD:

Have each guest write what they wish their mother had told them about marriage prior to their wedding. Draw cards out of a basket and read aloud. Allow the guests to decide who wrote each card. Place in an album for the bride-to-be.

ENVELOPES FOR THANK YOU NOTES:

As the guests enter the home, have a basket of envelopes from Thank you notes (of the bride's choosing) and a pen. Each guest will address an envelope complete with their home address. This will save the bride time and ensure that she gets her thank you notes written.

WEDDING SHOWER TABLE DÉCOR

Theme: Decide if the wedding shower will have a theme and decorate accordingly.

Flowers are always appropriate. Placing two to three dozen colored roses or tulips in a large crystal vase is eye catching for the center of the serving table. Using a variety of square glass vases and "bunching" or "clustering" flowers interspersed with crystal candle sticks or votives makes a beautiful presentation.

The Hostesses each have a variety of talents. If one is especially gifted in decorating, ask if she would be willing to decorate the serving table. The others will oversee the remaining responsibilities.

Food is a part of the décor, so keep that in mind when selecting your menu and serving pieces. You want color, texture, and interest in the recipes prepared and in the way in which they are displayed.

Keep It in the Family: Pay tribute to the bride's relatives by putting their old wedding photos on display for a creative bridal shower idea. Guests will love taking a look at the styles of decades past. To make the serving table even more whimsical and picture-perfect, affix the images to teapot lids using 6-inch pieces of artistic wire. Intersperse vases with soft pink and off white flowers among the family wedding photos. Using a lace runner will give your table a more vintage look.

Centerpieces can be simple and cost-efficient. Here are a few ideas:

- **Straws and Flowers**: You will need two bunches of mini carnations (or flower of choice) in a color that fits your décor, a large square clear glass vase (size or sizes to fit the serving table), and colorful small plastic straws. Tip the square vase on its side and fill it up with new straws. Stand upright and add tap water halfway up. Insert individual stems of mini carnations (or flower of choice) into openings of randomly selected straws. Multiple vases on a table make a stunning and fun display.

- **Spools of Twine**: You will need different sizes of twine balls with holes in the middle, small waterproof glass containers that will fit down in the holes of the spools, mini Chrysanthemum flowers (or flowers of choice) and a rectangular wooden tray. Insert the small glass containers into each spool of twine. Fill with water and place a cluster of flowers in each one. Arrange the twine spools on the wooden tray. Votives can be placed among the spools for a more cozy feel.

- **Field of Daisies**: You will need 8-10 Gerbera daisies, wooden twigs from your yard, wheat grass, ceramic bowl of your choosing, and a sharp knife. Turn the ceramic bowl upside down and place a square of wheat grass on top. Trim the excess along the edge of the bowl with a sharp knife. Flip the bowl right side up and insert the wheat grass disc into the bowl. Insert twigs to create a standing nest or cage for the flowers. Poke daisies into the grass using the twigs as support to keep them upright. Add water. You can make multiples for a large serving table or intersperse with other décor on table.

- **Candles**: Add radiant elegance to your bridal shower serving table by using the soft glow of candles floating in crystal clear round glass bowls. Fill the bowls with water and along with the floating candles, add pearls, acrylic crystals, water-proof LED lights, colored sand, or fresh flowers. A combination of any of these would be beautiful. Place the clear glass bowls atop a decorative round mirror to create a warm and inviting look. Add warmth to your table by interspersing votive candles among the clear glass bowls.

BABY SHOWER ETIQUETTE

When should the shower be held? A baby shower should be held four to six weeks before the due date, unless the Mother-to-be wants to have it after the child is born. If you are counting by weeks, 28-32 weeks is an ideal time to host a baby shower.

How many showers can be given? Multiple showers are okay, but make sure you invite different guests to each party. Only close family members of the honoree can be invited to more than one shower.

Is a theme necessary? No. But a theme can be helpful in assisting with the type of decorations chosen.

Who should be invited? Since the hostess bears the expense of the party, it is up to her to determine the number of the guests she is comfortable accommodating. The hostess should give the honoree the number and ask whom she would like to invite.

How many should be invited? A shower is to be an intimate gathering where the honoree has the opportunity to speak with each guest. Limit the guest list to family and close friends. No one coming should be surprised to find out that there is a baby on the way.

What should be printed on the invitation?

- Name of Mother-to-Be and Hostess
- Location
- Date and Time
- Directions
- Phone number of main hostess
- R.S.V.P. (include information about how to R.S.V.P.) or Regrets Only
- Theme of the Shower (if applicable)
- Dress Code (if desired)
- When addressing, use formal name. Example: Dr. and Mrs. William S. Brown

Can registry information be placed in the shower invitation? Yes, it is fine for the hostess to include registry information with, but not on, the invitation. A registry list is a suggestion; but remember the choice of gift is always up to the giver.

When should the invitations be mailed? Four to six weeks prior to the date of the shower.

R.S.V.P. or Regrets Only? The phrase R.S.V.P means Respond Please and Regrets Only means that if you do not reply, it will be taken as an acceptance—you will attend. The guests should respond to the hostess when either of these responses is requested on an invitation, but often they do not.

How much should I spend on a gift? As with any gift, how much you choose to spend should have more to do with your relationship with the recipient and what you feel comfortable spending than with an arbitrary dollar amount. If you are not a family member of the honoree, a basic rule of thumb is to spend no less than $30 and no more than $50 on a baby shower gift.

BABY SHOWER RECIPES

Menu Selection: The menu chosen will depend on the time of day that the shower is given. Example: If the shower is from 9 a.m. to 11:00 a.m., a brunch menu would be appropriate. Below are a few good recipes for a brunch menu:

Hope's Coffee Slush

- 3 cups brewed coffee, cooled
- 3 pints half and half
- 2 tablespoons pure vanilla
- 2 cups granulated sugar

Mix thoroughly the ingredients above. Place in two large plastic zipper-lock bags. Press out the air, seal securely, and lay flat on shelf in freezer. A half hour before serving (may require 45 minutes in the wintertime) remove from freezer. As ingredients soften begin to break into pieces, creating slush. Serve in slushy consistency. Note: Replace one pint half and half with heavy cream for richer slush.

Sorority House Casserole

- 1 pound breakfast sausage
- 6-8 slices Italian bread
- ¾ stick butter, softened
- ¾ cup mild Cheddar, shredded
- ¾ cup sharp Cheddar cheese, shredded
- 7 eggs, beaten
- 2 cups half and half
- 1 teaspoon onion powder
- 1 ½ teaspoons salt
- 1 teaspoon pepper
- 1½ teaspoons prepared mustard

Preheat oven at 350°F. Cook sausage, drain and crumble. Spread both sides of each slice of bread with softened butter. Place in 9x13 baking dish. Sprinkle with sausage and cheddar cheese. In a large bowl, combine remaining ingredients and pour over bread, sausage, and cheese mixture. Top with ½ cup shredded Cheddar cheese. Cover and refrigerate overnight. Bake for 40-45 minutes until golden brown. Serves 12.

Fruit Kabobs

Using five fruits of choice, cut into bite-size cubes. If using apples or fruit that will turn brown, toss in a tablespoon of lemon juice. Place alternately onto a wooden skewer and serve with a dip recipe.

COCONUT DIP:

1½ cups vanilla yogurt, 4½ teaspoons unsweetened shredded coconut, and 4½ tablespoons orange marmalade. Thoroughly combine the ingredients in a small bowl. Serve with fruit kabobs.

CHOCOLATE DIP:

One (8 ounce) package cream cheese, softened, ½ cup confectioners' sugar, ⅓ cup baking cocoa, 1 teaspoon vanilla, 2 cups whipped heavy cream. In a large bowl, beat the softened cream cheese until light and fluffy. Beat in cocoa, sugar, and vanilla. Once combined, beat in whipped cream. Serve with fruit.

Lemon Blueberry Mini Muffins

BATTER:

- ½ cup butter, softened
- ½ cup shortening
- 3 cups sugar
- 4 large eggs, room temperature
- 4 teaspoons pure vanilla
- Juice and zest of two lemons
- 2 teaspoons pure lemon extract
- 2 cups sour cream
- 4½-5 cups all-purpose flour
- 2-¼ teaspoons baking powder
- 1 teaspoon baking soda
- ¾ teaspoon salt
- 1½ cups fresh blueberries

Preheat oven at 375°F. Line two 24-cup mini muffin tins with paper liners. In mixing bowl, cream butter and shortening until smooth and creamy. Add sugar, blend well. Add eggs one at a time. Add vanilla, lemon juice, zest, lemon extract, and sour cream. Blend well; fold in flour, baking powder, baking soda, and salt. Mix well. With a large spoon gently fold in blueberries. Using a muffin scoop, scoop batter into paper-lined muffin tins. Batter should be firm and not topple. If it topples it may need a small amount of flour added. Bake until lightly browned around the edges and muffins are set to the touch, 15-20 minutes.

LEMON GLAZE:

- Zest of two lemons
- 4 tablespoons butter, melted
- ¼ cup lemon juice
- 3 teaspoons pure lemon extract
- ½ to ¾ cup half and half/milk
- 2 cups confectioners' sugar

Melt butter in glass mixing bowl. Add milk and confectioners' sugar, blend well. Fold in zest, lemon juice, and lemon extract. Brush glaze over muffins while warm. Serves: 60-70 mini muffins.

BABY SHOWER GAMES AND CREATIVE IDEAS

BABY BLOCKS:

Using plain wooden blocks, acrylic paint and brushes, have each guest design a block for the new baby. Each one will be personal and colorful.

DIAPER ADVICE:

Using a box of newborn disposable diapers and a permanent marker, allow each guest to write a word of advice or encouragement to the mother-to-be.

BECAUSE I SAID SO:

On a slip of paper or small index card, ask each guest to write down a parenting saying or advice that they associate with their parents. Place them in a basket. Mix them up, and allow each guest to select one. Have fun guessing whose card was chosen and whether or not the guest has or would say it to her own child.

BABY BINGO:

Go to the www.pampers.com website where you can download Baby Bingo game cards. How to play: Print out one bingo card per guest. Remember, each person's card must be unique! Before you start receiving your baby shower gifts, hand each guest their card. Each card has a unique combination of baby shower gifts. Each time you open one of yours, guests must cross it out on their card. The first person to cross out a diagonal, horizontal, or vertical line wins a prize!

BLESSING CARD:

Have each guest write a special blessing or a favorite scripture verse that would be an encouragement to the mother-to-be.

WHAT "I WISH" CARDS:

Have each guest write what they wish their mother had told them about child birth or what they wish their mom had told them about parenting. Draw cards out of a basket and read aloud. Allow the guests to decide who wrote each card. Place in an album for the mother-to-be.

ENVELOPES FOR THANK YOU NOTES:

As the guests enter the home, have a basket of envelopes from Thank you notes (of the mother-to-be's choosing) and a pen. Each guest will address an envelope complete with her home address. This will ensure that the mommy-to-be will get her notes written before the baby is delivered.

BABY SHOWER TABLE DÉCOR

Theme: Decide if the baby shower will have a theme and decorate accordingly.

Flowers are always appropriate. Placing two to three dozen colored roses or tulips in a large crystal vase is eye catching for the center of the serving table. If a girl, a spectrum of pink interspersed with dashes of white will remind those gathered of the little one to come.

Silver Rattles, Stuffed Animals, and Books can be used along with the floral arrangement to add a personal touch.

Trucks and Trains can be used for a little boy's arrival. If the parents of the daddy-to-be have kept any toys from their childhood, these would be very special used as a part of the table décor.

Dolls and Strollers can be used for a little girl's arrival. If the parents of the mommy-to-be have kept any toys from their childhood, these would be very special used as a part of the table décor.

Food is a part of the décor, so keep that in mind when selecting your menu and serving pieces. You want color, texture, and interest in the recipes prepared and in the way in which they are displayed.

Shower Hostesses each have a variety of talents. If one is especially gifted in decorating, ask if she would be willing to decorate the serving table. The others will oversee the remaining responsibilities.

You are My Sunshine. Arrange bright yellow and white fresh flowers in glass jars. Colorful scrapbooking paper is good for making cute round tags with quotes or phrases that match the theme to attach to each jar. Using a gender-neutral color scheme of bright yellow, grey & white with chevron patterns will bring a touch of sunshine to the shower. A fabric runner matching the color scheme will add interest to the serving table.

Diaper Cake. These fun centerpieces are popular at baby showers because they double as practical gifts and centerpieces. The cakes are not difficult to make. It might require a little time, but you will save money in the end. The exact amount of supplies needed for a diaper cake depend upon how large you want the cake to be and how much money you want to spend on the project. Most diaper cakes use about 50 to 75 newborn or size 1 diapers. Below is a list of supplies:

- Diapers (disposable or cloth)
- Rubber bands
- Clear stretch jewelry cord
- Ribbon
- A cake topper (a stuffed animal, ribbon, board book, etc.)
- A sheet of cardboard, cake board, or a cake plate

Begin by preparing the diapers. Many diaper cakes are made with disposable diapers, but you can swap them for cloth diapers if that's what the mother-to-be prefers.

- One at a time, roll the diapers up tight starting from the front of the diaper and rolling it toward the back. Secure with a rubber band.

- Cut a piece of clear stretch jewelry cord to the fit the circumference of the base layer of the diaper cake.

- Place items like baby lotion, baby wipes or toys in the center of the cardboard or cake plate and start inserting the rolled up diapers one by one until you've created a circular shape.

- Wrap the piece of stretch jewelry cord around the diapers to keep the base layer together.

- Add a second layer of rolled up diapers and secure with a piece of stretch cord. Make sure the diapers are close together. If you can see any gaps between diapers or exposed rubber bands, secure a piece of ribbon around the layer to disguise it.

- Follow these steps for building the remaining tiers.

Once all the tiers are secure and complete, decorate the diaper cake with board books, teething rings or other small items. Tuck them inside the ribbon or fasten them to the tiers with tape. This an opportunity to really personalize the project for the baby's mom and dad, so don't be afraid to get creative. If the baby's gender and name are known, you could include that as well. The idea is to make the diaper cake eye-catching and practical at the same time. You may also wish to include rattles, board books, teething rings, baby wash, baby lotion, diaper rash cream, baby wipes, baby bibs, or other items inside your diaper cake.

PARTY ETIQUETTE

Party Etiquette and Shower Etiquette are quite similar. Much of the dos and don'ts depend upon the type of party being given. To ensure a successful party, planning is imperative.

Do not invite more people than you can comfortably seat.

When to mail invitations or call to offer an invitation:

- Three to six weeks for an anniversary party.
- Same day to two weeks for a casual dinner/party.
- One month ahead for a Christmas party.
- Three to six weeks for a formal dinner party.
- A few days to three weeks for an informal dinner.
- Three weeks for a graduation or birthday party.
- A few days to three weeks for a housewarming party.

Make the invitation simple and make sure it includes all the pertinent information: type of party, date, time, address, dress, etc.

A time schedule for preparing for your party may seem like folly, but whether the party is for six or sixty, it is a necessity. What to do:

- Write down a complete menu far in advance. Make a grocery list from the menu recipes chosen.
- Make note of which foods can be made in advance and frozen or wrapped and stored in the refrigerator.
- Prepare all the recipes that can be prepared in advance and store according to instructions.
- Note the serving dishes you will need for the menu planned. Make certain you have a serving piece for each dish.
- Determine if your party will be a buffet or a sit down dinner. Plan accordingly.
- Set the table a day or two in advance.
- If special decorations are involved, plan and prepare ahead for these.
- Make tea a day or two ahead. Coffee can be placed in coffee pot hours ahead and turned on before the dessert is served.
- A day or two ahead, check your ice source and begin to store extra ice in order not to run out the night of the party.

Décor: This will depend on the theme and purpose of the party—decorate accordingly.

The more "together" you are, the more relaxing the evening or event will be for your guests. Planning and working ahead will ensure that you as the hostess will enjoy your time as much as the friends and family you invited. We are to open our homes, sharing all God has given us with others.

"Contribute to the needs of God's people; pursue the practice of hospitality." Romans 12:13 AMP

Cajun Grilled Beef Tenderloin

- 1 (3½ pound) beef tenderloin
- ¼ cup hot sauce
- ¼ cup low-sodium teriyaki sauce
- 3 tablespoons Worcestershire sauce
- 1 tablespoon Creole seasoning
- Cooking Spray
- Sandwich buns
- Mustard-Horseradish Cream Sauce
- Arugula

Place tenderloin in a large zipper-lock plastic bag. Combine hot sauce and following three ingredients. Pour over tenderloin. Seal bag; marinate in refrigerator 1-2 hours. Turn bag occasionally. Remove tenderloin and discard marinade. Coat grill rack with non-stick spray and heat one side of grill while leaving the other side turned off. Place tenderloin on the unheated side. Close grill lid and cook for 30- 40 minutes, turning once mid-way through cooking time. Let stand 10 minutes before slicing. Serve topped with Mustard-Horseradish sauce or on buttered buns with arugula and Mustard-Horseradish Sauce:

MUSTARD-HORSERADISH SAUCE:

- ¼ cup prepared horseradish
- 1 cup heavy whipping cream
- ¼ cup Dijon mustard
- 1 tablespoon fresh lemon juice

Using a spoon and a fine wire-mesh strainer, press all the juice from horseradish. Set aside and discard juice. In a glass bowl, beat whipping cream with an electric mixer at high speed until soft peaks form. Fold in horseradish, mustard, and lemon juice. Cover and chill for an hour.

Oven-Roasted Squash

- 2 medium-sized yellow squash, sliced
- 2 medium zucchini, sliced
- 1 red bell pepper, thinly sliced
- 4 garlic cloves, minced
- 2 tablespoons olive oil
- 1 teaspoon salt
- ½ teaspoon pepper
- 1 ½ tablespoons balsamic vinegar
- 3 tablespoons pine nuts, toasted
- 8 fresh basil leaves, cut in thin strips

Preheat oven to 400°F. In a bowl, combine first 4 ingredients; drizzle with oil and sprinkle with salt and pepper. Toss and place vegetables on an ungreased jelly-roll pan. Bake uncovered for 10 to 20 minutes. Remove and toss with vinegar, pine nuts, and basil. Serve immediately.

Week Six

LESSON PLAN

I. LEADER OPENS IN PRAYER

II. DEVOTIONAL

- Esther—*A Woman for Such a Time As This*. Read the book of Esther in order to prepare. For help in preparation, refer to the Devotional section in today's lesson.

- **Biblical Principle**: God uses women with a willing heart to accomplish His divine purposes.

III. LESSON—Choose one or all of the topics in today's lesson based on the time allotted for class.

- If the leadership is uncomfortable teaching today's topic, or knows of a qualified guest for teaching on household cleaning, consider inviting the guest to address today's topic. The more practical the lesson, the more effective it will be. Feel free to substitute your own cleaning recipes for any recipes offered in the book.

If the leadership chooses to teach on today's topic of cleaning, have a variety of cleaning helps on display to refer to during the lesson. Examples:

- Organizational tote or bucket full of cleaning products (a tote much like the one you took to college to hold shower products). I keep a tote under the kitchen cabinet for my household cleaning and one in each bathroom.

- A cleaning tool for wood blinds, Swiffer duster for furniture and floors, micro-fiber cloths, and cleaning products which the leadership has found to be effective.

The leader introduces the topic for today by using the teaching sheets in today's lesson and by personal research using Google and the words Home Cleaning. <u>Note</u>: Leave time for making cleaning product recipe.

- Cleaning agents—have some products on hand the leadership has found to be effective. Example: Dawn® dishwashing soap. I have found Dawn® to be the most effective in cutting through grease. The leadership should share the products that have worked for them.

- Using the lesson sheet titled *A Cleaning Plan*, explain the importance of having a cleaning plan: weekly, monthly, and quarterly. There are some cleaning jobs that don't have to be done every week, and some that do. The leadership should share their cleaning routines.

- When addressing the cleaning of each room, divide the rooms according to list below:

    1. Bedrooms and Bathrooms—Cover creative ways a child can learn to clean his own bedroom and bathroom. Example: Cleaning charts—chores and allowances. Refer to *Age Appropriate Chores for Kids* in today's lesson.

    2. Kitchen, Laundry Room, and Mud Room.

    3. Living Room, Family Room, Game Room, Hearth Room, and Dining Room.

- Discuss the importance of doing fall and spring cleaning—those cleaning projects that need to be tackled twice a year. Example: Cleaning baseboards, vacuuming around the edge of the carpeting, washing down all the woodwork, cleaning windows inside and out, along with washing screens, etc. (See handouts for suggestions).

- Make homemade cleaning product recipe. Provide container for transporting it home.

- The leadership should share the "secrets" they have discovered over the years related to cleaning.

- **Optional**: Offer a hands-on activity. Examples: Show the young women how to effectively clean wood blinds with a wood blind cleaning tool. Demonstrate how to clean the inside and outside of dirty windows—T-shirts are some of the best rags to use for glass—no lint. Show how to wax wood floors. Whatever you choose, be practical!

IV. TIME IN THE KITCHEN
- Today's Time in the Kitchen will be spent making homemade cleaners.

V. WEEK SIX LESSON SHEETS
- Introduction—*A Necessity of Life*
  A Cleaning Plan
  Cleaning 101
  Ten Speedy Spring Cleaning Tips
  Let's Take it a Room at a Time
  Special Household Cleaning Projects
  Flooring Care
  Carpet Stains
  Age-Appropriate Chores for Kids
  Devotional on Esther

VI. EQUIPMENT FOR WEEK SIX
- Cleaning products used by leadership, as well as, buckets and containers for holding cleaning products, cleaning rags/cloths, etc.

- Ingredients required for making cleaning product recipe

Homemade Spray Cleaner

MIX TOGETHER IN A SPRAY BOTTLE:

1 cup white vinegar

1 cup water

Use the vinegar and water spray to clean countertops, range surface, and all backsplashes. For bathrooms, use to clean countertops, floors, and exterior of toilet. For hard-to-clean soap scum, take vinegar and water mixture, heat in microwave until barely hot. Spray shower walls and door, let stand 10 to 15 minutes and then scrub. Will soften soap scum.

HOMEMADE CLEANING PRODUCTS[21]

The four products for healthy cleaning are: Hydrogen peroxide, white vinegar, baking soda, and rubbing alcohol.

- **Hydrogen Peroxide** and cream of tartar made into a paste is good for cleaning porcelain and stains.

- **Undiluted white vinegar** can be used to scrub the inside of toilet.

- **Baking soda's** mild abrasive action makes it a good substitute for harsh commercial scouring powders. Sprinkle on a cloth and tackle the ring around the tub, clean vanities, or the kitchen sink.

- **Baking soda** will solve your stopped-up drain problems. Just pour ½ to ¾ cup into the drain, use just enough hot water to wash the solution down. Let stand for 2 hours or overnight, flush thoroughly with hot water; it deodorizes as well.

- **Rubbing alcohol** is better than Windex.

Equal parts of white vinegar and alcohol in a spray bottle works great on glass, mirrors, chrome fixtures, and ceramic tiles. *Peroxide* is a great bathroom cleaner. Using a spray bottle, make your cleaning solution. Mix 1 cup white vinegar, 1 tablespoon baking soda, and 1 cup water. Shake to mix. For a more pleasant scent, add 15 drops of either tea tree, lavender, eucalyptus, lemon, or peppermint essential oils to the water and vinegar

A Recommended Book: *Everyday Cheapskate's Greatest Tips* by Mary Hunt contains recipes for cleaning solutions for every part of the house.

---

[21] Pantry Recipes for Homemade Cleaning Products." http://organizedhome.com/clean-house/pantry-recipes-homemade-cleaning-products.

Introduction
A NECESSITY OF LIFE

Recently while at the gym, I saw a commercial where the little girl says, "My mom said that there is no use cleaning the house until I leave for college." This may sound like a grand idea. Why bother cleaning when those living in the house, apartment, or dorm room with you are just going to mess it up? If you think about not cleaning at all for the span of a child's growing up years or for the entire four years of college, that is pretty disgusting. Who wants to live in that filth?

We talked about de-cluttering in Week One. Truly, de-cluttering your home or apartment makes cleaning much quicker and easier. The less "stuff" you have to move out of the way in order to clean, the quicker the process. Start with picking up and putting away everything that is not in its "normal" place; then you can activate your cleaning plan.

Just as doing laundry is more efficient when you have a plan or system in place—so is cleaning. Systems may change with the seasons of life. Different seasons will require different cleaning systems and schedules.

When in school or working full time, the cleaning may need to be divided between a few evenings and the weekend. Once you marry and have children, you may have to divide the areas of your home and clean as you can according to the children's sleep schedules, school schedules, and your daily commitments. Once they are grown and out of the home, you may want to hire a maid! Why not?

I used to think the entire house had to be cleaned in one day. But, as I have gotten older and have gone through different seasons of life, I no longer worry about accomplishing that. I have a system which works for me. Weekly, I divide the downstairs of the house into three areas over three days. Because no one lives upstairs, I clean the upstairs once a month. This system works for me.

Where would we be without systems? How chaotic driving, banking, and shopping, just to mention a few, would be without systems. As grand as it sounds not to clean your home until the children are grown or a student completes their college education, is not practical. No one wants to live in chaos and filth. Finding the system and schedule that will work best for you—whether wife, mom, or student, is the key to keeping your home, apartment, or dorm room clean without becoming frustrated and overwhelmed.

A CLEANING PLAN

With the right cleaning strategy, you can keep your time spent cleaning to a minimum and give yourself the maximum time for friends, family, and things that matter most. You may choose to clean for an hour every morning, two hours after work, or all of Saturday morning. Just have a strategy and schedule that fits into your life.

Concentrate on one room at a time; do not run all over the house pushing dirt around here and there. Stick with one room until it is sparkling clean. You will have the reward of having completely cleaned one space and then you can move on to the next room.

There are everyday chores such as making beds, cleaning the kitchen floor, doing dishes, etc. Then there are the big tasks such as cleaning out closets, kitchen drawers, cleaning ovens, etc. You should have a routine for the regular cleaning chores and a schedule for the bigger cleaning jobs. Below is a general plan for cleaning a home daily and seasonally.

EVERYDAY CLEANING

- Remove all dirt from your floors with a small vacuum, broom, dust mop, or Swiffer duster.
- Wash dishes and wipe off countertops and cooking appliances.
- Empty kitchen trash can, if necessary.
- Wipe down bathroom sinks and bathtubs.
- Make beds and straighten rooms.

CLEANING AS NEEDED

- Vacuum carpets and hard-surface floors thoroughly with vacuum cleaner or dust mop.
- Vacuum upholstery and draperies with upholstery attachment to vacuum.
- Dust and/or polish furniture.
- Clean the stove and wipe out the refrigerator.
- Wash kitchen and bathroom floors.
- Clean toilets, fixtures, and bathroom mirrors.
- Change bed linens, every week or two.
- Empty all waste baskets.

SEASONAL

- Surface clean rugs and carpets, using a carpet-cleaning solution or an absorbent powder.
- Remove all wax, apply new wax, and buff hard-surface floors.
- Wash throw rugs.
- Shampoo upholstery furniture.
- Wash or vacuum lamp shades, wash walls, and woodwork.
- Dust books, pictures, and lamps.
- Clean mirrors, TV screens, picture frames, and art objects.
- Clean ovens, microwave, refrigerator, freezer, and other appliances.
- Wash bathroom carpeting and shower curtain.
- Organize closets.
- Turn mattresses, wash pads and pillow covers, and air or wash pillows.
- Clean storm windows, screens, and windows.
- Wipe ceiling fan blades and motors with a damp cloth.

YEARLY

- Vacuum rug pads and the back of rugs.
- Shampoo carpets, clean rugs, and turn rugs to equalize wear.
- Wash curtains, blinds, shutters, shades, and clean draperies.
- Clean closets and cabinets.
- Wash or dry-clean bedspreads, blankets, and slip covers.
- Clean out garage, basement, and workshop.

EMERGENCIES

- Remove spots and stains while they are fresh.

CLEANING 101

Systems and supplies are the main ingredients in keeping your home clean. A well-stocked cleaning closet is a girl's best friend. You will be more likely to start your cleaning and finish the task if you have all that you need on hand. The following is a list of tools and supplies you need to efficiently clean your home.

GATHER YOUR TOOLS AND SUPPLIES

- **Baskets or Rubber Container**—Used for carrying supplies from one room to another and for collecting items that have been left in the wrong room.

- **Scrub Brushes**—Available in an assortment of sizes—the type needed will be determined by the job to be done.

- **Buckets**—A bucket for mopping and a two-sided bucket to hold your cleaning supplies and rags; keeps them all together, saving you time and energy.

- **Chamois**—These are expensive, but when properly used, last indefinitely. Nothing absorbs water better than soft leather, so it is perfect for drying cars and windows. After using your chamois, wash in a detergent solution, rinse thoroughly, squeeze out the water, stretch it to full size, and place it on a flat surface to dry.

- **Cleaning Cloths**—Can be made from old t-shirts, worn out wash cloths, sheets, diapers, or towels. Cotton, linen, white, or light-colored fabrics are best. Guardsman's® One-Wipe cloth, is great.

- **Hydrogen Peroxide**—Sanitizes surfaces without damaging them.

- **Mops/Swiffer Dusters**—Mops should have detachable heads for easy cleaning.

- **Rubber Gloves**—Protect your hands. Always wear gloves when using cleaning solutions.

- **Scouring Pads**—Made of synthetics and steel wool. Keep a variety on hand.

- **Sponges**—Have plenty on hand. Wash occasionally in a load where bleach is being used or run through dishwasher cycle.

- **Stepladders**—Have one that is at least three feet tall.

- **Window Squeegees**—Speeds window washing and are great when used on shower doors and bathroom tile.

- **New Two-Inch Paint Brush**—Great for dusting off lampshades. Also good for cleaning chairs, railings, and pictures.

GATHER YOUR CLEANING AGENTS

- **All-Purpose Cleaners**—Remove grease and grimy dirt.

- **Ammonia**—Available in clear or sudsy form. It is a grease cutter, wax stripper, window cleaner, and general soil remover. It is not a stain remover. Note: You can buy scented.

- **Baking Soda**—Most versatile cleaning product available. Used in dry form, it acts as a very mild scouring powder that will not scratch delicate surfaces. Use it to scour dirty surfaces by adding water to make a paste. Combined with other ingredients, it makes a very good cleaning solution that always deodorizes.

- **Bleach**—Helps remove stains and whitens laundry—also excellent for killing germs.

- **Lemon Juice**—Bottled or fresh; provides a mild acid reaction needed in cleaning solutions.

- **Liquid Dishwashing Detergents**—Used for cleaning tasks in addition to washing dishes.

- **Vinegar**—White vinegar can be used to clean fabrics and other household projects.

- **Waxes, Polishes, and Oils**—Used to shine and protect wood, leather, brass, chrome, silver, glass, and other surfaces.

TEN SPEEDY
Spring Cleaning Tips [22]

- **Remove clutter first**—Clear off items from tables, floors, and other surfaces before you start cleaning so you can zoom through each room.

- **Rely on a few ingredients**— Clean floors with 1 cup vinegar and 1 gallon water (Do not use this solution on wood flooring). Spray a mixture of half vinegar, half water to clean countertop and sinks.

- **Use one cleaning tool at a time**—Grab what you need to handle the same chore, like vacuuming, throughout your home, then switch tools.

- **Use micro-fiber cloths**—With dry micro-fiber cloths, dust furniture. Wet and wring out another for wiping down mirrors and glass surfaces.

- **Only clean what is dirty**—Spot clean visible dirt; skip cleaning walls, inside windows, and hardwood floors if they don't look dirty.

- **Call in help**—Consider handing some cleaning projects off to the pros; they do it faster, better, and have all the right equipment. Best jobs to hire out: carpet shampooing, sealing tile grout, and window washing.

- **Be efficient**—Instead of removing everything from shelves and cabinets, move items to the right to clean the left side. Then move items to the left to clean right side.

- **Give yourself a deadline**—Set a timer for ten, twenty, or thirty minutes, and tell yourself you'll finish a task in that amount of time.

- **Avoid scrubbing**—Spray cleaner in bathroom sinks, the microwave, and refrigerator and let stand five to ten minutes to soften hardened-on gunk.

- **Take advantage of overnight hours**—Before going to bed, set your oven to clean. Similarly, pour toilet cleaner in toilet bowls, then just brush and flush in the morning.

---

[22] Donna Smallin, "10 Ways to Speed Up Spring Cleaning," Better Homes and Gardens (May 2011): 94. 116

LET'S TAKE IT
a Room at a Time

CLEANING WALLS

Most walls are painted with latex, which is easy to wash after it has cured or set for a period of time. Clean walls with a commercial all-purpose cleaner, or use the following recipe for a homemade cleaner: Mix ½ cup of vinegar, 1 cup clear ammonia, ½ cup baking soda, and 1 gallon warm water. Apply solution to the wall with a sponge and rinse with clear water. If your wall has a texture, use old socks rather than a sponge. The socks will not tear like a sponge.

CLEANING WINDOWS

You can avoid washing your windows if you keep your blinds or curtains drawn, but life without light is gloomy. So, if you like light and want to look out at the world, you will need to clean your windows twice a year, usually in the spring and in the fall. Recipe for window cleaner: Mix ⅓ cup ammonia in 1 gallon of warm water. Apply with a sponge/squeegee or pour the solution into a spray container and spray it directly onto the windows. Wipe with a lint-free cloth, a chamois is best. Vinegar may be substituted for ammonia. Squeegees work well to remove excess water and then dry with chamois. Note: White coffee filters are great for cleaning windows and glass without leaving streaks or residue behind.

BATHROOM:

Bathrooms tend to become both dirty and messy. The obvious solution to bathroom clutter is first discard all unused items, then create storage for the things most bathrooms are not designed to store, such as hair dryers, makeup, electric shavers, and magazines. Using Rubbermaid containers, trays, and organizers can help with the bathroom clutter. The most efficient way to clean your bathroom is to clean it often.

- **Bathtub Rings**—A suggested method to keep bathtub rings from gathering on your tub is to add bubble bath to your bath water or a capful of detergent to the water. Towel dry.

- **Hair Removal**—Remove all hair from the tub and sink before cleaning in order to keep hair out of the cleaning cloth.

- **Cleaning Solution**—For tubs and sinks: This solution cleans porcelain as well as cultured-marble, ceramic tile, and fiberglass. Mix ½ cup vinegar, 1 cup clear ammonia, and ¼ cup baking soda in 1 gallon of hot water. Caution: Wear rubber gloves, and work in a well-ventilated area when using this powerful solution. Apply the solution to the fixtures with a sponge, scrubbing if necessary, and rinse with clear water. Dry with clean cloth.

- **Yellowed or Discolored Porcelain**—Clean with a paste made of cream of tartar moistened with hydrogen peroxide or a paste made of borax moistened with lemon juice. Scrub the paste into lightly stained areas with a brush and rinse well (old toothbrushes work well).

- **Ceramic Tile**—Stained or mildewed grout is very noticeable and makes your whole bathroom look dirty. A toothbrush or nail brush is the best tool for cleaning grout. To remove the mildew, dip the brush in chlorine bleach and gently scrub the affected grout. If spots persist, hide them by camouflaging them with white shoe polish. If you get the white polish on the tile, let it dry and wipe off with a damp rag.

- **Drains**—Moderately clogged drains can be treated by pouring ½ cup baking soda, followed by ½ cup vinegar down the drain. These ingredients when mixed create a foaming action. Let sit for three hours and rinse with clear water.

- **Shower Curtains**—Need to be cleaned on a regular basis to remove built-up scum, water deposits, and mildew. Most shower curtains are washable; fabric curtains and some plastic ones can be washed in the washer. Use regular detergent when you wash fabric curtains and follow the manufacturer's instructions for water temperature and wash/rinse cycles.

- **Plastic Shower Curtains**—When machine washing, use the gentle cycle and cool water. Wash plastic curtains in ½ cup detergent and ½ cup baking soda, along with two large bath towels. To prevent a machine-washed shower curtain from wrinkling, add a cup of vinegar to the rinse cycle. Washing the curtain in a bathtub will cause fewer wrinkles than machine washing. A good solution for cleaning plastic shower curtains is ½ cup vinegar, 1 cup clear ammonia, ¼ cup baking soda, and 1 gallon warm water. Apply the solution to the curtain with a sponge while it is lying flat. Wear rubber gloves when using this solution. Let the solution stand for several minutes to loosen scum, then scrub with a brush or sponge adding more cleaner if necessary. Rinse well with warm water to which a few drops of mineral oil have been added to make the curtain soft and flexible. Shake off excess water and hang to drip-dry, **or just buy a new one!**

- **For mildew on shower curtains**—Spray with disinfectant regularly. Shake excess water off curtain after every use.

- **Shower Area**—Spray periodically with a mildew inhibitor and disinfectant to cut down on mildew.

- **Leave the shower door slightly open** to allow air to circulate; this will discourage the growth of mildew.

- **Glass Shower Doors**—Sparkle when cleaned with a sponge dipped in white vinegar. A solution of white vinegar and water will remove hard water deposits.

- **Lemon Oil** is great for removing the water spots on the metal frame around shower doors.

- **If grout or caulking** breaks away, re-caulk immediately to prevent water damage.

- **Toilets**—A grin and bear it chore! In-tank cleaners are not a substitute for regular cleaning. Clean and disinfect your toilet bowl with ½ cup chlorine bleach. Pour it into the bowl and let it stand 10 minutes; scrub and flush. Wear rubber gloves and do not mix chlorine with other cleaners.

KITCHEN:

Kitchens get messy because they can be a "catch-all" place and because cooking can be messy! Below you will find some helps in keeping your kitchen clean on a regular basis.

- **Countertop Surfaces**—All kitchen countertops are made to be tough and durable. A variety of surfaces are available requiring different methods for cleaning. There are several popular countertops surfaces, among them are quartz, granite, marble, soapstone, solid surfaces, and butcher block. Each one should be treated differently:

  Quartz: Quartz has a nonporous surface that resists both scratching and staining. It is also impervious to heat and acid. No sealing is required. To clean quartz countertops you will not need anything more sophisticated than a gentle soap solution. Buff dry with a soft absorbent towel.

  Granite: Granite, a natural stone, is strong and durable. It will require sealing to avoid stains. It is almost impervious to heat. For cleaning, surface can be wiped with warm soapy water and rinsed. You can also use a 50/50 solution of isopropyl alcohol and water. Do not use vinegar, Windex, or bleach on granite.

  Marble: Marble is a natural stone and is waterproof and heatproof. It is not the best choice for kitchens due to its penchant for staining and scratching. To clean, you may use a marble cleaner or a squirt of non-abrasive dish soap with warm water in a spray bottle and spray counter generously. Scrub gently and wipe the soapy solution off with a clean wet cloth. Rub the counter dry and buff with a soft absorbent towel.

  Soapstone: Soapstone is a natural stone and is fairly impervious to heat. It should be wiped down with a damp cloth and treated with mineral oil regularly. After mineral oil treatment, you may use any household cleanser such as Ajax or Comet.

  Solid-Surfaces Materials: These materials are sold under brands that include Avonite, Corian, and Swanstone, and are all man-made material. Although they resist staining, they can easily be damaged by heat. Clean these surfaces with a damp microfiber cloth. A mild dish soap or ammonia based cleaners can also be used. Towel dry the surface to prevent water spots.

  Butcher Block: Butcher block countertops are very sanitary and waterproof when sealed. A thin layer of Mineral oil can be applied once a month for the first year, after that you can apply it once every six months or when surface appears dull. Clean by mopping up spills immediately with a damp cloth or paper towel. Adding a drop of liquid soap to your wet cloth will help loosen any sticky or greasy spills, making them easier to wipe up. Never use harsh cleaners like Windex, Formula 409, or any other chemicals.

- **Floors**—The first step to cleaning any floor is to get up all the dirt by vacuuming, sweeping, or using a Swiffer dust mop. A vacuum with a small brush attachment or crevice tool is effective in cleaning around baseboards, under refrigerators, etc. Knowing the material your floor is made of is important. Floors can be easily damaged by using the wrong cleaning method or product.

- **Dishwasher**—Baking soda cleans your dishwasher inside and out. Dip a damp cloth in soda and clean smudges and fingerprints from the exterior; (enamel surfaces) the same method will also remove stains from the liner. Use a synthetic scouring pad to clean stubborn stains and glass cleaner for chromium trim. For stainless surfaces use a combination of dish soap and baby or mineral oil. Going with the grain of your stainless, place a little bit of dish soap on an all-cotton cloth, moisten with a modest amount of warm water then wipe along the grain. When you finish cleaning an area, dry any water streaks with a clean towel or cloth. Time to polish. Dab a small amount of mineral or baby oil onto a dry towel. Follow the grain of your stainless steel. The results will make you happy.

- **Freezers and Refrigerators**—Regularly clean out and wash refrigerator and freezer to keep fresh and clean. For exterior, follow cleaning process described in manual.

- **Ceramic Cook-tops**—This is a glass cook-top with electric heating elements under the glass. Wait until the top cools to wipe up spills; never use a wet sponge or cloth on a hot panel. Abrasive cleaning products will scratch the surface. The best way to clean a ceramic cook-top is to sprinkle a nonabrasive cleanser or baking soda over the surface and rub with a synthetic scouring pad or sponge. Rinse well with clear water, and buff dry with a soft cloth.

- **Gas and Electric Stovetops and Ovens**—The exteriors of most gas and electric ranges are baked on porcelain enamel with chrome trim. Wipe the surface around the heating elements after each use. Use a synthetic scouring pad for stubborn soil. Harsh abrasives or steel wool will damage the stove's enamel or stainless finish. Gas burners should be washed occasionally. Clear the holes with a fine wire or pipe cleaner. Electric ovens are usually self-cleaning. All control knobs for stoves and ovens can be removed and washed in soapy water, dried, and placed back on appliance.

- **Stainless Surfaces**—Use a combination of dish soap and baby or mineral oil. Place a little bit of dish soap on an all-cotton cloth, moisten with a modest amount of warm water. Find the grain of your stainless and wipe along the grain. When you finish cleaning an area, dry any water streaks with a clean towel or cloth. Time to polish. Dab a small amount of mineral or baby oil onto a dry towel. Follow the grain of your stainless steel. The results will make you happy!

LIVING AREA:

- Remove all the clutter first. Everything in its place!

- Begin with higher objects such as ceiling fan, wall mounted televisions, light fixtures, fans, hanging lights, sconces, lamps, etc., using a Swiffer duster. Dust lampshades with a small dry, soft paint brush moving from top to bottom. Occasionally, clean these items with a cleaning solution according to instructions given on the object for removing dirt and grime.

- Dust all wood surfaces. I recommend using furniture polish once a month and a Swiffer duster the remainder of the month. This helps to prevent build-up. For furniture pieces that cannot be polished, use a slightly damp rag for removing dust.

- Shake out curtains, and when necessary, wash according to care label. Draperies will need to be vacuumed regularly or dry-cleaned.

- Clean all spots on carpeting, allow to dry completely, and vacuum.

BEDROOMS:

- Bedrooms tend to gather dust due to skin particles and because they are "lived in."

- Change sheets every week or every other, according to need. My grandchildren shower every night before bed and put on clean pajamas, because they go to bed clean, every other week is sufficient. If sick, you may want to change your pillowcases more often.

- Begin with higher objects, such as ceiling fan, wall mounted televisions, light fixtures, fans, hanging lights, sconces, lamps, etc. using a Swiffer duster. Dust lampshades with a small dry, soft paint brush, moving from top to bottom. Occasionally, clean these items with a cleaning solution according to instructions given on the object for removing dirt and grime.

- Dust all wood surfaces. I recommend using furniture polish once a month and a Swiffer duster the remainder of the month. This helps to prevent build-up.

- Shake out curtains and when necessary wash according to care label. Draperies will need to be vacuumed regularly or dry-cleaned.

- Clean all spots in carpeting, allow to dry completely and vacuum.

SPECIAL HOUSEHOLD
Cleaning Projects

MIRRORS

In order for the mirrors in your home to reflect well on you, they must be clean. Choose from one of these mirror cleaners to have beautiful, sparkling mirrors:

MIRROR CLEANER:

Mix ⅓ cup ammonia in one gallon of warm water. Apply the solution with a sponge/squeegee or pour into a pump bottle and spray sparingly onto mirror. Buff with a lint-free cloth, chamois, or paper towel. Vinegar may be substituted for ammonia.

MIRROR CLEANER:

Mix 2 cups isopropyl rubbing alcohol (70 percent), 2 tablespoons liquid dishwashing detergent, and 2 cups water. Stir until the solution is completely mixed and pour into a pump bottle. Spray the mixture sparingly on the mirror and buff with a lint-free cloth or paper toweling. Note: White paper coffee filters are great for cleaning mirrors without leaving streaks of residue behind.

TELEVISION SETS:

Your television collects dust and airborne particles. It is recommended that you use micro-fiber cloth on television screens. Note: With the new LED, HDTV, plasma LCD and QLED televisions, specialty cleaning instructions are given inside the instructional manual.

PICTURES:

Paintings and photographs framed behind glass require little care. When you clean the glass over a painting or picture, be careful not to allow any moisture to get behind the glass. When using furniture polish on picture frames, spray it on a cloth and carefully apply to the frame. Using a Swiffer duster works as well as polish.

BLINDS:

The best way to clean wood blinds is to begin with vacuuming the dust from each slat. With blinds turned in the down position, take a slightly damp cloth, and wipe each slat left to right. Depending on the degree of dirt, rinse the cloth every two to three slats and change water regularly. Turn blinds in the upward position and clean the other side. Natural wood blinds with decorative yarn tapes; should never be immersed. In most hardware stores, you can find a special duster designed for cleaning wood blinds.

CURTAINS:

Carefully read the care label on your curtains before determining method of cleaning; follow the manufacturer's instructions.

DRAPERIES:

Most draperies are lined and are usually made of fabrics that are much heavier than those used for curtains. It is usually best to dry-clean draperies. Vacuum all draperies before sending them out to be dry-cleaned. If you want to wash draperies, test a corner of the fabric in a bowl of warm water and detergent to see if it bleeds. When washing in a machine, use only the gentle cycle. Carefully read the care label on your draperies.

SHADES:

Light diffusing and opaque shades are normally made of fabrics that are washable; some have a protective vinyl coating that makes them easy to clean. Others are not washable and must be dry-cleaned. Vacuum shades regularly with the small brush attachment. Lower the shades completely before vacuuming to clean the full length. Do not forget the very tops of the shades and valances. To remove finger marks, use a damp sponge or a quick spray of all-purpose cleaner. Carefully read the care label on your shades.

SHUTTERS:

Vacuum all shutters regularly with the small brush attachment. Wipe them occasionally with a damp sponge to remove smudges and fingerprints. Use warm, soapy water with a damp cloth to wash painted shutters; wash each louver separately on both sides. Shutters that are finished with varnish, lacquer, or wax can be cleaned with commercial aerosol polishing/waxing products. Choose a product that is appropriate for the finish of your shutters.

FLOORING CARE

CARPET:

The easiest way to tackle vacuuming a carpeted room is to divide the room into sections. You can be sure to cover every inch of carpeting if you divide it into quarters and vacuum an entire quarter before moving on to the next. Vacuum once a week or more in areas of heavy traffic. Frequent vacuuming prolongs the life of your carpet. Every six months, vacuum around the edge of the carpeting along the baseboards. On occasion, do a deep cleaning of carpets to deal effectively with stains and spots.

CERAMIC TILE, GLAZED:

Highly glazed ceramic flooring is almost carefree floor covering. It requires little more than regular vacuuming and damp mopping. When damp mopping, use an all-purpose cleaner along with a synthetic scouring pad. Dry the floor with a soft cloth to avoid streaks. A bucket of water with 1 cup of white vinegar will make the floor glisten.

CERAMIC TILE, UNGLAZED:

Unlike shiny, easy-to-care for glazed tile, unglazed tile is porous and must be sealed to resist stains. Unglazed tile floors need to be sealed with a commercial sealer and a water-based wax. Do not clean your unglazed ceramic-tile floor with acids, strong soaps, or abrasives. Vacuuming followed by damp mopping should be sufficient.

MARBLE:

Non-polished marble is very porous and must be sealed with a commercial sealer. Polished marble is less porous but can still be stained. Marble floors look great after being damp mopped using clear water and an all-purpose cleaning solution in warm water, or a mixture of 1 cup fabric softener and ½ gallon water. If the floor appears to be dull after several washings, mop with 1 gallon water and 1 cup of white vinegar solution. It will glisten, and this beats re-waxing.

VINYL NO-WAX:

This flooring is a breeze to maintain. All you have to do is keep it clean. Vacuuming and damp mopping should be all that is needed. Use an all-purpose cleaning solution on vinyl floors and always read the product label for precautionary measures and instructions. It might be good to test any cleaner before applying it to the entire floor. If your no-wax floor loses its shine in high traffic areas, use a glossy renewing product available from the manufacturer of your floor.

WOOD:

Wood floors are elegant. The care of floors will depend upon the product that was used to seal the floor: varnish, shellac, polyurethane, or lacquer. Only the polyurethane requires no further treatment, including waxing. The integrity and beauty of wood floors not finished with polyurethane can be maintained by using solvent-based cleaners and polishes. <u>Note</u>: Water should never be used on wood floors, except those treated with polyurethane; these can be washed with a lightly damp mop. For varnished, shellacked, or lacquered floors, the fastest way to clean is with a one-step cleaner/polish.

Vacuum the floor, then pour the solvent-based liquid on a small area and rub lightly with a clean, dry wax applicator. Work a small section at a time; stroke the floor in the direction of the grain. Blot up any excess liquid with a clean cloth. Apply a liquid or paste solvent-based wax to wood floors twice a year. Make sure the room is well ventilated when using solvent-based products.

CARPET STAINS

Carpet cleaning solution contains 1 teaspoon mild detergent, 1 teaspoon white vinegar, and 1 quart warm water. Below are some tips for spots and stains:

- **Carefully blot or scrape the entire stained area** before applying any cleaning solution. Remove as much of the spill as possible. If you start cleaning too soon, you will make a bigger mess because the cleaning solution will spread the stain over more of the carpet.

- **Test the carpet** in an inconspicuous area making sure the cleaner does not damage or discolor carpet.

- **Do not rub a spill** for you may spread the problem to a larger area of carpeting. When you apply spot cleaner, work from the outside of the stain toward the inside to avoid spreading the stain.

- **After applying the cleaning solution**, blot up all the moisture in the carpeting. A clean white bath towel is best for drying carpet and brushing the nap back up to a standing position.

- **After blotting the carpet**, if you feel there is still too much moisture, place a ¾-thick stack of white towels over the spill and weight them with a heavy object or stand on the towels.

- **If the spot remover used alters the color** of the carpet, try touching up small places with artists' acrylic paint. If that doesn't work, try a felt-tip marker or a permanent-ink marker of the appropriate color. Go slowly, blending the colors into the fibers.

- **To raise depressions** left in carpet by heavy furniture, try steaming. Hold a steam iron close enough for steam to reach the carpet. Do not let the iron touch the fibers, especially if they are synthetic, because they could melt. Lift the fibers by scraping with the edge of a spoon.

REMOVING SPECIFIC STAINS FROM CARPETING

- **Blood**—Absorb as much of the blood as you can. Mix 1 teaspoon mild detergent, 1 teaspoon white vinegar, and 1 quart warm water. Apply the solution to the spot. Let the carpet dry. Apply a dry-cleaning fluid and let dry. Vacuum completely.

- **Butter**—First, scrape up as much butter as possible or absorb as much of melted butter as possible. Apply dry-cleaning fluid or Blue Dawn® in warm water. Rub lightly. Let the carpet dry. If the spot remains, reapply the fluid/Blue Dawn®. Dry thoroughly and vacuum.

- **Candle Wax**—The easiest way to remove candle wax from your carpet is to press an ice cube against the drip. The wax will harden and can then be pulled off. Treat any remaining traces of wax with dry-cleaning solution. Let the carpet dry and vacuum.

- **Candy**—Candy that contains no chocolate is easily removed from carpeting. Scrape up as much of the candy as possible. Mix 1 teaspoon mild detergent, 1 teaspoon white vinegar, and 1 quart warm water. Apply the solution to the spot. Let the carpet dry. If spot remains, reapply the solution. Let carpet dry and then vacuum.

- **Chewing Gum**—Chewing gum can be a very sticky mess. Press an ice cube against the blob of gum. The gum will harden and can then be pulled off. Treat any remaining traces of the chewing gum with dry-cleaning fluid. Let the carpet dry and vacuum.

- **Chocolate**—The longer chocolate stays on your carpet, the more difficult it is to remove. Scrape it from the carpet. Mix 1 teaspoon mild detergent, 1 teaspoon white vinegar, and 1 quart warm water. Apply the solution to the spot. Rinse with clear water, dry completely and vacuum gently.

- **Coffee**—Be sure to blot the coffee spill immediately. Using the same solution used for chocolate stains, apply the solution to the coffee stain. Let the carpet dry and then apply dry-cleaning fluid and let dry. Vacuum carpet completely.

- **Crayon**—For dropped crayons that have been stepped on and ground into the carpeting, scrape excess away and remove the rest by placing a blotter over the crayon stain and pressing it with a warm iron until the blotter absorbs the melted crayon. Move the blotter frequently so that it does not get oversaturated. Apply dry-cleaning fluid, and let the carpet dry. Reapply if necessary and then vacuum.

- **Fruit**—Fruit stains can be very hard to remove if they are allowed to set. But if you act quickly, the following method usually prevents a permanent stain. Scrape up spilled fruit and absorb fruit juice. Use the same solution mentioned under coffee and chocolate and apply to the spot. Let the carpet dry. If the spot remains, reapply the solution. Let the carpet dry and vacuum gently.

- **Ink**—Fast action is very essential when dealing with ink spots. Immediately apply dry-cleaning fluid. Let the carpet dry. If the spot remains, reapply the dry-cleaning fluid. Let the carpet dry thoroughly and vacuum.

- **Lipstick**—To remove lipstick, scrape away as much as possible. Apply dry-cleaning fluid and let dry. Then mix a solution of 1 teaspoon white vinegar, 1 teaspoon mild dishwater detergent, and 1 quart of warm water. Apply the solution to the spot. Let the carpet dry. If the spot remains, reapply the solution. Let the carpet dry and vacuum gently.

- **Milk**—Blot up the spilled milk. Apply the solution of detergent, vinegar, and water to the spilled area. Let the carpet dry and vacuum gently.

- **Mud**—Allow the mud tracked onto your carpet to dry. Brush or scrape off as much as possible. Use the carpet solution and apply to the spots. Let the carpet dry completely and then vacuum.

- **Nail Polish**—Apply dry-cleaning fluid, acetone, or polish remover to the spilled polish. Test the solvent you plan to use on an inconspicuous part of the carpet. Never apply solvents directly onto the carpet. If the stain remains, use carpet solution and apply to the spot. Let dry and then vacuum gently.

- **Soft Drinks**—The carbonation in drinks will help you clean spilled drinks quickly, but you must act fast. Some of the dyes found in drinks can stain your carpet permanently. Blot up the spilled drink. Using carpet solution, blot the spot thoroughly. Let the carpet dry. If spot remains, apply solution once again. Dry completely and vacuum gently.

- **Tea**—The tannic acid in tea is a potent dye, so move quickly when tea is spilled on your rug. Blot up the tea spill. Using carpet solution, apply to the spill. Let the carpet dry. Apply dry-cleaning fluid. Let the carpet dry and vacuum gently.

- **Urine**—Blot up urine immediately. Using carpet solution, apply to area. Let the carpet dry and vacuum gently.

- **Vomit**—Treat immediately. Blot up as much as possible, then dilute immediately with baking soda and water or club soda. Apply a solution of ammonia (1 part) and water (10 parts). Rinse with cold water. Let dry, and then vacuum.

Note: Dry-cleaning solution called for in many stain cleaning instructions can be found at local hardware stores.

AGE-APPROPRIATE
Chores for Kids [23]

A FAMILY IS A TEAM:

Everyone shares in the responsibility of keeping the home. Children are never too young to learn to help. Both my girls taught their children at a young age to fold washcloths and from there proceeded to bigger items. If you start at a young age giving them simple responsibilities, helping around the house will become natural to them.

2-4 year old

- Help dust
- Put napkins on table
- Help put away toys
- Put laundry in hamper
- Help feed pet

4-7 year old

"Help" is the important word at this age. Many of the chores will be done as a helper and slowly kids can graduate to doing them independently.

- Set the table or help set the table
- Put away toys/things
- Help feed pets
- Water plants
- Help make bed
- Dust
- Put laundry in hamper
- Help put dishes in dishwasher
- Water the garden
- Help wipe up messes
- Help with yard work (rake with child's rake or plant flowers, etc.)
- Help clear table
- Help put away groceries

[23] Age-Appropriate Chores for Kids]: "Free Printable Behavior Charts." www.freeprintablebehaviorcharts.com.

8–10 year old

- Make bed
- Water plants
- Clean room with direction
- Set the table
- Clear the table
- Dust
- Vacuum
- Feed pets
- Help make dinner
- Put laundry in hamper
- Help wash the car
- Help wash dishes
- Help load/empty dishwasher
- Rake leaves
- Take out the trash

---

11 year old and older

- Take out garbage
- Set the table
- Clear the table
- Clean room with direction
- Put away groceries
- Clean the bathroom with direction
- Clean the kitchen
- Dust
- Vacuum
- Mow lawn
- Feed pets
- Water plants
- Put laundry in hamper
- Help with laundry and eventually start doing own laundry
- Help make dinner/make small meals on own
- Help wash the car/wash car
- Make bed
- Help with yard work
- Shovel snow
- Wash dishes/load or empty dishwasher

ESTHER
A Woman for Such a Time as This

Biblical Principle: God uses women with a willing heart to accomplish His divine purposes.

Read the Book of Esther.

Biblical History for Lesson—The book of Esther begins with King Ahasuerus(Xerxes)—a pagan king— and a banquet he was giving for his people, one that lasted for seven days. He invited people from the greatest to the least. King Ashasuerus had great wealth—couches made of gold and silver, marble floors, many jewels, and fine linens. The drinks were served in golden goblets; the royal wine was plentiful. At the same time the king was giving a banquet, Queen Vashti was having a little party of her own. The king got very intoxicated and sent for the queen; he desired to show off his prized trophy. Apparently, she was very beautiful! She refused to come, which made him very angry. He called all of his wise men and asked them what he was to do.

In Esther Chapter 1:16-20, one of the men, Memucan, said, "Queen Vashti has wronged not only the king but also all the princes and all the peoples who are in all the provinces of King Ahasuerus. For the queen's conduct will become known to all the women causing them to look with contempt on their husbands by saying, 'King Ahasuerus commanded Queen Vashti to be brought in to his presence, but she did not come.' This day the ladies of Persia and Media who have heard of the queen's conduct will speak in the same way to all the king's princes, and there will be plenty of contempt and anger. If it pleases the king, let a royal edict be issued by him and let it be written in the laws of Persia and Media so that it cannot be repealed, that Vashti may no longer come into the presence of King Ahasuerus, and let the king give her royal position to another who is more worthy than she. When the king's edict which he will make is heard throughout all his kingdom, great as it is, then all the women will give honor to their husbands, great and small" (NAS). The king liked what his wise men suggested, so he sent out an edict. Persian law was irrevocable when the king signed it in to law—it was law!

With time, the king got over being angry with Queen Vashti and realized that he deeply missed her, but he had to abide by the law he had set forth. His wise men suggested that a beautiful young virgin be sought for the king. So, young beautiful women were brought from all over the kingdom for the king's choosing. The one who pleased the king would take Queen Vashti's place.

We are going to treat this story as if it were a play and pick up the story in Scene One.

SCENE ONE

Mordecai appears on the scene. He was one of many Jews who refused to uproot his family from Babylonia and return to Jerusalem. Therefore, they were taken captive by the Persians when they moved in and took over Babylonia. Mordecai was bringing up his uncle's daughter, Esther. It says of her, "Now the young lady was beautiful of form and face, and when her father and mother died, Mordecai took her as his own daughter." Esther 2:7b NAS

We already see God's hand of mercy, grace, protection, and provision on Esther as she is chosen to be one of the young women to go before the King.

- Mordecai loved Esther, and in order to watch over her, we see him coming to the gate of the king's palace every day to keep a watchful eye on her.

- The young women spent a year in preparation before they were presented to the king—six months with oil and myrrh, and six months with spices, and the cosmetics for women.

- We would all be looking pretty good if we had that type of pampering!

- The young women were called before the king and allowed to take with them anything they desired.

- Esther didn't find it necessary to take anything, just her beauty. Both her beauty of character and her physical beauty were enough.

> Esther's turn came to appear before King Ahasuerus. "She was summoned by name. Now when the turn of Esther, the daughter of Abihail the uncle of Mordecai who had taken her as his daughter, came to go into the king, she did not request anything except what Hegai, the king's eunuch who was in charge of the women, advised. And Esther found favor in the eyes of all who saw her." Esther 2:15, NAS

Our heavenly Father delights in us, as the king delighted in Esther, and He calls us by name, as the king called her by name.

As I am envisioning Esther, I am imagining her to have an inward beauty as well as an outward beauty. She was appealing to all who encountered her, a reflection of the God of the universe, and set apart.

> "The king loved Esther more than all the women, and she found favor and kindness with him more than all the virgins, so that he set the royal crown on her head and made her queen instead of Vashti." Esther 2:17 NAS

We see God's favor on Esther in being the king's choice.

In keeping a watchful eye on Esther, Mordecai came to the king's gate daily. One day as he sat at the gate, he overheard two of the palace guards expressing their dislike for the king and plotting to overthrow him. Mordecai reported this information to Esther.

She then tells the king about the plot against his life and gives Mordecai all the credit for uncovering it. "Mordecai foiled an assassination plot against the king and the report of this service was duly recorded in the king's diary." NAS Ryrie Study Bible

Once the plot was investigated and found to be true, the guilty were hung.

SCENE TWO

Entering the stage is Haman, an egotistical man, possibly related to the Amalekites and if so, he was a descendent of Esau, who was an enemy of the descendants of Jacob. Haman was advanced in rank by the king and given great authority over the princes who were with him.

> "When Haman saw that Mordecai neither bowed down nor paid homage to him, Haman was filled with rage." Esther 3:5 NAS

- Haman knew that if this one influential Jew would not bow down to him, no Jew would bow down, so he plotted, with the help of his wife and friends, to eliminate the Jews.

- Haman convinced the king that the Jews were a threat to his kingdom and that he should write a decree telling every province to kill all the Jews on the thirteenth day of the twelfth month. "A copy of the edict to be issued as law in every province was published to all the peoples so that they should be ready for this day" Esther 3:14 NAS

- Upon hearing about the edict, Mordecai was grieved. He replaced his clothes with clothing that signified grief: sackcloth.

Esther then sent her servant to Mordecai to ask why he refused to remove his sackcloth. "Mordecai told him all that had happened to him, and the exact amount of money Haman had promised to pay to the king's treasuries for the destruction of the Jews. He also gave him a copy of the text of the edict which had been issued for their destruction, that he might show Esther and inform her, and to order her to go to the king to implore his favor and to plead with him for her people." Esther 4:7–8 NAS

> Esther sent word back to Mordecai telling him that only those summoned by the King could go before him. "And I have not been summoned to come to the king for these thirty days." Esther 4:11 NAS

Mordecai's response included within it a very famous verse that sums up why God had placed Esther within the king's palace. Esther 4:13–14 says, "Do not imagine that you in the king's palace can escape any more than all the Jews. For if you remain silent at this time, relief and deliverance will arise for the Jews from another place and you and your father's house will perish. And who knows whether you have not attained royalty for such a time as this?"

God had placed Esther there within those walls to accomplish His purpose on behalf of His children.

Dianne's Personal Testimony—<u>Note</u>: The leader may want to share her testimony of a time in her life when she knew God was asking of her a specific task at a specific time for His glory and honor. *When Mark and I felt God calling us away from the business world into full-time vocational ministry, we only knew where we were to go; we knew nothing of the purpose God had for us in going. It wasn't until we felt God calling us away that we began to realize that He had placed us in a specific church, and in a strategic position, for such a time as* *this. Our purpose in being there was made clear to us in our stepping down. God had a specific calling and a specific purpose, and all He asked of us was to be willing. Esther was willing!*

> Esther knew what she was called to do; and desired to fulfill the assignment given her, even if it cost her life. She asked her people to pray and fast for three days. "Go assemble all the Jews found in Susa, and fast for me; do not eat or drink for three days, night or day. I and my maidens also will fast in the same way. And thus I will go in to the king, which is not according to the law; and if I perish, I perish." Esther 4:15–17 NAS

So, all the people, along with Mordecai, did as Esther requested.

SCENE THREE

Esther dressed in her best robe and went before the king. "It happened when the king saw Esther the queen standing in the court; she obtained favor in his sight; and the king extended to Esther the golden scepter which was in his hand. So Esther came near and touched the top of the scepter. The king said to her, 'What is troubling you, Queen Esther? And what is your request? Even to half of the kingdom it will be given to you.'" Esther 5: 2–3 NAS

God honored the fasting and prayers of His people by giving Esther favor in the king's presence.

- She responded by asking the king if he and Haman would attend a banquet she was giving the following day.
- We saw Haman's hatred of Mordecai escalating, and at dinner that night, he boasted to his wife and friends that Queen Esther had invited only him and the king to her banquet.

Yet, the honor was not enough; it did not satisfy him due to the hatred he had in his heart toward Mordecai. He could not rejoice in the invitation because of the sin in his own heart. His wife and friends had an idea. "Then Zeresh his wife and all his friends said to him, 'Have a gallows fifty cubits high made and in the morning ask the king to have Mordecai hanged on it; then go joyfully with the king to the banquet.' And the advice pleased Haman, so he had the gallows built." Esther 5:14 NAS

SCENE FOUR

That night, the king could not sleep and requested the chronicles of his reign be brought to him. As he was reading, he just happened to read how Mordecai uncovered the plot of the two eunuchs—doorkeepers—to kill the king. He asked his servants, what had been done for Mordecai for saving the king's life, and they replied, "Nothing has been done for him." Esther 6:3 NAS

It just so happened about that time, Haman had arrived in the court, wanting to get there early in order to have time before the banquet to talk with the king about hanging Mordecai. The king saw him and said, "What is to be done for the man whom the king desires to honor?" Haman's first thought was that the king must be referring to him; we see how much pride he had!

So, Haman says, "For the man whom the king desires to honor, let them bring a royal robe, which the king has worn, for him to wear, and the horse on which the king has ridden, and on whose head a royal crown has been placed; and let the royal robe and the horse be handed over to one of the king's most noble princes and let them array the man whom the king desires to honor and lead him on horseback through the city square, and proclaim before him, 'Thus it shall be done to the man whom the king desires to honor.'" Esther 6:6–7 NAS

Now, for the shock of a lifetime, the king said to Haman, "Take quickly the robes and the horse as you have said, and do so for Mordecai the Jew, who is sitting at the king's gate; do not fall short in anything of all that you have said." Esther 6:10 NAS

About this time, Haman had to be saying to himself, "Do what and for whom?"

- Mordecai was robed and paraded before the people.

- Haman returned home and began to whine to his wife about his day.

- Suddenly, the king's men showed up at the front door and took him away to the queen's banquet.

- At the banquet, Esther was asked by the king, "What is your request and why have you invited me here?"

> Queen Esther proceeded to tell him, "If I have found favor in your sight, O king, and if it pleases the king, let my life be given me as my petition, and my people as my request; for we have been sold, and my people, to be destroyed, to be killed, and to be annihilated. Now if we had only been sold as slaves, men and women, I would have remained silent, for the trouble would not be commensurate with the annoyance of the king." Esther 7:3-4 NAS

This statement peeked the king's curiosity and he asked Queen Esther, "Who is he, and where is he, who would presume to do thus?" This was the moment Esther had prepared for, and the purpose for which she was there. She responded, "A foe and an enemy is this wicked Haman!" She exposed the enemy of God's people.

The king was so angry he had to leave the room. When he returned, he found Haman throwing himself upon Queen Esther begging for his life; this made the king even angrier. He proceeded to tell his men to hang Haman on the very gallows that he had prepared for Mordecai, and they did.

SCENE FIVE

In Chapter 8, King Ashasuerus gave Haman's house and his possessions to Queen Esther. Mordecai received the king's signet ring and was placed in charge of the house of Haman.

> Queen Esther petitioned the king to revoke his edict. "If it pleases the king and if I have found favor before him and the matter seems proper to the king and I am pleasing in his sight, let it be written to revoke the letter devised by Haman, which he wrote to destroy the Jews, who are all in the king's provinces. For how can I endure to see the calamity which shall befall my people, and how can I endure to see the destruction of my kindred?" Esther 8:5–6 NAS
>
> The king addressed Queen Esther and Mordecai. "Behold, I have given the house of Haman to Esther, and him they have hung on the gallows because he had stretched out his hands against the Jews. Now, you write to the Jews as you see fit, in the king's name, and seal it with the king's signet ring; for a decree which is written in the name of the king and sealed with the king's signet ring may not be revoked." Esther 8:7–8 NAS

Once again, we see God's favor, His protection, and His blessings on Esther and Mordecai, as well as His fulfillment of His plan for His people. "In each and every province and in each and every city, wherever the king's commandment and his decree arrived, there was gladness and joy for the Jews, a feast and a holiday." Esther 8:17 NAS

Esther was prepared and because of that God used her mightily!

Discipling Leader: Discuss the following questions with the class:

- How has the story of Esther's life impacted you?
- What will you do differently as a result of studying the life of Esther?

If time allows, utilize the Discussion Questions and the Examining the Heart Questions.

DISCUSSION QUESTIONS

1. Whose care was Esther placed in within the king's palace? *Hagai*

2. How did Hagai feel toward Esther? "Now the young lady pleased him and found favor with him. So he quickly provided her with cosmetics and food, gave her seven choice maids from the king's palace and transferred her and her maids to the best place in the harem."

3. What were Mordecai's instructions to Esther? *Not to reveal her nationality.* "Esther did not make known her people or her kindred, for Mordecai had instructed her that she should not make them known."

4. Why did Mordecai tell her not to reveal her nationality? *He feared for her life.*

5. Who came daily to check on Esther? *Mordecai.*

6. How does the king celebrate his marriage to Esther? *He celebrates with a great banquet and by declaring it as a holiday.*

7. Has Esther declared her nationality to the king up to this point? Why or why not? *No, she has not, because she had promised Mordecai she would not.* "Esther had not yet made known her kindred or her people, even as Mordecai had commanded her; for Esther did what Mordecai told her as she had done when under his care."

8. In respecting Mordecai's request, what characteristic describes Esther? *The characteristic of obedience; she was obedient to her authority—Mordecai.*

9. What was it Mordecai refused to do that made Haman so mad? *He refused to bow down to him.*

10. What did Mordecai do upon hearing about the decree? What did the Jewish people do? *Mordecai tore his clothes and put on sackcloth. He went out into the city and began to wail loudly and bitterly. The Jewish people fasted, wept, wailed, and many put on sackcloth and ashes.*

11. What was Esther's response when told about the decree by her maidens and eunuch? "Then Esther's maidens and eunuchs came and told her, and the queen writhed in great anguish. And she sent garments to clothe Mordecai that he might remove his sackcloth from him, but he did not accept them."

12. How did God reward Esther's obedience? *She was honored by the king and respected by the people. Her uncle, Mordecai, was saved. The king listened to her petition and revoked his decree, therefore saving her people, the Jews.*

Examining the Heart

1. Do you have an inner beauty that is reflective of your heavenly Father, a beauty that sets you apart?

2. Have you ever had a time when you knew without a shadow of a doubt that God had put you within a certain place for His specific purposes?

3. Have you developed the discipline of fasting and prayer in your Christian life? Read Matthew 6:16–18.

4. Are you spiritually prepared, should God say to you, "I have called you *for such a time as this*?"

Week Seven

DECORATING MADE SIMPLE

Week Seven

LESSON PLAN

I. LEADER OPENS IN PRAYER

II. DEVOTIONAL

- Mary—*A Woman of Honor*. Read Luke 1:26–56, Matthew 1:18–24, Luke 2:1–23, and Luke 2:21–40 in preparation for lesson. For help in preparation, refer to the Devotional section in today's lesson.

- **Biblical Principle**: A woman fully submitted to God's will for her life is a woman to be honored.

III. LESSON—Choose one or all of the topics in today's lesson based on the time allotted for class.

- **Leadership**: It is important to emphasize that we are not advocating acquiring a home full of furniture, but a home or apartment that honors the Lord—one that is warm and inviting, a place for family, friends, and guests to gather. **Contentment** is the key. God has given each of us the home and the economic level we have, and we are to be content with what God has given us. Also, we are to be good stewards of what He has given us, so learning how to do our own decorating and painting will enable us to do just that!

- You have the option with this lesson to bring in a professional decorator/painter to share budget-friendly decorating and painting tips. Be sure your guest keeps it simple and gives the participants ideas they can recreate and afford on their single or young married budgets.

- One of the discipling leadership team may be especially gifted in design and willing to teach this week. Handouts are included on the following topics: home decorating, how to hang pictures and display artwork, effective bookcase arranging, effective lighting, proper placing of furniture in a room according to scale, and basic painting information.

- The leader teaching may want to bring in samples of decorating/lighting items and ideas she has used in her home. She might also include fabric swatches, ideas for picture arrangements, different types of lighting, lamps, accessories, creative framing ideas, mantle arrangements, a variety of books used to fill in a bookcase area, etc. <u>Note</u>: Be sure the ideas given can be recreated and accomplished on a young woman's budget. Look around the hostess' home and give examples of the scale of a room, mantle arrangements, book casing, decorating, painting ideas, etc.

- Bring in pictures (personal or some from decorating magazines) to illustrate the decorating ideas discussed this week. These are easier to view if each picture is placed in a clear plastic pocket and put into a notebook.

- The discipling leader may also want to refer to decorating magazines, catalogs, websites, and their years of experience to show the different styles of decorating, room arrangements, book casing, lighting, etc.

Below are **Optional** activities for today's lesson:

- **Optional**: If one of the participants in the class is especially gifted in decorating or painting furniture or other decorative pieces, have her bring some of her own work to show and explain how she accomplished the look.

- **Optional**: If a guest decorator teaches, consider having the participants bring in photos of areas in their homes or apartment where help is needed with decorating or painting ideas. The leadership and/or guest speaker can give suggestions. One or more of the participants in the class may want to share some creative decorating or painting projects they have done in their homes.

- Leave time during the lesson for questions; they will have plenty!

IV. TIME IN THE KITCHEN

- If time allows, consider preparing one of the recipes in the Time in the Kitchen section.

V. WEEK EIGHT LESSON SHEETS

- Introduction—*Efficiency Décor*
  Reflecting Your Style
  Home Decorating—Taunton House Decorating Book by Heather J. Paper
  Arranging Furniture for Your Home
  Effective Lighting for Your Home
  Proper Ways to Hang Pictures and Display Artwork
  Effective Bookcasing for Your Home
  Decorating Resources
  Devotional on Mary

VI. EQUIPMENT FOR WEEK EIGHT

- Magazines and pictures to illustrate decorating ideas.

- Any items used to demonstrate decorating ideas, mantle arrangements, etc.

- If teaching on painting: Painting equipment, tarp, brushes, tape, etc. A color wheel, paint sample chart, etc.

- If recipe is prepared, provide all the ingredients.

- You will need plates, forks, or spoons to taste the prepared dish.

Introduction

EFFICIENCY DÉCOR

Some friends and I were at lunch one day reminiscing about our first year of marriage and our very first apartment. Everyone agreed that some of their fondest memories were those spent in their first apartment as newlyweds. On the way home that day, I began to think about our first place. Mark found it, and he was so proud. I hadn't seen it prior to our wedding because I lived in Nashville, and our home-to-be was in south Florida. We flew to Florida the morning after our wedding. Once we arrived, we retrieved our luggage, picked up the car, and set out for our new home, an *efficiency* apartment. Perhaps you are like me; I had no clue what an *efficiency* apartment was! As we pulled up the short drive, I noticed that there were two front doors rather close to one another. I asked if this was a duplex. Mark answered, "Not quite."

He unlocked the door and welcomed me into our new home. Let me give you a quick tour. I say quick because I discovered that an *efficiency* apartment is one-quarter of a small house! I stepped into the living room to see our bed/couch (living room and bedroom all in one), the only closet, the bathroom, the kitchenette, and the back door all at once. I told you it would be a quick tour! How clever of someone to design the living room that instantly makes it into a bedroom just by removing the rectangular back cushions! It must have been a man who designed it so he could watch TV in bed. To say I was shocked would be an understatement. Now, I wasn't expecting a mansion for after all we were a young married couple.

We were in south Florida to work and save money for graduate school, not to live in luxury—but an *efficiency* apartment? Needless to say, the decorating took very little time or effort. The only furniture we had was two plastic parson's tables. I know, what is a parson's table? Here it is: a plastic square top in which is stored the four plastic legs. When removed and pushed into the compartments in each of the four corners underneath, you instantly have a coffee table with four chunky legs that stands about twenty-four inches high. Wow! Of course I had to decorate the tops of our cute chunky white plastic coffee tables, so I purchased a glass globe that sat atop a wood base and was filled with red and gold *dried* flowers—the flowers of the 1970s. All matched perfectly with our black and cream coverlet that was provided over our bed/couch—not at all what I would choose now!

Your taste, like mine, will change over the years, but I want to encourage you to step out and trust yourself to know what you like and what you don't like in color, fabric, furniture styles, etc. Establish an apartment or home that reflects you, not your parents! If you feel insecure in this area and don't have a natural eye for decorating, find a friend or acquaintance who does.

Whatever your living quarters, know that it is your home, and you need to make it feel like home and reflect you as a person. You don't have to break the bank to accomplish this! Shop smart and when choosing colors, choose what you like. When choosing furniture, choose what you can afford, the fabric you like, and something that is comfortable. Home sweet home does not have to look like a showroom at a furniture store. It just needs to be warm and inviting!

REFLECTING YOUR STYLE

"She makes for herself coverlets, cushions, and rugs of tapestry. Her clothing is linen, pure and fine, and purple (wool). Give her of the product of her hands, And let her own works praise her in the gates (of the city)."
Proverbs 31:22, 31 AMP

Your home needs to reflect your life style, your taste, and your heart. When beginning the decorating process, here are some do's and don'ts ...

DON'T...

- **Compare your home or apartment** to the homes of friends, family, or acquaintances. If you are married this can harm your spouse's self-esteem; he will feel that he does not sufficiently provide for you and your family. If you are single, this will rob you of contentment.

- **Copy someone else's taste in design**. You can repeat an occasional decorative idea, but be yourself—do your own thing! You live in your home, let it be a reflection of you.

- **Go into debt in order to have a full house**—full of furniture and fully decorated. The old adage is true, "good things come to those who wait." A full house can cause an empty bank account!

- **Buy sales items** that do not complete or compliment your décor just because they are a "good deal." Coming home with a lamp or an accessory thinking that you will find a place to display it is a waste of money that could have been spent on a more beneficial decorative item to complete or compliment your design.

- **Be discontent** with what you have—discontentment reflects an ungrateful heart!

- **Be impatient** by wanting everything immediately—if you get all you want as soon as you move into your home, will you enjoy them or be onto your next "want"?

DO...

- **Make a list of items** you need to complete the decorating of the room you are working on and stick to your list.

- **Pray**—I pray before I go shop, and it is amazing how many times the Lord leads me to a good deal, one that fits my budget. He knows what is best for me and what I can afford.

- **Shop smart!** Save your money in order to buy better quality furniture—it will last for years!

- **Be content!** Discontentment breeds discontentment, robbing you of joy and peace. God will not honor an ungrateful, discontented heart. Contentment brings peace and joy!

- **Be patient**—You will better appreciate those things you were willing to wait for.

- **Be yourself**—God made you with your own unique taste; trust what you like.

Proverbs 31:27a says, "She looks well to how things go in her household." AMP

HOME DECORATING [24]

Taunton House Decorating Book by Heather J. Paper

Creating comfortable living quarters is more than a matter of shopping for a new piece of furniture. Whether you are starting from scratch or simply doing a little redecorating, it's important to first take a look at the big picture. Determine whether your family members live formally or if they are more laid back. Take a look at the colors and styles you like most. Be sure to figure kids and pets into the equation.

PERSONAL STYLE

The way you like to live will have a strong influence on the way you decorate your home. Are you more relaxed in a traditional setting, with wingback chairs and a camelback sofa? Or are you the type who likes the sleek contemporary style? If you are unsure, try this simple exercise: thumb through several decorating books looking for rooms that you find appealing; there will be some common decorating threads among them that will give you a sense of where to start. You may even find that you like elements of different styles, putting you in the eclectic category.

COLOR CUES

The choice of color palettes is purely personal. Similar to furniture styles, colors can speak volumes about your individual tastes. Pick up a stack of paint chips and you will see why choosing a palette can seem like an insurmountable task. In order to make the decision easier, here are a few clues. We all have a favorite color, so start by simply considering the various tints and shades within the color family you like. Also, think about the room and how it will be used. Is it a living room where you will entertain often? If so, consider neutral hues that will make most guests comfortable. The biggest clue is your wardrobe. Take a look at the colors you wear each day. Chances are if you are comfortable wearing them, you will be comfortable living with them.

A SMOOTH BLEND

In the process of decorating a room it is possible to spend too many hours trying to match colors. In fact, that is not necessary or desirable. It is more important that colors blend. For example, if you have two or three blues within a room, they will be right at home together if they are of similar tones and intensities. If you are uncertain if your colors will work together, try this simple test: gather the colors together, step back, and look at them through squinted eyes. If they seem to become a single shade, then you have a beautiful blend of colors.

HARMONY

It is imperative that there be at least one or two common threads of color. You can use multiple patterns within a room as long as you can connect them somehow, and they are in harmony.

[24] Heather J. Paper, Home Decorating (Taunton Press, 2005).

THE FAMILY ROOM

Creating a successful arrangement in the family room may be the easiest of all. Simply start with your largest seating piece—the sofa—and orient it toward the room's focal point, typically the home-entertainment center (the television). More often than not, this multipurpose storage piece is placed against the largest wall. Complete the seating group, making sure that each piece of furniture is no more than eight to ten feet apart, for easy conversation. Because you should be able to view the television without craning your neck, swivel chairs are often a good solution. Also, keep in mind that this is often where casual meals are served. Sit in each seat, making sure that there's a nearby place to sit a glass or dish. If not, you will need to add a small table or two.

LIVING ROOM

There is no hard and fast rule in terms of room arrangements, even in the living room. But a few guidelines will help you create a comfortable and inviting atmosphere. When placing your main seating pieces, keep in mind that people are most at ease sitting across from each other or at tight right angles. It is hard to converse if you are sitting too closely together side by side; even if your sofa can easily accommodate four people, plan on seating no more than three. For additional seating, use benches, ottomans, and nearby dining room chairs. Small upholstered cubes are a good choice as well. When not in use they can tuck away under a console table. Some cocktail tables come with cubes that nest underneath the tabletop until they are needed. Once you have lived with your furniture plan for a while, reassess how it is working. If it feels like you have too much furniture, don't hesitate to move a piece or two to another room. It is all a part of finding the right comfort level.

SCALE

Simply put, scale refers to the relationship among furnishings within a room. Visual weight as well as size comes into play. Many people flank a sofa with two end tables. If you don't want a matched set (in this age of eclecticism, that's the case more often than not), be sure that your selections are compatible in scale, with each other as well as with the sofa between them. For one end of a plush sofa, you might choose a set of nesting tables two inches taller than the sofa's arm; on the other end, you may opt for a small chest that's two inches lower. They both work with the height of the sofa and from a visual point of view too. The multiple legs of the nesting tables balance the mass of the chest at the opposite end.

WALL ART

We are long past the day when wall art consisted solely of paintings, posters, and prints. Today, we are more inclined to let our imaginations run wild, hanging anything that can be supported by a nail in the wall. From decorative plates to architectural elements—even store signs, boat oars, or a crisscross pair of skis—wall art is truly in the eye of the beholder. What if the objects of your desire are not conducive to being hung on a wall? There is often a way around that; small items such as pottery and figurines fit neatly on wall-hung shelves.

ARRANGING FURNITURE

Arranging furniture is one of the most daunting—yet most important—design decision you can make. These common scenarios will teach you the basics of furniture placement.

- Whether your room is big or small, having the right furniture arrangement will make it more enjoyable. Knowing how to arrange furniture can help you navigate how a room will be used.

- When arranging living room furniture; leave room for traffic and an entry drop spot.

- The living room furniture arrangement should provide for visiting guests, but still feel cozy when it's only you and your family.

- Cozy key seating pieces up to the fireplace facing each other. Arranging furniture around a fireplace, especially in the winter, makes your living room feel inviting.

- Use end tables as landing spaces on both ends of the sofa.

- Pair chairs to balance the visual weight of the sofa and to maximize seating.

- If you have no free walls and a centered fireplace, float seating in the center of a room filled with doors and windows.

- Face chairs and sofa toward each other to encourage conversation. Anchor the conversation grouping with a rug and a large coffee table.

- Frame the space with additional seating and cabinets for storage positioned around the perimeter of the room along the walls.

- If you're not sure how to arrange furniture in a living room, orient seating so it takes advantage of whatever view your room has to offer, whether it's a TV or a bank of windows. Create your own focal point by hanging a large piece of art on a wall or create a vignette of favorite objects on a console or bookshelf. If you can't decide between arranging the furniture around the fireplace or the TV, choose both and mount the TV above the fireplace.

- For face-to-face conversations, place seating no more than 8 feet apart. In a large living room, use furniture to create comfortable islands. Face two sofas in the center of a room, and place a group of chairs and side tables at one end to create a separate conversation area. A furniture arrangement that encourages conversation is the best kind for making memories in your home.

- Leaving enough space between pieces is vital in arranging furniture. Allow 30 inches between furniture you need to be able to walk around and 14 to 18 inches between a coffee table and sofa, so drinks are within reaching distance. This should still be held true when planning a large living room furniture arrangement. If a piece of furniture is too far away, it may look like it's floating in the room without purpose.

- The key to a good furniture arrangement is all in the details—especially side tables and coffee tables. Consider your room size and furniture arrangement when choosing the right coffee table. Use round pedestal tables as side tables between chairs and sofas. The curves of round tables make them easier to navigate around. When space is tight, use nesting tables for flexible use when needed.

- In an irregular room with one wide traffic lane, use the perimeter of the room for a computer desk and storage console. Choose chairs with casters so that they are easy to move. Float the furniture to focus on the fireplace and the television. Ensure that the living room furniture is arranged near both the fireplace and television.

- Always place the television so the screen faces away from the sunlight. The viewing distance for a standard TV is 8 to 12 feet, and the best viewing angle is not more than 30 degrees. For traffic flow, create paths that flow behind viewers and not between them and the screen.

- Family rooms can oftentimes be storage hubs, so a good living room furniture arrangement makes room for cabinets, drop zones, and drawers. Consider freestanding pieces in a smaller room and wall-to-wall built-ins in a larger room. Always allow for some storage near the TV for media items.

- Lighting is a key factor in the overall mood of your room and plays a big part when planning how to arrange living room furniture. Windows let in ample natural light, while chandeliers, sconces, and lamps keep the room bright at night. Improve lighting by installing in-floor electrical outlets to service floating furniture arrangements.

EFFECTIVE LIGHTING
for Your Home [25]

How you light your home is an important part of decorating. Lighting interior design contributes greatly to the look and feel of a room. There are many types of lighting that can be used in various rooms.

- **Ambient or General Lighting**—Illuminates the whole room. Recessed and track lighting are the most popular. Certain wall sconces are another example. It is recommended that you install a dimmer switch with your track and recessed light so that you have the added flexibility in adjusting the brightness.

- **Task Lighting**—Provides sufficient light to help you perform the task at hand, reading, cooking, shaving, etc. Task lighting should be glare free, and it should make things easy to see without tiring or straining your eyes.

- **Accent Lighting**—This light is focused lighting that is used to illuminate a sculpture, piece of art, or architectural element in a room. Accent lighting is about three times as bright as ambient lighting.

- **Natural Light**—This light comes through windows, doors, and skylights. Depending on the time of day, season, or weather, it can vary in brightness and intensity. Rooms can be arranged to take advantage of the position of the sun at different times of day. This type of lighting is also called kinetic lighting because the light from outside moves. It is one of the less reliable types, as it is affected by the seasons and the weather, but natural lighting can produce an effect unequaled by any artificial light source, when used properly.

Do not be afraid to use multiple types of interior lighting in a room. In fact, this is highly desirable and will create very dramatic effects. Using several strategies at once in a room allows you to turn any light off, changing the look and feel with the flick of a switch. This can be effective for creating different moods in different rooms at night.

- Lighting can also be effective in making a room look larger or smaller. Example: If a room seems too narrow, then wash one wall with light to visually expand it.

- If a ceiling is high, but you want the room to have a cozier and intimate feel, do not allow much light to escape beyond the height of the light/lamp shade. Try up-lighting the ceiling to make a room appear larger.

You will find hundreds of home lighting options for your home. Think of lighting from two aspects *functional and aesthetic*. Functionally, home lighting needs to provide the correct type of light in sufficient quantity for the intended purpose. Aesthetically, it can be configured to create the desired mood through intensity and color.

Lighting in Rooms

LIVING ROOM

1. Place a lamp behind every reader's shoulder, about twenty-four inches above the floor.
2. Highlight a framed piece of art with halogen track lighting or by attaching a picture light.
3. Use accent lights to illuminate book or display shelves.
4. Install recessed lighting as your general lighting or to bring out beautiful wall textures.
5. Use dimmer switches to change lighting atmosphere.

DINING ROOM

1. A chandelier over a table sets a beautiful setting.
2. Highlight a framed piece of art with halogen track lighting or by attaching a picture light.
3. Install halogen strip lighting in your china cabinet to highlight china or collectibles.
4. If a chandelier is not your taste and you have a long table, try a trio of pendant lights.

BEDROOM

1. Place table lamps on your bedside tables. For children's rooms, avoid halogen lamps, which get very hot.
2. Wall sconces can provide good general lighting without being too bright.
3. If there is not much space, consider recessed lights or pendant lights.
4. Don't forget candlelight if a romantic setting is what you have in mind.

Candice Olson, celebrated interior designer and TV host, says, "The most important part of any decorating project is lighting." According to Olson, without it, décor falls short of the sparkle factor and then the project budget is wasted. [26]

PROPER WAYS TO HANG PICTURES
and Display Artwork

STEP ONE:

Measure the distance between the wire at full tension and the top of the frame.

STEP TWO:

Measure the height of your frame and divide the result in half.

STEP THREE:

From the floor, measure up the wall to fifty-eight inches and make a light pencil mark.

STEP FOUR:

From the pencil mark, measure upward the distance recorded in step 2 and make a second light pencil mark.

STEP FIVE:

From this pencil mark, measure downward the distance recorded in step 1.

STEP SIX:

Place nail and hanger here.

BASICS ON HANGING PICTURES AND WALL ART

An arrangement of favorite framed photographs, wall art, or collectibles can add personality and warmth to any room. When done correctly, wall art can change the focal point or the entire look of any room.

- **Pictures should hang just above eye level.** Eye level is often defined as art center aligned at fifty-eight inches from the floor. While this is a good guideline for larger pieces, it can leave smaller pieces stranded on a wall. It is acceptable to hang a small print at seated eye level, so that the seated person can enjoy the view.

- **If most of the time people are standing in the room**, then the eye level should be directed at the viewers who are standing. In a room where the viewers will spend the majority of the time seated, like a living room, eye level would be from a seated position.

- **Creating a group of art or photos on a wall** is an excellent way to create an interesting focal point. This task, however, requires extra planning. It is suggested that you map out the way you would like to arrange your pictures on the floor first. This way, you can move them around without leaving holes in the wall.

- **The secret to arranging art on the wall is simple ...** balance, balance, balance! Use a measuring tape to be sure that the distance between several pictures that will hang in a row is equal. Four small pictures on the left can be balanced with two medium-sized pictures on the right. Be patient, take your time, measure, and plan.

- **Consider lighting to emphasize your arrangement.** When lighting is directed to the arrangement, it commands even more attention. This type of lighting should be subdued and not cause a glare. Be careful of lighting that is too bright.

- **Add diversity to the arrangement.** Use frames and mats that are different sizes and shapes, but complement one another.

- **Pay attention to balance in your entire room.** Be careful not to put everything in one part of the room. Leaving the other walls bare will throw the balance of the entire room off.

ARRANGING ART GROUPINGS:

- **Working horizontally**, as on a sofa wall or hall entrance—Prints grouped in odd numbers are visually balanced, giving volume without crowding.

- **Even number arrangements**—Large spaces: Tightly group an even number of pictures to balance a large space, such as a high wall in a room with vaulted ceilings. Small spaces: Tightly group an even number of pictures in a small space, such as a gallery kitchen or a tight stair landing, to give a window effect. Enhance the effect by using light colors and slender frames. In both cases, the trick to evenly numbered collections is tight grouping so that pieces appear as one statement rather than a series of small comments.

- **Symmetrical art placement**—If you have a selection of pictures that are similar in subject matter, size, and framing consider a symmetrical grouping to create a mirror-image balance. Symmetrical collections are often used to create the popular gallery effects, above large pieces of furniture, such as sofas and above mantles.

- **Asymmetrical wall arrangements**—If you have a selection of dissimilar pictures with at least one common element, such as subject matter, use an asymmetrical grouping for balance. When hanging two larger pictures together, try lowering one and raising the other so that the top and bottom do not match. Group larger and smaller pieces to create interest and energy. Example: Hang a large focal piece, such as a garden scene, with two smaller pieces, such as gardening tools or seed packets. Combine horizontal and vertical pieces in the same grouping. Hang a tall architectural print with two panoramic skyline photos.

- **Spacing pictures**—Tightly spaced is two inches or less between prints. Normal spacing is four to six inches apart. Trick to use: place your hand with fingers closed between the prints.

BASIC GROUPINGS OF ART WITH FURNITURE:

- **Fill two-thirds of the wall space**—When placing art above furniture such as sofas, chair groupings, or console tables, eyeball the amount of space between the furniture and the ceiling, and then allocate two-thirds of that space for pictures.

- **How high to hang**—Hanging a picture too high above a piece of furniture can leave both pieces feeling disconnected. A good guideline is five to nine inches above the furniture.

- **Spacing art**—When hanging a print above a sofa, remember to leave arm space above the sofa back.

- **Pictures and oversized furniture**—Oversized furniture calls for robust prints to strike a balance. For visual weight, consider a grouping of two to three prints that carry strong visual weight through color or wider molding and mat combination.

EFFECTIVE BOOKCASING *for Your Home*

- Less is more these days, so do not overload your bookshelves.

- Mix antique books and accessories with new coffee table books of interest.

- Stand up pretty porcelain plates, toile trays, and framed antique drawings on top of books and position them in between vertical stacks of books.

- Create a zigzag pattern of large objects and colorful books from upper shelf to lower shelf, to keep the eye interested and moving from top to bottom.

- Vary the texture of items on the shelves. Mix woven baskets, painted wooden folk art, metal and wooden boxes, and framed art work among shinier porcelain items to enliven the shelves.

- Think large scale when choosing bookshelf accessories and books. Coffee table books that are too large can be stacked horizontally to fit. A single large inexpensive basket has more impact than an expensive collection of miniatures. Save the miniatures for a small tabletop where they can be stars in their own right.

- Consider painting or wallpapering the back wall of your bookcases a fun pattern, deeper tone, or a contrasting color to make the accessories pop visually.

- Tuck a small pot of ivy into an interesting cachepot, box, or basket and place into your shelf arrangement.

- If space allows, consider placing a small lamp on a shelf. It adds warmth to the room.

RESOURCES FOR DECORATING

MAGAZINES

- Architectural Digest
- Better Homes and Gardens
- Bridge for Design
- Country Home
- Country Living
- Do It Yourself
- Family Handyman
- Flea Market Décor
- House Beautiful
- Interior Design
- Martha Stewart Living
- Real Simple
- Southern Living
- Taste of Home
- This Old House
- Traditional Home

CATALOGS

- Ballard Designs
- Crate and Barrel
- Frontgate
- Garnet Hill
- Horshow
- Pottery Barn

PAINTING 101[27]

Be sure to choose the proper type of paint for the job. The two major types of interior paint are latex, which is water-based and can be cleaned up with soap and water, and alkyd, which is oil-based and must be cleaned with paint thinner. Latex is the easiest to use.

Paints come in four finishes with varying degrees of shine: flat, satin, semi-gloss, and gloss:

- **Flat**—No sheen; best on walls in low-use areas, like dining rooms, living rooms, and bedrooms; washable but not scrubable.

- **Satin**—Slight sheen; good for walls and trim in higher use areas like hallways and kids rooms; washable and scrubable. This is the most popular sheen; it is durable and elegant.

- **Semi-gloss**—Medium sheen; good for walls and trim in high abuse areas like kitchens, bathrooms, laundry rooms; washable and scrubable.

- **Gloss**—High sheen; best for trim and cabinets; washable and scrubable.

When painting the walls and trim, use lower sheen on the walls and a higher sheen on the trim.

OIL-BASED PAINT:

Commonly used on molding, cabinets, and furniture. It provides a protective coating and creates a smoother finish than water-based paint.

Advantages of Oil:

- Goes on smoother
- Covers more thoroughly in one coat
- Shrinks less
- Takes longer to dry so you have more working time
- Holds up well in high-traffic areas

Disadvantages of Oil:

- More likely to crack, fade, and yellow over time
- Fumes can be overwhelming
- Clean-up solvents like mineral spirits and turpentine are necessary for cleaning brushes. These hazardous chemicals need to be managed carefully.

OTHER IMPORTANT CONSIDERATIONS:

- Oil-based paints should never be poured down a drain.

- Many cities have a local hazardous waste collection center that accepts old paint and stain. No matter which formula you reach for, oil or latex, use a laundry or bath sink for minor clean-up. Paint can ruin kitchen disposals.

---

[27] "Paint Glossary: All About Paint, Color, and Tools: Home Improvement: Home and Garden." www.hgtv.com/interior painting.

LATEX:

Often called acrylic latex because it contains a plastic resin made of acrylics or polyvinyl, which adheres better.

Advantages of Latex:

- Doesn't yellow over time
- Environmentally friendly
- Dries faster
- Much easier to clean up by using soap and water
- Latex is far more forgiving, primarily for cleanup, making it a great choice for the weekend warrior
- Many painters are finding latex is more widely available than oil
- Disadvantage of latex: it swells the grain of wood, making sanding between coats a necessity

More Painting Tips:

- All paints contain chemicals, so wear gloves when tackling large projects to minimize direct skin exposure.
- If you're painting a wall or doing some simple effects, reach for latex. If there's wood involved, you may want to consider oil-based paint.
- When in doubt, tell the experts at your local paint/hardware store what you're doing and they'll be happy to offer advice.

ALL ABOUT PAINT:

To tell if your current wall color is water-based or oil-based, douse a white cloth with rubbing alcohol and rub it on the wall (in an out-of-the-way spot). If the paint softens and begins to transfer onto the cloth, it is water based. If the alcohol does not remove any color, it is oil-based.

- **Primer**—Used to seal bare surfaces and provide a base for paint to grab on to. If you have spackled your walls, priming is a must to keep spackling from bleeding through the paint. Use water-based primer on new drywall, previously painted walls (including those that have been patched, repaired or stained), galvanized metal, and non-ferrous metals. Use oil-based primer on severely stained or damaged walls, on paneling, under wallpaper, and on wrought iron, ferrous metal, and raw wood.

- **Sheen**—Paint's sheen gives it a certain finish and quality. There are several options: matte-flat, eggshell, and satin.

- **Matte-Flat**—Smooth finish has little or no sheen. Helps hide surface imperfections but may suffer damage more easily than other finishes. Best for low-traffic areas.

- **Eggshell**—Velvety sheen, easy to clean. Great middle-of-the-road option between flat and high gloss. Gives a flatter look than glossy paint but still provides hard-wearing and protective coating.

- **Satin**—Silky, pearl-like finish, stain resistant. Creates protective shell that resists moisture and mildew. Good for kitchens, bathrooms, and high-traffic areas.

- **Semi-Gloss**—Sleek, radiant, and high resistance to moisture. Good for cabinets, doors, and windows.

- **High Gloss**—Very durable and easy to clean. It's a glass-like finish and is good for trim and molding.

- **Water-Based Paint**—Latex paint is often called water-based, commonly used on walls and ceilings; it is less toxic and easier to clean up than the oil-based paints. Water-based paint comes in a variety of sheens including matte, eggshell, or high gloss. It is a paint that works well on surfaces previously painted with latex or flat oil-based paints. It usually doesn't adhere well to high-gloss finishes and cannot be used on bare steel because it will rust it. Water-based paint can be used on top of wallpaper, but there is a risk that the water in the paint may cause the paper to peel away from the wall.

TOOLS:

- **Paintbrushes**—Which is best? Use a nylon-bristle brush for water-based paint and natural bristles for oil-based paint. Do not use natural bristles with water-based paint; the water can make the bristles limp. Foam brushes are good for intricate work such as painting molding or window casings. These brushes usually last for only one use because they're hard to clean and easy to tear.

- **Paintbrush Shape**: Angled-sash Paintbrush—The bristles are shaped at an angle to make it easier to cut into corners and paint moldings. And, Straight-end paint brushes—The bristles are cut at the same length.

- **Types of Bristles**—The best brushes have bristles that are flagged and tipped. Flagged bristles are slightly split, so they'll hold more paint and spread it more smoothly. Tipped bristles are slightly tapered to help release an even, controllable amount of paint. Typically, the more expensive the brush, the easier the paint job!

CLEANING PAINTBRUSHES:

For latex paint, use soap and water to clean paint from the brush immediately after painting. If the painting dries on the brush, you'll need special solvents to remove it. If your house is on a public sewer system, you can clean the brushes in your sink, but be careful not to dispose of paint in an area where it might seep into the groundwater.

For oil-based paints, you'll need a solvent such as paint thinner or mineral spirits. Pour about two inches of thinner into a metal container and swirl the dirty brush in, until the paint comes off. Press the brush against the side of the container to remove excess thinner and clean off the remaining thinner with the rag, then rinse with soap and water. If oil-based paint dries on your brush, soak it in paint thinner for a few minutes before cleaning. Most paint brushes can be wrapped in plastic wrap or original covering.

Hang brushes with bristles down to maintain their shape.

PAINTING PADS:

These can be very useful for cutting around trim. The pads come with small wheels that allow you to paint up to the edge of the trim without getting paint on the trim.

ROLLER COVERS

Paint rollers are time savers on any paint project. Using the correct roller cover can make your painting a lot smoother.

- **Nap**—The correct nap length of roller cover all depends on the texture of the surface to be painted. For a rough surface, use a roller with a long nap length. For smooth surfaces, use a shorter nap length.

- **Fiber**—Mohair is good for applying enamel paint. Lamb's wool covers are excellent for alkyd paints, but not for latex. Synthetic fibers are the most versatile but cannot be used with epoxies and polyurethane.

- **Core**—Cardboard cores are not very durable because they absorb the paint; they get soft and often lose their shape. Typically, the greater the cost the higher the quality.

ROLLER COVERS

- **For latex paint**, scrape as much paint off the roller as possible. Partially fill a sink or large bucket with warm water and roll the applicator back and forth. If necessary, use detergent with the water to remove difficult paint. Rinse the roller until the water is clear. Let dry. Once dry, rollers can be stored in a clean plastic zipper-lock bag for future use within the week.

- **For oil-based paint**, scrape as much paint as possible off the roller. Roll the applicator in a paint tray containing mineral spirits or paint thinner then wash the roller in soapy water. Rinse thoroughly and let dry. If doing a job over two to four days, you can wrap the brush/roller in cellophane, place in a plastic zipper-lock bag, and store in the refrigerator between jobs. With oil-based paint jobs, the brushes used can also be wrapped in plastic wrap, placed in a plastic zipper-lock bag, and stored in the refrigerator overnight. If paint is collecting in the bristles of the brush to the point of affecting the look of the paint job, clean and let dry. It is always good to have at least two identical brushes on an oil-based paint job, in order to have one drying while using the other. If the paint begins to collect gobs of paint and cause difficulty in painting, go ahead and clean the brush thoroughly.

- **No-hassle paint touch-ups**: Instead of getting the roller out to do a touch up, take an old washcloth, dip it in the paint can and bounce it over the spot a few times. The washcloth leaves the same kind of texture as a roller sleeve and you can throw it away when you are done.

MARY
A Woman of Honor

Biblical Principle: A woman fully submitted to God's will for her life is a woman to be honored.

Read Luke 1:26–56, Matthew 1:18–24, Luke 2:1–23, Matthew 2:1–23, and Luke 2:21–40.

Biblical History for Lesson—Luke, a physician, writes with the compassion and warmth of a family doctor as he carefully documents the perfect humanity of the Son of Man, Jesus Christ. He emphasizes Jesus' ancestry, birth, and early life before moving carefully and chronologically through His ministry. At the very beginning of his gospel, Luke tells his audience that he was not an original apostle or even an eyewitness to Jesus' words and works. Many believe Luke came to faith in Christ through the ministry of the apostle Paul, whom he befriended and accompanied on some of his missionary journeys. Luke is the only non-Jewish writer of a New Testament book. Luke's gospel includes many details of Jesus' life omitted from the other three gospels. Only Luke records a detailed account of Jesus' birth and the events surrounding it, including the angelic announcement to Jesus' mother, Mary, that she would give birth to the Messiah. Only Luke includes the boyhood of Jesus. (Stanley, 2005)

We will pick up the story in Luke 1:26.

- Mary was fearful at what the angel had said to her. She could see no way humanly that this could be possible.

- In the Jewish culture, a young unmarried girl who became pregnant risked disaster. Unless the father of the child agreed to marry her, she would probably remain unmarried for life—shunned among her people.

- If her father rejected her, she could be forced into begging or prostitution in order to earn a living.

"God chose Mary to bear the Savior of the world, but she also had to bear the public shame of being an unwed mother." NAS Ryrie Study Bible

Gabriel responded to her fear and said, "Do not be afraid, Mary, for you have found favor with God. And behold you will conceive in your womb and bring forth a Son, and shall call His name Jesus. He will be great, and will be called the Son of the Highest; and the Lord God will give Him the throne of His father David. And he will reign over the house of Jacob forever, and of His kingdom there will be no end." NKJV

The angel, Gabriel, said to her, "The Holy Spirit will come upon you, and the power of the highest will overshadow you; therefore, also, that Holy one who is to be called the Son of God. Now indeed, Elizabeth your relative had also conceived a son in her old age; and this is now the sixth month for her who was called barren. For with God nothing will be impossible." NKJV

When we face difficulties in life, we must not forget the truth of the above verse: Nothing and that means absolutely nothing is impossible for God. He can do anything. Nothing is too hard for him!

> Herbert Lockyear in *All the Women of the Bible* said, "When Mary willingly yielded her body to the Lord saying, 'Behold the handmaid of the Lord, be it unto thee according to thy word,' the Holy Spirit, by His gentle operation, took Deity and humanity and fused them together and formed the love-knot between our Lord's two natures within Mary's being. Therefore, when Jesus came forth it was as the God-man, 'God manifest in flesh,' or 'that holy thing which shall be born of thee shall be called Son of God.' Son of Mary—humanity! Son of God—Deity. We may not understand the mystery of when Mary yielded up her body that Christ should be formed within it, but believing that with God nothing is impossible we accept what scripture says as to the birth of Christ." [28]

One Christian writer is quoted as saying of the virgin birth, "Jesus Christ himself is such a miracle that it is no straining of faith to believe that His birth was also a miracle."

I love Mary's response to what God asked of her through the angel, Gabriel. Read her response in Luke 1:38 in the following versions:

- "Behold the maidservant of the Lord! Let it be to me according to your word. 'I am the Lord's servant, may it be to me as you have said.'" NIV

- "Yes, I see it all now. I am the Lord's maid, ready to serve. Let it be with me, just as you have said." The Message

- "Behold the bond slave of the Lord; may it be done to me according to your word." NAS

Mary's response was one of a servant's heart—humble, submitted, and surrendered to what God was asking of her, to bear His son, the Savior of the world. She willingly yielded her body to God.

> "The customary age for betrothal among Mary's people was thirteen or fourteen, so she was probably a young girl when her parents arranged her engagement to Joseph. The angel Gabriel visited her shortly after her engagement and announced that she would bear the Savior of the world. Jewish society treated unmarried pregnant women with shame and scorn, yet Mary remained strong in her faith. Expecting the worst from Joseph, her family and society, she gratefully accepted God's will for her life." (Stanley, 2005)
>
> Charles Stanley says, "What would have happened had Mary not believed Gabriel's words? Would she have disqualified herself to be the mother of Jesus? The fact is she did believe, and God did fulfill His word in her." (Stanley, 2005)

Gabriel had informed Mary that her cousin, Elizabeth, was also pregnant and in her sixth month. Mary goes to see Elizabeth, a journey of about eighty-one miles. She stayed with her for three months.

- As Mary enters Elizabeth's home, the baby in Elizabeth's womb leaps. She is filled with the Holy Spirit and addresses Mary as the, "Mother of my Lord."

[28] Herbert Lockyear. *All the Women of the Bible*. (Grand Rapids: Zondervan Publishing, 1988).

- Elizabeth tells Mary that she is blessed because she believed that the Lord would do what he said he would do.

- God was affirming His will and purpose for Mary through Elizabeth.

Dianne's Personal Testimony—<u>Note</u>: The leader may want to share her testimony of a time in her life when she experienced affirmation of God's specific calling in her life. *God has been so gracious to affirm, through others, what He has led me to do. When He put it on my heart to start this ministry, my pastor's wife encouraged me to step out and trust God; so I did. God used her to affirm the ministry He had called me to do. In no way am I comparing this ministry that God has given me to what God asked of Mary! But God does affirm His calling for us through others.*

Read Mary's song in Luke 1:46–56. Some refer to it as her hymn. I love the translation of Mary's song in the Message Bible:

> "I'm bursting with God-news; I'm dancing the song of my Savior God. God took one good look at me, and look what happened—I'm the most fortunate woman on earth! What God has done for me will never be forgotten, the God whose very name is holy, set apart from all others. His mercy flows in wave after wave on those who are in awe before him. He bared his arm and showed his strength, scattered the bluffing braggarts. He knocked tyrants off their high horses, pulled victims out of the mud. The starving poor sat down to a banquet; the callous rich were left out in the cold. He embraced his chosen child, Israel; he remembered and piled on the mercies, piled them high."

As we read through Mary's song over and over again, we can see her quoting verses from the Old Testament; she knew God's Word! (See Psalm 103:17, Psalm 98:1, Psalm 118:15, Job 5:11, Psalm 107:9, Genesis 17:19, Psalm 132:11, and Genesis 17:17).

> "This lyric expresses Mary's inward and deeply personal sacred and unselfish joy, and likewise her faith in Messianic fulfillment. It is also eloquent with her reverential spirit. Her worship was for her Son, for her spirit rejoiced in Him as her own Savior. Her hymn also spoke of her humility, for she was mindful of the fact that she was but a humble village maiden whose low estate the Lord regarded" (Lockyear, 1988).

As I studied Mary's story, I was moved by her faith at such a young age. Her faith was apparently quite incredible for her age; God recognized that and chose her to bear His son. Our heavenly Father desires for each of us, as His children, to have the faith Mary had, no matter our age.

As a result of studying Mary's life, we must ask ourselves a few questions:

- Do I have great faith?

- Do I have such a great faith that if God asked of me something so miraculous, so divine, and unbelievable, I would trust Him, believe Him, and be willing to submit and surrender to what He is asking of me?

- Would I willingly bear shame and ridicule for my Savior? Oh, that I would answer, "be it unto me as you have said." Oh, that I would have a faith like the faith of young Mary!

Charles Stanley says of Mary, "Mary was an ordinary girl with extraordinary godly character that gave her an uncommon faith. Completely trusting in her God, in every way Mary was a good and faithful servant." (Stanley, 2005)

Dr. Stanley assigns two of his life principles to Mary. First, "Obey God and leave the consequences to Him." Secondly, "God does not require us to understand His will; just obey it, even if it seems unreasonable." Mary believed, trusted, and obeyed. (Stanley, 2005)

After visiting Elizabeth for three months, Mary returned home to await the arrival of her baby.

> "And it came to pass in those days that a decree went out from Caesar Augustus that all the world should be registered. So all went to be registered everyone to his own city. Joseph also went up from Galilee, out of the city of Nazareth, into Judea, to the city of David, which is called Bethlehem (See Micah 5:2), because he was of the house and lineage of David, to be registered with Mary, his betrothed wife, who was with child. So it was that while they were there, the days were completed for her to be delivered. And she brought forth her firstborn Son, and wrapped Him in swaddling clothes, and laid Him in a manger, because there was no room in the inn." Luke 2:1–7 NKJV

Oh, the celebration Mary, Joseph, and all of heaven must have had at the birth of Jesus Christ. Mary, like Hannah, bore her son in order that he would be given back to God. She knew he was special, set apart, and created for a specific purpose.

Jesus was divine, yet Mary gave him life. She carried him in her womb, gave birth to him, nursed him, and raised him in the meager home of a carpenter.

Because of her willingness to obey God and surrender to His will for her life, Mary was a woman who was blessed with living in the divine presence of God.

Below are characteristics we learned about a young, humble, teenage woman named Mary:

- She believed God.

- She trusted God.

- She had a great faith at a young age.

- She was willing to bear shame, public humiliation, and ridicule in order to fulfill God's will for her life.

- She knew God through knowing His Word.

- She was a woman of godly character.

- She rejoiced in the midst of difficult circumstances.

Have the class prayerfully consider the above list of characteristics and whether they apply to their lives. After considering the characteristics displayed by Mary, ask the Lord:

- Am I like Mary?

- Am I attentive to His voice?

- Am I graciously accepting of His will for my life?

- Am I willing to obey whatever it is that the Lord, might ask of me?

Encourage the class to listen for His answers and pray over each of the above questions.

Discipling Leader: End the lesson with the verse below. Explain the verse and its application to the life of a believer. Discuss what it looks like to "walk by faith" as Mary did.

"For we walk by faith, not by sight." 2 Corinthians 5:7 NKJV

End today's lesson with discussing the following questions with the class:

- How has the story of Mary's life impacted you?

- What will you do differently as a result of studying the life of Mary?

Discipling Leader: Add personal comments. If time allows, utilize the Discussion Questions and the Examining the Heart Questions.

DISCUSSION QUESTIONS

1. Who was sent by God to a young Jewish woman? *The angel, Gabriel.*

2. To whom did God send him? *To a virgin named Mary, engaged to a man named Joseph, of the house of David.*

3. How does Gabriel address Mary? "Rejoice highly favored one, the Lord is with you; blessed are you among women."

4. What was Mary's response? "How can this be, since I do not know a man?"

5. In the Jewish culture of that day, how was pregnancy outside of wedlock viewed? What was the punishment? *It was shunned and against the law. The punishment was permanent shame and if her father rejected her, the young woman would be on the street forced to make a living by whatever means she could.*

6. Mary goes to visit her cousin, Elizabeth. What were the results of her visit? *Elizabeth recognizes her as the mother of her Lord and confirms what God is asking of Mary.*

7. Mary is resolved to trust God. She returns from seeing Elizabeth to wait on God for the birth of His son. Under what circumstances was Jesus born? *In a simple stable in Bethlehem among the animals.*

8. God chose a lowly young woman, an innocent young man, and a lowly stable as the setting for the birth of Jesus. How does the knowledge of these facts influence your view of God? *He looks for the faithful and the willing to use for His glory and purposes. His ways are not our ways as it says in Isaiah 55:8-9.*

9. What were the blessings in Mary's life as a result of her obedience? *She had the honor and privilege of being the mother of the Savior of the world. She was a first-hand witness of the ministry of Christ on earth.*

Examining the Heart

1. Can you imagine being addressed by an angel of God, being told you were favored by God and chosen by God for His purpose and plan?

2. Now, put yourself in Mary's place. How would you have responded, knowing the culture, the shame, and ridicule that were to come? What would your answer have been? Would it have been, "May it be done to me according to Your word?"

3. When you think of Mary's faith being a 10 on a scale of 1-10, where would your level of faith fall?

4. Are you willing to make yourself available to God for whatever he would want to accomplish in and through your life?

You, like Mary, can live in the divine presence of God. All you have to do is believe, trust, and have faith in a God who loves you and has a plan and a purpose for you. All He desires of you is a willing, surrendered heart and spirit, submitted to Him fully!

Week Eight

TIPS ON GARDENING, FLOWERS, AND CANNING

Week Eight

LESSON PLAN

I. LEADER OPENS IN PRAYER

II. DEVOTIONAL

- Lydia—*An Hospitable Woman*. Read the story of Lydia in Acts 16:13-15 (9-12) in order to prepare. For help in preparation, refer to the Devotional section in today's lesson.

- **Biblical Principle**: Women changed by the truth of the gospel will exercise their spiritual gifting for the glory of God.

III. LESSON—Choose one or all of the topics in today's lesson based on the time allotted for class.

- Gardening—Many young people these days are interested in eating more healthy, and therefore, desire to grow their own food. Many have not been raised around a parent with a green thumb, so they want to learn the basics of growing herbs and plants, and how to have a beautiful yard and patio area.

- The leadership may want to invite a guest speaker to teach on today's topic, if they do not feel comfortable teaching on gardening and other related topics.

- If the leadership teaches, consider these topics: English Gardening and creative potting, finding the right shrubs for your yard, how to grow your own garden, and growing herbs, etc.

- Put together a list of Farmers Market locations in your city and pass out to participants.

- Pass out one index card per participant. Ask the class participants to write down questions for the Week Nine's Woman to Woman panel. Collect before the end of class.

IV. TIME IN THE KITCHEN

- Prepare one of the canning recipes in today's lesson or a favorite canning recipe of the leadership. Example: The Barbeque Sauce would be an easy recipe to prepare.

V. WEEK EIGHT LESSON SHEETS

- Introduction—*Blackberry Pickin'*
Grow, Grow, Grow a Garden
Your Local Farmer's Market
Canning Tips
Canning Recipes
Tips for Gardening, Flower Beds, and Potted Plants
Resource Books
Devotional on Lydia

VI. EQUIPMENT FOR WEEK EIGHT

- Provide ingredients for preparing a canning recipe from today's lesson and containers for participants to take home a sample.

- Bring gardening tools and equipment needed to demonstrate planting potted flowers.

- Show pictures of ideas for planting English Gardens.

- A pack of white index cards. Pass out one card per participant. Ask them to write down questions for the Week Nine's Woman to Woman panel. Collect before the end of class.

Introduction

BLACKBERRY PICKIN'

Now that I'm older, I find myself reflecting back on my childhood experiences and memories. Ones that vividly stand out are the summers spent with my grandparents—hours from home and family. I remember the summer in Ohio when I went to church camp with them. My grandpa decided that I needed to attend the children's church service. He was determined I was going to go. I set out from our little cabin to cross this incredibly huge campground; well, it seemed huge to a little five-year-old girl. I went reluctantly, but not far! I hid behind the first tree I came to, thinking he and Grandma wouldn't see me. But they did see me, and Grandpa was not happy with my disobedience. I could be a fairly hard-headed little one! His solution to my refusal to go and my outright disobedience was a good old-fashioned spanking! In fact, it was the only time my Grandpa spanked me. But I went!

I also remember the summer in Springfield, Ohio following my third-grade year. What a fun summer! Grandma and Grandpa had planted a garden in their backyard. I can still smell the bright colored marigolds planted around the edge of the garden, supposedly to keep critters out. My grandparents were very meticulous people. I remember their freezer and how detailed and orderly it was. In fact, Grandpa had placed a diagram on the inside of the lid displaying where each item was located. Looking into the freezer, many items were wrapped neatly in freezer paper and secured with freezer tape. Others were placed in clear freezer containers, stacked, and labeled with his beautifully neat handwriting, something I did not inherit! It was a work of art. That summer, I spent hours either on the screened-in porch or in the basement playing with a wicker picnic basket, complete with four colorful place settings of plastic dishes—silverware, napkins, and all.

Evansville, Indiana, was the summer of my seventh-grade year. Grandpa hadn't been the pastor very long at Evansville First Church, so we hadn't been in the city previous to my stay. My Grandma was working part time at Sears, so Grandpa would come home and cook hamburgers for the two of us at lunchtime. He was a great cook and a sweet man. I cherish those lunches with him.

One Sunday, Grandpa suggested we go blackberry picking. Now, keep in mind, it was the middle of the summer. I am, and was as a child, very hot natured. We set out into the woods that hot Sunday afternoon to find blackberries, and to say I had an attitude from the onset would be putting it mildly. I was HOT and determined to make their lives and our blackberry pickin' time miserable! Looking back, I can see that I missed an opportunity to make a great memory with my grandparents, but then what do we know at thirteen? A little sweating, a little itching, and a few thorns was a small price to pay for a sweet memory! While living in Evansville, a member of the church had given them a parcel of land in which to plant a garden. I remember picking corn and digging up potatoes and carrots. That was also the year Grandpa planted Big Boy tomatoes along the back side of his garage and decided to use a new product on the market called Miracle Grow—talk about BIG BOYS! Those were the biggest tomatoes I had ever seen.

I have many fond memories of my grandparents, the summers spent with them and their many gardens. You too can make memories for your family gardening together!

Grow, Grow, Grow a Garden

According to an article in *Home Life Magazine*,[29] many American families are growing their own fresh fruits and vegetables to save money and avoid pesticides. Below are seven steps to growing your own garden:

1. Plan the place. Choose a central location easily accessible.

2. Find level ground that gets plenty of light and has good drainage (slopes down).

3. Begin by creating 4'x10' plots—as many as you desire in order to grow your garden.

4. Pick your plants. Consult the *Farmer's Almanac* or *Rodale's All-New Encyclopedia of Organic Gardening* for charts listing crops, their yields, and planting times. Some good choices are nutrient-rich vegetables: asparagus, garden beans, broccoli, beets, peppers, parsley, basil, lettuce, squash, cabbage, and strawberries.

5. Plant your crops. Drop seeds into trenches, and set seedlings in generous holes, allowing space for their roots. Be sure to water as you go, and label each plant or row.

6. Maintain growth. Take a half hour every few days to weed and water.

7. Harvest the bounty. Harvest promptly and regularly or plants will quit producing. Share the fruits of your labor!

Your Local Farmers' Market

If gardening is not your thing but you desire to eat healthy, go visit your local farmers' market or locate a farm like the Jones Vegetable Urban Farm, a community-based nonprofit organic farm, located in Birmingham, Alabama. Edwin Marty, executive director, at the farm says, "I don't think there is any way that anyone could dispute that a tomato grown locally is going to taste absolutely better than one shipped from across the country." Edwin Marty, and those like him, promote buying and eating area-grown produce. Eating freshly picked local produce means you get the freshest produce as well as a great benefit from the nutritional boost it gives.

Edwin went on to say, "The food that you are going to buy from local farmers is going to have so many more nutrients because it is picked ripe. It's picked when it is ready to be eaten, when the sun's energy has given it the maximum amount of flavor and sweetness."[30]

According to book author and Certified Nutritionist, Christine Avanti, in the past decade, the number of farmer's markets has exploded across the country. There are now more than 8,500 nationwide and 900 are open during the winter. That's a 250-percent increase since 1994.

---

[29] Andrea Bailey Willits, "Grow," Home Life Magazine (March 2011): 19–20. 174.
[30] Sara Askew Jones, "Healthy Living—Eat Local," Southern Living Magazine (June 2008): 109–111.

She says, "Your local farmers' market is hands-down the best place to buy fresh, locally grown food—food that's not a product of the processed food industry. I guarantee you that the fresh produce, the fresh-laid eggs, the pasture-raised beef, poultry, and pork, the jars of honey, the fresh baked bread—whatever you buy at the farmers' market—will taste better than anything you could buy at the supermarket."[31]

The benefits of buying local are: freshness, great flavor, seasonal variety, and as if that is not enough, when you buy from area farmers, more of your food dollars stay in your community. So if you do not want to grow your own—Go, go, go to your local farmers' market or vegetable urban farm and pick away!

HEALTH BENEFITS OF EATING FRESH

1. Eating raw cruciferous vegetables (such as cabbage, cauliflower, or broccoli) may help protect against the development of bladder cancer.

2. According to a new study, eating a high amount of vegetables (428 grams per day in the research) may reduce the risk of developing type 2 diabetes.

3. You avoid exposure to deadly pesticides and health risks related to their usage in planting.

4. Additives and preservatives are not being ingested into your system.

MEMPHIS FARMERS' MARKET LOCATIONS:

Shop at the nearest Farmers Market in your area. In doing so, you will definitely eat healthier.

1. **Agricenter Farmer's Market**, 7777 Walnut Grove Road, Cordova, Tennessee. Open May through October on Monday—Friday from 7:30–5:30, Saturday from 7–5:30. Closed Sunday.

2. **Collierville Farmer's Market**, 454 W. Poplar Avenue parking lot, Collierville United Methodist Church. Open Mid-May—October on Saturday from 8–1.

3. **Memphis Farmer's Market Central Station**, S. Front Street @ GE Patterson in Historic District. Open April—October on Saturday from 7–1.

4. **Cooper Young Community Farmer's Market**, 1000 Cooper Street. Open May—October on Saturday from 8–1.

Note: Leadership, consider putting together a list of Farmer's Markets located in your city and passing out the list to the class participants.

---

[31] Christine Alvanti, Skinny Chicks Eat Real Food (Emmaus, Rodale Publishing, 2012), 147–148.

CANNING TIPS

When I was a little girl, my grandparents canned the produce from their garden. It was a big part of their summer activities. What fun to pull out homemade strawberry jam, corn cut fresh from the cob, or green beans from the freezer when visiting them. Companies like Canal House help women with canning supplies, techniques, and recipes.

From an article on The Open Road Blog entitled, "Canning and Preserving, Courtesy of Canal House," the author states, "It's always a treat to receive a jar of homemade jam or preserves from a friend or neighbor at the end of berry season or during the holidays. But many home cooks—even those who are undeterred by stirring Risotto or unintimidated by flipping a Tarte Tatin—don't try canning and preserving at home. There's an unspoken assumption that pickling vegetables or jarring a batch of sauce or salsa requires a great deal of time and skill. But actually, canning and preserving are about as straightforward as they are soulful!"

She goes on to state, "Canning and preserving at home captures the essence of seasonal fruits and vegetables, making them available year round (with an extra dose of affection). Jam made with berries from a friend's garden, for instance, brings new meaning to your morning toast or a PB&J made for a child's lunch. You might try a salsa or pico de gallo recipe, especially if your tomato plants are growing like weeds in the July sunshine. Being able to open a jar of salsa at a wintertime football party, made from tomatoes that grew in your yard the previous summer, brings a soulful touch to otherwise casual snack food. Home chefs can make canning/preserving recipes their own, such as substituting blood oranges, grapefruits, tangerines, or even limes in orange marmalade recipes (although, for the record, citrus fruits are in season in the winter). While canning and preserving makes every day eating more upscale, it's not the complex, ambitious task that many people think it is. Give the Canal House Cooking canning and preserving recipes a try ... and then muster all your self-control not to open the jars before October. You'll love having these reminders of summer when you're unpacking your sweaters and holiday decorations. And you get to eat local, healthful food long after you've stopped shopping for citronella candles and sunblock." [32]

Owners of Canal House, Christopher Hirsheimer and Meredith Hamilton, were asked the following questions in an interview on Williams-Sonoma's blog titled, The Blender. "For someone who's new to preserving (canning), what would you recommend they start with? Any tips? Jam is great and easy, and you can start eating it right away—a fast return on your efforts. Make small batches of jam. You won't be overwhelmed by the whole process. Also, when you keep it small you won't overcook the fruit like when you have to boil down and reduce a large volume of liquid. When they are asked, "What will you be putting up this year? What are your favorite ingredients to preserve?" Their response is, "We always put up lots of tomatoes: tomato passata, tomato jam, oven-dried tomatoes, and on and on."

---

[32] "Canning and Preserving Courtesy of Canal House." http://www.openroadmedia.com/blog/2012-07-12/Can-ning-and-Preserving-Courtesy-of-Canal-House-Cooking.aspx

TOOLS FOR CANNING

- **Boiling Water Canner**—Made of porcelain-coated steel or aluminum. Comes with an airtight lid and a wire basket for holding canning jars

- **Home Canning Jars**—Found at Wal-Mart, Target, Williams-Sonoma, and local grocery stores

- **Canning Tools**—Found at Wal-Mart, Target, Williams–Sonoma, and local grocery stores. <u>Note</u>: For a more extensive list, see www.williams-sonoma.com (canning and preserving)

CANNING TOMATOES[33]

1. Visually examine canning jars for nicks, cracks, uneven rims, or sharp edges that may prevent sealing or cause breakage. Examine canning lids to ensure they are free of dents and sealing compound is even and complete. Check bands for proper fit.

2. Wash jars and two-piece caps in hot, soapy water. Rinse well. Dry bands; set aside. Heat jars and lids in a saucepot of simmering water (180°F or 82°C). Do not boil lids. Allow jars and lids to remain in hot water until ready for use, removing one at a time as needed.

3. Fill boiling-water canner half-full with hot water. Elevate rack in canner. Put canner lid in place. Heat water just to a simmer (180°F or 82°C). Keep water hot until used for processing.

4. Select fresh tomatoes at their peak of quality and flavor. Use firm tomatoes free of cracks, spots, and growths. Prepare only enough for one canner load. Wash tomatoes; drain.

5. Place tomatoes in wire basket and lower into a large saucepot of boiling water. Blanch tomatoes 30 to 60 seconds or until skins start to crack. Remove from boiling water. Dip immediately into cold water.

6. Slip off skins; trim away any green areas; cut out core. Leave tomatoes whole or cut into halves or quarters. For tomatoes packed in water, place tomatoes in a large saucepot, adding just enough water to cover. Boil gently 5 minutes. Remove canning jar from hot water with a jar lifter; set jar on towel. Add 1 tablespoon bottled lemon juice to each pint jar or 2 tablespoons bottled lemon juice to each quart jar.

7. Carefully pack tomatoes into hot jar, leaving ½-inch headspace. Ladle boiling water or cooking liquid over tomatoes, leaving ½-inch headspace. Add ½ teaspoon salt per pint jar or 1 teaspoon salt per quart jar, if desired.

8. Slide a non-metallic spatula between tomatoes and jar; press back gently on tomatoes to release trapped air bubbles. Repeat procedure 2 to 3 times around inside of jar.

9. Wipe rim and threads of jar with a clean, damp cloth. Remove lid from hot water using a lid wand. Place lid on jar, centering sealing compound on rim. Screw band down evenly and firmly, just until resistance is met—fingertip tight.

[33] Roger Doiron, "Canning Tomatoes Step by Step," Kitchen Gardener's International. http://kgi.org/canning-tomatoes-step-step

10. As each jar is filled, set it onto the elevated rack in the boiling-water canner. Water in canner should be kept at a simmer (180°F or 82°C). After all jars are filled and placed onto the rack, lower rack into canner. Water must cover the two-piece caps on the jars by 1 to 2 inches. Add boiling water, if necessary. Put lid on canner. Bring water to a boil. Start counting processing time after water comes to a rolling boil. Process pints 40 minutes, quarts 45 minutes, at a gentle but steady boil for altitudes at or below 1,000 feet above sea level. For higher altitude areas, consult your local extension office.

11. When processing time is complete, turn off heat and remove canner lid. Let canner cool minutes before removing jars. Remove jars from canner and set them upright, 1 to 2 inches apart, on a dry towel to cool. Do not retighten bands. Let jars cool 12 to 24 hours.

12. After jars have cooled, check lids for a seal by pressing on the center of each lid. If the center is pulled down and does not flex, remove the band, and gently try to lift the lid off with your fingertips. If the lid does not flex and you cannot lift it off, the lid has a good vacuum seal.

13. Wipe lid and jar surface with a clean, damp cloth to remove food particles or residue. Label. Store jars in a cool, dry, dark place.

CANNING RECIPES

Peach Preserves

3 teaspoons Fruit Fresh®

¼ cup water

1 cup sugar

1 quart sliced and peeled peaches

Mix Fruit Fresh® and water with sliced peaches. Pour sugar over fruit but do not stir. Let soak covered in refrigerator for 12 hours. The sugar will make a juice without adding more water. Cook on stovetop in a thick pot for 2 to 3 hours until juice becomes thickened and takes on the look of preserves. Fruit will be soft. Do not cook more than 6 quarts at a time. Each recipe makes a quart of peach preserves. Once completely cooked, place in quart size jars. Seal top with paraffin wax. Be careful when you melt the paraffin not to leave it atop stove after melted; wax can be flammable. Use 2 to 3 teaspoons of melted paraffin to top each jar of preserves. Secure with jar lid.

Olita's Sweet Pickles

1 gallon jar of whole dill pickles

5 pounds sugar

8 to 10 ounces minced garlic

10 to 12 cinnamon sticks

Drain juice from pickles and rinse. Slice pickles. Return to jar and layer pickles, sugar, garlic, and cinnamon sticks. Replace jar lid and tape around edges. Turn upside down daily for 14 days. Keep refrigerated after opening.

Bread and Butter Pickles

5½ cups pickling cucumbers, thinly sliced

1½ tablespoons kosher salt

1 cup sweet onion, thinly sliced

1 cup granulated white sugar

1 cup white vinegar

½ cup apple cider vinegar

¼ cup light brown sugar (packed)

1½ teaspoons mustard seeds

⅛ teaspoon ground turmeric

Combine cucumbers and salt in a large, shallow bowl; cover and chill 1½ hours. Move cucumbers into a colander and rinse thoroughly under cold water. Drain well, and return cucumbers to bowl. Add onion to the bowl. Combine sugar and remaining ingredients in a medium saucepan; bring to a simmer over medium heat, stirring until sugar dissolves. Pour hot vinegar mixture over cucumber mixture; let stand at room temperature 1 hour. Cover and refrigerate 24 hours. Store in an airtight container in refrigerator up to 2 weeks. Yields 4 cups of pickles.

Spaghetti Sauce

- 2 tablespoons olive oil
- 2 cups onion, chopped
- 2 cups green peppers, chopped
- 1 cup celery, chopped
- 4 cloves garlic, minced
- 2 pounds ground beef
- 3 cans (6 ounce) tomato paste
- 3 cans (8 ounce) tomato sauce
- 1 can (15 ounce) or fresh tomatoes, chopped
- 2 teaspoons basil
- 3 teaspoons oregano
- 1 teaspoon salt
- ½ teaspoon pepper
- 2 bay leaves

Sauté onion, green pepper, celery, and garlic in oil until onion is tender. Add ground beef; cook until browned. Drain off fat. Add remaining ingredients; simmer one hour. Remove bay leaves. Pour into can, freezer jars, or freezer plastic containers. Seal, label, and freeze. Yields: 6 pints. Note: Add 2 pounds cooked ground beef before serving sauce.

Heirloom Tomato Salsa

- 5 pounds heirloom tomatoes
- 2 onions, roughly chopped
- 4 large cloves of garlic, roughly chopped
- 1 cup fresh cilantro leaves, washed, and dried
- 1 tablespoon sea salt
- 1 to 2 jalapeño peppers, seeds, ribs, and stems removed, finely diced (wear gloves when working with these)
- ¼ cup sugar
- 1½ cups white vinegar

Place the tomatoes, onions, garlic, and cilantro in the bowl of a food processor and blend until it reaches the desired consistency. Put the blended mixture into a large, non-reactive pot, add the jalapeños, sugar, salt, and vinegar, bring to a boil, and then simmer until it reaches the desired thickness. While the salsa is cooking, sterilize your jars and lids in the hot water bath for 10 minutes. Drain and remove the jars, ladle the hot salsa directly into the hot jars leaving ¼ head space, wipe the rims with a clean, damp paper towel, apply the lids, and secure the bands. Process in a hot water bath canner for 20 minutes, then remove from the water and let the jars cool on a rack or several dishtowels to avoid extreme temperature changes, which can crack the jars. Once cooled, check the seals (the lids must be popped down) and store in a cool dark place for up to one year. If any of the lids have not sealed properly, store the jar in the fridge and use within one week. Yields: 6 pints or 12 half-pints.

Green Beans

Wash, string, trim, and cut green beans into ½ inch pieces. For canning raw: Pack the beans into canning jars to within ½ inch of top of jar. Add ½ teaspoon salt to each pint. Fill with BOILING water to within ½ inch of top of jar. Place cap on and screw tightly to seal. For canning hot pack: Boil beans in water for 3 minutes. Remove beans, reserving liquid, and place in canning jar to within ½ of top. Add ½ teaspoon salt to each pint. Fill jar to within a ½ inch of top with cooking liquid or boiling water. Place cap on and screw tightly to seal. Store in a cool place.

Barbecue Sauce

6 tablespoons brown sugar

3 tablespoons paprika

3 teaspoons salt

3 teaspoons dry mustard

1 teaspoon chili powder

⅛ teaspoon cayenne pepper

6 tablespoons Worcestershire sauce

3 cups tomato juice

¾ cup chili sauce

¾ cup vinegar

1 ½ cups onions, finely chopped

In saucepan, mix all ingredients and boil for 15 minutes over medium-high heat, stirring occasionally. Pour into sterilized canning jars to within a ½ inch of the top. Place cap on and screw tightly to seal. Place in a boiling *water bath* for 10 minutes. A *water bath* is a method of processing fruits, tomatoes, and pickles. For *water bath*: Use a large kettle or pail that is deep enough to cover jars at least one inch over the top and a little extra space for boiling. A wire rack is necessary for the bottom of the kettle or pail in order for the jars to be held at least one inch above the bottom of the pan. This will allow water to circulate. Cover the pan to keep water at a rolling boil during the process. As soon as water reaches a good boil, begin your *water bath* time of 10 minutes. Make sure the water is boiling during the processing period. When time is up, remove jars and allow to cool completely. Check lids to make sure they are tight and secure. Store in a cool place.

TIPS FOR GARDENING, FLOWER BEDS, AND POTTED PLANTS

African Violet—Pour the water from boiled eggs on your African violets. They will thrive on the extra calcium.

Ants—If you place black pepper in the haunts of ants, they will flee! Also, did you know that ants will not cross a chalk-drawn line?

Arrangements of fresh tulips stay fresher when copper pennies are tossed into the water.

A teaspoon of sugar to soapy lather will remove gardening stains from your hands.

Azaleas—One tablespoon of vinegar to one gallon of water when you are watering azaleas and other acid-loving plants such as hydrangeas and gardenias will correct any yellowing of the plants.

Azaleas—Azaleas thrive when you spray them every three weeks with a solution of water and ammonia. Use 1 level teaspoon ammonia to one gallon of water for the spray.

Blackberries make a great addition to the garden. They can be grown easily along a fence or wall. Space plants 4 to 5 feet apart. Johnson's Nursery or Petals from the Past are good sources for purchasing blackberry plants. Place order at www.johnsonnursery.com or www.petalsfromthepast.com. [34]

Black Spot and Mildew—Garlic bulbs planted near rose bushes will help the bushes develop resistance to black spot and mildew.

Blueberries in a Container—Purchase a rabbit eye blueberry (favorites are "Delite" and "Tifblue") from your local nursery. Plant it in a large container filled with good soil and peat moss; then water thoroughly. Place it in partial to full sun and mulch well to help the plant retain moisture. Containers dry out quickly in heat of summer, so check daily. Use an azalea fertilizer in the spring and fall. This plant will look great and add color to your porch year round, as well as provide blueberries for you to enjoy for a month or so in the summer [35]

Box Planter—Begin with a small, hardy shrub such as a dwarf Alberta spruce, as a permanent anchor. Renew the spaces around the spruce with a variety of fresh seasonal annuals. Use small annuals that won't overwhelm the shrub and slow-release fertilizer when you plant. [36]

Day Lilies—There are over 50,000 named daylily selections. Some of the favorites are Tuscawilla, Red Volunteer, Orange Volunteer, Vanilla Fluff, and Strawberry Candy.

Drain Spouts—To save topsoil and prevent erosion of lawn and garden from drain spouts, place a large flat stone under the spout to spread the rain water over a larger area.

Dwarf pineapple lilies add a lush appearance to the front of a border. These beautiful plants originated in South Africa. They got their name from the pineapple-shaped tufts of green leaflike bracts that form atop their flower spikes. Choose from several varieties. Add an unusual texture and look by trying pineapple lilies in your flowerbeds.

---

[34] Rebecca bull Reed, "Home and Garden- Family of Flowers," Southern Living (May 2008): 50–54.
[35] "A Harvest by the Door," Southern Living (May 2008): 18.
[36] Kate Carter Fredrick, "Outdoor Containers—Four Seasons," Better Homes and Gardens (March 2010): 130–134.

Food—A good slow-release fertilizer will feed plants for up to three months.

French Hydrangeas—These beautiful southern plants have voluptuous blossoms. They prefer morning sun with light afternoon shade. Soil pH can affect the color of the blossoms. Acid soil produces the bluest blues; white alkaline soil can turn blossoms pink. Hydrangeas make a great cut flower for indoor arrangements. Cuttings: Take 6 to 8-inch cuttings, wet the end, dip in rooting powder, and then stick each cutting into moist potting soil. Keep soil moist and plant in shade. Cutting should root in six to eight weeks. Place in garden bed. Hint: For pink blooms sprinkle, one tablespoon lime around the base. For blue, sprinkle 1 tablespoon aluminum sulfate at the base.[37]

Frost Dates—To learn when the last frost date in your area should occur before planting spring plants, visit www.victoryseeds.com/frost

Gardenias—A sprinkling of Epsom salt around the roots will reward you with longer blooms.

Great Tool—Water your garden with a Rain Wand. Its aluminum extension and nozzle let you apply a shower of water to your plants and control the amount with an easy-grip shut-off handle. Can be purchased at any nursery or garden store.

Great Vines—Vines offer great solutions for color, fragrance, and shade in tight spots. Good choices include Tangerine Beauty cross vine with orange-red flowers; Carolina Jessamine with fragrant, yellow blooms; and trumpet honeysuckle with red and yellow flowers.[38]

Hanging Baskets—Water your hanging plants with ice cubes to eliminate any dripping.

Healthier Geraniums—Coffee grounds added to soil when you are planting geraniums increase growth and blossoms.

House Plants—Before you leave town on a trip, place your houseplants on bricks in the bathtub filled with water. Enough water will be absorbed into the bricks to keep the plants in good condition (only for pots with drainage).

Making a Flower Bed—Composted cow manure or mushroom compost adds nutrients; pulverized bark or soil conditioner improves texture; and topsoil adds volume for building up the bed.

Marigolds—Signet Marigold is an excellent flowering plant for window boxes, herb gardens, and in front of mixed borders. Hundreds of tiny flowers will appear all summer amid scented foliage. Planting only a half-inch deep, these plants will yield flowers into the fall.[39]

Moles—If you have problems with moles in the yard, place coffee grounds in their runs.

Mosquitoes—You can reduce the number of mosquitoes breeding in your yard by emptying all sources of water from buckets and plant saucers. Keep roof gutters clear of debris so water does not collect. Fill low spots in yard and flowerbeds where water tends to stand. Mosquito Bits (granules) or Mosquito Dunks (solid) are good products for ridding your yard of these pesky critters. A sprig of fresh mint rubbed on face, arms, and legs repels mosquitoes.[40]

---

[37] Gene B. Bussell, "Home and Garden Plants We Love—Summertime Blues," *Southern Living* (June 2008).
[38] "Home and Garden—Things to Do," *Southern Living* (March 2008): 62.
[39] Steve Bender, "Home and Garden Plants We Love—Try This Marigold," *Southern Living* (May 2008): 85–87.
[40] "Flowers You'll Love: Around the Garden," *Southern Living* (August 2007): 55–56

Pansies—These flowers may be the most versatile garden annual. They have a vast array of colors, thrive in chilly weather, and do equally well in beds and containers. In the spring, you can plant well before the frost and in the fall, you can plant them in September while the days are still warm. You will enjoy their color right into November, if not longer. [41]

Perennial Color—Purple Cone flower is a great choice for your garden and you will enjoy it year after year. Varieties include the Ruby Star, Bravado, White Swan, and White Luster. All prefer well-drained soil. Improve drainage by adding some organic matter, such composted manure, finely shredded pine bark or mushroom compost. After planting water them well until established. [42]

Pick tomatoes, peppers, and tomatillos early in the morning the day you plan to eat them. Use sharp clippers to harvest these to avoid tearing the vines.

Pruning—When pruning azaleas, forsythias, spiraeas, and quince, they should be trimmed once they have finished blooming. If you wait until summer to cut them back, you will remove next year's flowers.

Quick Spring Arrangement—Daffodils look great when placed as a bunch in a small vase. When cutting the daffodils, cut the stems at an angle under water to improve water uptake. These flowers secrete a substance that prevents other flowers from taking in water, so mix them only with other daffodils. Place the arrangement in a cool area away from vents and direct sunlight; be sure to change the water every couple of days. For freshness, add oral preservative. [43]

Rabbits and Squirrels—Moth balls sprinkled by tomato plants and other fruits will keep squirrels and rabbits away. [44]

Roses—As the days become warmer and leaves begin to appear on your roses, fertilize with Schultz Liquid Rose food 10-12-12 or a granular feed such as Vigoro Rose Plant Food 12-6-10. Amend the soil around your rose bushes by adding mushroom compost or composted manure is great for rose bushes.

Unwanted Grass—For unwanted grass on your patio or walkway, pour table salt between the stones and/or bricks.

Weeds—To stop weeds and grass from running wild between your patio bricks, douse them with a little ammonia and they will promptly die.

White Vinegar—Fill a spray bottle with vinegar and spray to kill weeds in garden, yard, and pots. Flowering plants should be trimmed once they are finished blooming. If you wait until summer, you will hinder the plant from producing foliage in the coming year.

Wilted Cut Flowers—A teaspoon of household dish detergent to one quart of water will revive wilted cut flowers. [45]

---

[41] Eric Liskey, "Outdoors Plantings—Pansy Power," Better Homes and Gardens (March 2010): 112–114.
[42] Rebecca bull Reed, "Home and Garden—Family of Flowers," Southern Living (May 2008): 50–54.
[43] "Home and Garden—Things to Do," Southern Living (March 2008): 62.
[44] Wimmer Cookbooks, Why Didn't I Think of That? (Memphis, Wimmerco.com 1993), 80.
[45] Melanie Gaines, "Summer Pleasures: Colorful Cuttings," Decorating Step-by-Step (May 2007): 128.

Barbara Mundall of *Better Homes and Garden Magazine* says, "One of the most difficult challenges gardeners face is getting the garden to look good for more than one moment in time. Her solution, a valuable lesson for all gardeners, is to cultivate a diversity of plants, including species that bloom later and sport attractive, long-lasting foliage. As the earliest plants finish blooming or die back, ferns unfurl and hostas begin to poke their shoots through the soil. Then rhododendrons, peonies, and hydrangeas add season-long succession of blooms, ensuring that when spring finally arrives, it will be in no hurry to leave."[46]

RESOURCE BOOKS

A Field Guide to Trees and Shrubs by George A. Petrides

Ball Blue Book—The Guide to Home Canning and Container Gardening for All Seasons by Barbara Wise

Encyclopedia of Garden Plants by Christopher Brickell

Herbs and Spices: The Cook's Reference by Jill Norman

Herbs from the Ground Up by Sal Gilbertie

Landscape for Privacy by Marty Wingate

Organic Gardening by Michael and Christine Lavelle

Raised-Up Vegetable Gardening Made Simple by Raymond Nones

Real Food: For Mother and Baby by Nina Planck

Real Food: What to Eat and Why by Nina Planck

Residential Landscape Design by Mike Dooley

The American Horticultural Society—A-Z by Christopher Brickell

The Backyard Homestead by Carleen Madigan

The Cook's Herb Garden by Jeff Cox and Marie Pierre Moine

The Farmers Market Cookbook by Nina Planck

The Vegetable Gardner's Bible by Edward C. Smith

The Vegetable Gardener's Container Bible by Edward C. Smith

Timeless Landscape Design—The Four-Part Master Plan by Hugh Dagner

---

[46] Barbara Mundall, "Outdoors in the Garden—Spring Times," Better Homes and Garden, (March 2010): 95–99.

LYDIA
An Hospitable Woman

Biblical Principle: Women changed by the truth of the gospel will exercise their spiritual gifting for the glory of God.

Read the story of Lydia in Acts 16:13-15. Read Acts 16:9-12 for background information on how Paul and the disciples got to Philippi, the town where Lydia lived.

Biblical History for Lesson—Paul embarked on several missionary journeys, following the leading of the Holy Spirit. In Acts chapter 16, we see his travels as a disciple of Christ along with Silas and Luke. They set out for Asia, but the Holy Spirit stopped them from going. The Spirit of Jesus did not allow them to go there. So, they changed plans and went through Mysia to the seaport of Troas.

> Paul had a vision as he was preparing to sleep one night, "That night Paul has a vision: A man from Macedonia in northern Greece was standing there, pleading with him, 'Come over to Macedonia and help us!'" So, Paul along with his disciples, headed for Macedonia. Paul was seeking God's will and direction, and God led him to the place where he would use him to spread the gospel.
>
> "We boarded a boat at Troas and sailed straight across to the island of Samothrace, and the next day we landed at Neapolis. From there we reached Philippi, a major city of that district of Macedonia and a Roman colony. And we stayed there several days." Acts 16:11-12 NLT

Inscribed on the arches outside the city of Philippi in the district of Macedonia was a prohibition against bringing an unrecognized religion into the city. Certainly, Paul, Silas, and Luke were running a risk in sharing the gospel.

But because Paul listened, was attentive to, and obeyed the leading of the Holy Spirit, he boldly preached the gospel, and lives were changed. There was one woman in particular whose life was changed; her name was Lydia. Lydia was a part of a group that met for prayer outside the city by the river because there was no synagogue in their area and because of the prohibition against religion. For those gathered there, the riverbank was secluded, offering privacy, quiet, and water for Jewish purification rites.

> In Luke 16:14, Luke said of Lydia that she "worshipped God." In Luke's description of her, he said she was from Thyatira, a merchant of expensive purple cloth, and a worshipper of God. He used Lydia as an example of a significant woman in God's story.

Let's meet this significant woman...

> "On the Sabbath we went a little way outside the city to a riverbank, where we thought people would be meeting for prayer, and we sat down to speak with some women who had gathered there. One of them was Lydia from Thyatira, a merchant of expensive purple cloth, who worshiped God. As she listened to us, the Lord opened her heart, and she accepted what Paul was saying. She and her household were baptized, and she asked us to be her guests." Acts 16:13-14 NLT

The Greek word here for "listen" implies a continuing process. In other words, Lydia had been listening for some time to those at the riverbank and growing in her love and devotion for God. That day on the river's edge, Paul led her further along the road of intellectually understanding who God was and how he sent Jesus as a substitute for her sins.

As Lydia listened to Paul preach the gospel, her heart was moved. She accepted Christ as her Lord and Savior, was baptized, and instantly changed! Lydia was embarking on the next step of her spiritual journey with Jesus.

It is important to understand that the gospel penetrates the heart and changes lives.

Lydia then petitioned Paul and his disciples to be her guests in her home for the night. She said, "If you agree that I am a true believer in the Lord, 'Come and stay at my home.' And she urged us until we agreed." NLT

Note: There was no mention of a husband or a father in Lydia's story. This was unusual as women in biblical times were often identified by their relationship to a man, i.e. a father, husband, an adult son, or a brother. It is likely that Lydia had no surviving adult male relatives. She was probably widowed or perhaps divorced. Divorce was common and very easy to attain under Roman law. In most cases, divorce was not a result of scandal or stigma. Lydia sought no male counsel prior to inviting Paul and his disciples to stay in her home, indicating there was no male in her life to consult.

Lydia's hospitality and her acceptance of Paul and his ministry required courage. Having a group of foreign men stay in a woman's home in that day and time, might potentially cause scandal. If word got around that she was hosting meetings where people worshipped a new Jewish Messiah, it could have ruined her reputation and her business. Receiving Paul and Silas into her home after they were released from prison and asked to leave town was an act of bravery.

As a seller of luxury textiles dyed purple, Lydia was no doubt a successful woman in her community of Thyatira. It was only the wealthy in that culture who wore garments dyed purple or trimmed with purple. Tyrian purple, a dye extracted from the murex shellfish, was especially costly.

The expenses involved in Lydia's occupation as a merchant of luxury textiles indicates she was a woman of some wealth. It is believed that not only was she wealthy, but no doubt she had servants of her own—yet she desired to serve Paul and his disciples by opening her home to them. She was demonstrating the spiritual gift of hospitality.

Luke referred to Lydia by name, noting that she was truly a significant woman in God's story and in the lives of His disciples. God used Lydia to provide shelter, food, and clothing for His disciples.

God fulfilled his promise to provide for Paul, Luke, and Silas through her gift of hospitality.

What Lydia gained from her hospitality:

- She was personally discipled by God's disciples.
- She had the privilege of being used by God to provide for His called ones.
- She had the joy of being a part of the disciples' ministry while they were in Philippi.
- A church was established in Philippi because of Lydia's open heart.
- She became a vital part of a community when she accepted Christ. A community that loved her unconditionally.
- God used her and continues to use her as an example of an obedient hospitable woman—what she had was given for God's use.

IN CLOSING...

Let's look at Acts 16:40, "When Paul and Silas left the prison, they returned to the home of Lydia. There they met with the believers and encouraged them once more. Then they left town."

Paul and Silas had been arrested and placed in jail. When the officials realized that they were Roman citizens, they released them. Where did they want to go for rest and refreshment? Lydia's home!

The Macedonian missionaries ended up at Lydia's home again; they knew that they would be welcomed and cared for until the time God would move them on.

> God instructs believers: "When God's people are in need, be ready to help them. Always be eager to practice hospitality." Romans 12:13 NLT

We are called to follow Lydia's example of hospitality, offering to others a safe, warm, and inviting respite.

Discipling Leader: Discuss the following questions with the class:

- How has the story of Lydia's life impacted you?
- What will you do differently as a result of studying the life of Lydia?

If time allows, utilize the Discussion Questions and Examining the Heart Questions.

DISCUSSION QUESTIONS

1. What was the vision Paul had that led him to Philippi in the district of Macedonia? *That night Paul has a vision: A man from Macedonia in northern Greece was standing there, pleading with him, 'Come over to Macedonia and help us!'*

2. On what day of the week did Paul and his disciples meet a group of women on the riverbank outside of Philippi? What were they doing? *On the Sabbath. They were praying.*

3. What woman was described as "a merchant of expensive purple cloth? What else did Luke say about her? *Lydia from Thyatira, a merchant of expensive purple cloth, who worshiped God.*

4. Apparently, Lydia had spent a great deal of time at the riverbank listening to the teaching of God's Word. What happened to Lydia as she listened to Paul preach the gospel? *As she listened to us, the Lord opened her heart, and she accepted what Paul was saying.*

5. Lydia was an hospitable woman. What did she offer to do for Paul and his disciples? *If you agree that I am a true believer in the Lord, she said, "come and stay at my home." And she urged us until we agreed.*

6. What spiritual gift was Lydia demonstrating? What was it in Lydia's life that changed her heart and made her willing to minister to Paul, Luke, and Silas? *She was demonstrating the spiritual gift of hospitality. The Word of God and His Spirit changed her heart and brought forth the gift of hospitality that God had placed within her.*

7. What admonishment is given believers in Romans 12:13? *When God's people are in need, be ready to help them. Always be eager to practice hospitality.*

8. In order to be hospitable, you must be intentional. What are some ways you can be intentional in showing hospitality to those around you? *Discuss.*

Examining the Heart

1. Am I acknowledging my spiritual gifts and utilizing them for God's glory?

2. Am I intentional in opening my home to minister and encourage others?

Week Nine

WOMAN TO WOMAN

Week Nine

LESSON PLAN

I. LEADER OPENS IN PRAYER

II. DEVOTIONAL—*Living as a Wise Woman*. Prepare a large index card or a blank sheet of white paper according to instructions below and give one to each participant.

- The devotional time in this lesson is optional based on the time allotted for the panel today.

- If time allows: Write the following verse on the front side of each index card:

- "If any of you lacks wisdom, let him ask of God, who gives to all generously and without reproach, and it will be given to him." James 1:5 NAS

- On the back side, write the following:

    1. How would you define the word: wisdom?

    2. Name an older woman you consider to be wise.

    3. What are three words you would use to describe this woman of wisdom?

    4. Explain how she has impacted your life.

Allow the participants a few minutes to the fill out the cards, then discuss the verse and their responses to the four requests above.

Following the discussion of the above cards, explain the importance of having older, godly, and wise women involved in our lives. Move on to the panel time, introducing the women serving today.

III. LESSON

- **For Married Young Women**: A few weeks before this week's lesson, secure three women of varied ages to serve on a panel today. The women serving on the panel should be: a young woman in her mid-to-late 30s and married for at least ten years, a woman in her mid-to-late 50s, and a woman married at least forty years.

- Prior to class, text or email the panel members the questions turned in by class participants.

- Explain that the women on the panel were chosen because of their wisdom, the amount of years they have been married, and for the godly insight they are able to impart to the class.

- **For Single Young Women**: Introduce the panel for College/Single participants. The panel should consist of three women of varied ages—married and single. The participants attending the class will turn in questions for the panel a week or two in advance; these may cover a variety of topics based on the stage of life/age of class participants.

- Time at the end can be allotted for additional questions prompted by today's discussion.

- **Discipling Leaders**: When reading the questions aloud to the panel, consider your panel participants and who might be best qualified to answer each one. Once all the questions are answered, open the floor for any additional questions the young women might have thought of during the panel time.

- **Break**: Plan a break about half way through the class time for a snack and bathroom break. Use the last half of the class for answering any questions sparked by today's discussion. Then according to remaining time, ask any or all of the questions below of your panel:

  1. **For Married Young Women's Panel**: Assuming you could go back in life, what would you do differently in your marriage?

  2. **For Single Young Women's Panel**: As a single young woman, what were some specific qualities you looked for in the young men you dated? Assuming you could go back in life, what would you do differently in your choices of men to date?

  3. **For Both**: If you could give one word of advice to these young women as to social media, what would that be?

  4. **For Both**: What encouragement would you give these young women as to the priority of a devoted walk with Christ and a daily quiet time?

Thank the panel for coming and close in prayer.

IV. TIME IN THE KITCHEN
- Discipling leadership provides snacks and drinks for today.

V. WEEK NINE LESSON SHEETS
- Introduction—*Wise Counsel*
  Living and Loving with Purpose
  Single and Living Intentionally
  Intentional Living as Wife and Mom
  Reading Resources

VI. EQUIPMENT FOR WEEK NINE
- Snack foods and drinks for the break time.

- Plates, forks, cups, etc., for snacks brought today.

- Small thank you gift for each panel member.

Introduction

WISE COUNSEL

*Y*ears ago, when God chose to begin writing my and Mark's life story quite differently from what I had imagined it would be, I was struggling emotionally and spiritually. I needed to talk to a woman who was older, wiser, and one that I admired and who could be trusted with my feelings. So, I sought the counsel of an older woman in our church. At the time, she directed the prayer ministry and had a private office; so we met there on a Sunday afternoon.

Carolyn, fondly known as Miss Higgy (for Higginbotham), was always smiling and addressed everyone she saw as, "Sweetie." That day, I rounded the corner to her office to be greeted with a big smile and, "Well, Sweetie, come on in. Sit down. Before you share with me what is on your heart, let me pray for us." She prayed, and as I began to share with her, a dam broke wide open and tears were flowing like water out of a broken pipe! I poured my heart out to her. I felt bad for Miss Higgy as I desperately tried to explain my struggle through tears, sniffles, and an unsteady voice. She sat there patiently listening and handing me Kleenex after Kleenex. I was amazed that she could understand a word I said, but she seemed to comprehend my struggle.

When I had finished talking and dried my tears, she said to me, "Sweetie, I want you to stay away from the 'What if's' and the 'If only's.' Those are Satan's playground. He will cause you to struggle with doubt and fear, and he will have you questioning God, instead of trusting Him." I'm not sure how she knew that in months past, I had said to Mark many times, "If only we had…" or "What if we had done this instead of that, things would be different." Despite my tears and unsteady voice, the Spirit allowed her to know the word I needed to hear that day. She was so right! I had allowed Satan a foothold through questioning God and His plan for our lives.

---

*S*ince that day, I have thought about Miss Higgy's words of advice to me many times and I have used them time after time when counseling young women. Miss Higgy loved me, challenged me, and encouraged me. In the Bible we see older women loving and encouraging young women. Naomi loved and encouraged Ruth; Elizabeth loved and encouraged Mary.

God knew that young women would need the love, counsel, and encouragement of older women, which is why he placed a mandate or a challenge in the Bible for older women to teach and admonish young women. How grateful I am for Miss Higgy and other older women who have invested in my life through the way they lived, loved, and served.

It is a wise young woman who seeks time with and counsel and instruction from an older woman. Nothing in your life can hold as much value as the influence of an older woman who has experienced a long walk with Christ, many years of marriage, and a faithful trust in God, who has chosen to write her life story to be told!

LIVING AND LOVING *with Purpose*

Years ago, I read this statement in a book, "When we trust our lives to the unseen but ever-present God, he will write our lives into His story, and every last one of them will turn out to be a great read." Whether you are a college, single, or young married woman, God is writing your story and it will be a great read!

If you have ever read an autobiography, you have read the life story of the person featured in the book, written by that person. As children of God, He writes our story, and every one of us can be sure "it will be a good read." You can trust Him to write your story, direct your steps, and accomplish what He desires, according to His will and His timing.

God writes our stories to be told. We can learn from one another's stories. Let's look at some of the stories God has written in the lives of simple, gentle, quiet women used of God to impact thousands—women who lived, loved, and served others with great purpose. Perhaps their stories will have a profound impact on your life.

Amy Carmichael was a young woman who, at a very young age, felt called by God to the mission field. She followed God's guidance and eventually went to India to serve. There, she ministered to the people of that country for fifty-three years without a furlough. She founded an orphanage called the Dohnavur Foundation. It was a refuge for children in moral danger—unwanted children who were orphaned. She became the mother to hundreds of thousands of children. Amy was fondly known as Amma. She was a young woman who sacrificed all for the love of her Savior and His call on her life. Elisabeth Elliott said of Amy, "So she finished her course—Amy Carmichael, one of the tens of thousands of lovers of the Lord who staked everything on His faithfulness. Her life is another case in point of how grace goes to work on the raw material of individual nature. Was she a fool? Yes, for the same reason the apostle Paul was: for Christ's sake."[47] Amy allowed God to write her story and because she did, her life of obedience and courage is a model for all Christian women.

Jennifer Kennedy Dean wrote several books on prayer, challenging hundreds of thousands of Christians in the area of prayer. She said of prayer, "Prayer is the key to everything. What God wants to do on earth He does through prayer. Prayer is so much more than the words that come sandwiched between 'Dear God' and 'Amen.' We limit prayer's power by our misconceptions about what prayer is. My heart-felt passion is to teach others the deep truths about prayer that the Father is teaching me." In October of 2005, God orchestrated Jennifer's life in order to teach her more about Himself and the life of prayer by writing His story for her life—a story that would change everything. She says in her book, *Live a Praying Life*, "In October 2005, thinking we were finally about to get an answer for the dizziness that had been diagnosed as an inner ear infection,

---

[47] Elisabeth Elliot, *A Chance to Die*. (Revell Publishing, 1987).

instead we got the dreadful news that Wayne, my husband, had an advanced case of an aggressive brain cancer, for which there was essentially no hope for a cure. Two months later, he went to be with the Lord on December 13th. At some point in the very depths of grief, I asked the Lord, 'If you bear my burdens, then why do I feel this pain?' The Lord seemed to say to me: 'I stand between you and any blows headed your way. The blows meant for you land on Me. If the pain you feel hurts, just imagine the blow I absorbed for you. It should have been a knockout punch, but you will never feel the full force of a blow.' A praying life—a life lived in the flow of His power and provision— does not promise life without pain. It promises life without knockout punches." The Father's story, written through Jennifer's life, is there to teach us the power and depth of prayer![48]

I met Jennifer on June 10, 2019, at a Women's Ministry Expo. I shared with her the impact her books had on my life and my husband's life. Mark used her books over the years in discipling young men. In sharing about our losses, (mine, with losing Mark and hers, with losing Wayne) she said to me, "There is life on the other side of loss—it just takes time." Little did either of us know that just two days later, she would go to be with Jesus. She will be missed, but oh the blessing we have been given as a result of her obedience and her story!

Sherry Blankenship is a pastor's wife in St. Louis, Missouri. I first read her story in a book titled *Draw Near*. Her story is one that I am certain, if God had given her a choice, she would have chosen not to have it written the way He chose to write it. Sherry gave birth to triplets in September of 1981, two boys, Joshua and Jonathan, and a little girl named Anna Joy. This caught my attention as I began to read because our youngest daughter was born in September of 1981. Anna Joy was a wonderful little girl who was very fond of her two brothers. At the age of thirteen, she began to run a low-grade fever and was unusually tired. Having been a track runner, an A student, and full of life, this change in her behavior alarmed her mother. Sherry, being concerned, ordered blood work at their doctor's office. The doctor called following the first draw of blood and asked for a second set of blood to be drawn and tested. When the results came in, Anna was diagnosed with leukemia. Shocked and disheartened, they took Anna to St. Louis Children's Hospital. Her book is a record of her daily journal and journey with Anna over a year and a half of treatments, mountaintops, valleys, pain, and heartache. Yet in the midst of it all, God was there. Anna's life and radiance drew others to her heavenly Father as she lived out the story written for her. This young woman was called to suffer and ultimately die; her mother, Sherry, along with her dad and brothers, called to walk that hard road with her. But oh the testimony of God's faithfulness and grace that is found in the midst of this story. God wrote their story so that others can see and know the love of a mother for her child and the love and faithfulness of our heavenly Father.[49]

Mary was a young woman, sweet, innocent, full of life, and deeply in love with her heavenly Father and a young man named Joseph. She was filled with excitement and joy at the thought of their wedding to come. Oh, the planning that lay ahead of her. Her story was an exciting one, a story every young woman dreams of—a handsome young man, devoted to her and his heavenly Father. Their future looked so bright. Then God informed Mary of a new chapter he had written for her life. One she was unaware of prior to a visit from an angel named Gabriel. He informed Mary that God was about to rewrite her future; she had been chosen by God to bear His son. The angel said to her, "Rejoice, highly favored one, the Lord is with you; blessed are you among women." Mary's response was one that is an example to all women, when God writes our stories differently than we imagined. "I am the Lord's servant. May everything you have said about me come true." Because of Mary's willingness to submit to God's divine plan, she was given

---

[48] Jennifer Kennedy Dean, *Live a Praying Life*. (New Hope Publishers, 2010).
[49] Sherry Blankenship, *Draw Near*. (Tate Publishing, 2007). 199.

the honor of being the mother of the Savior of the world. She was a blessed woman, because she was an obedient woman. Charles Stanley says of Mary, "Mary provides a model of inspiration for ordinary women who can fulfill their deepest vocation by placing themselves at the service of others. She lived her life in relative obscurity, yet the world has celebrated her obedience to God for nearly two thousand years."[50]

Mary's story—God's story!

All four of these women are uniquely different from one another, living in various times in history. Mary's story was written nearly 2000 years ago and Amy's was written in the 1800's. Sherry's, Anna Joy's and Jennifer's were written in this day and time. Each woman is an example of a woman willing to submit her life to the Master author, as He writes her story with His pen and for His purposes.

No matter where you are in life, if you are willing to submit to God, he will write a story that will be a "good read"—a story with a grand ending!.

> "For since the world began, no ear has heard and no eye has seen a God like you, who works for those who wait for Him."
> Isaiah 64:4 NLV

> "Trust in the Lord with all your heart, and lean not on your own understanding; in all your ways acknowledge Him, and He shall direct your paths."
> Proverbs 3:5 NKJV

[50] Charles Stanley, Charles Stanley's Life Principles Bible, NKJV (Thomas Nelson Inc., 2005).

SINGLE AND LIVING *Intentionally*

by Leslie Hollowell

I came to an understanding years ago that "Many are the plans in a person's heart, but it's the Lord's purpose that prevails." Proverbs 19:21 NIV

I began at the early age of eight striving to determine the plans for my life. At this point, I was determined to be a detective and take my place as the fourth angel on Charlie's Angels. By age twelve, I was going to be a news anchorwoman. I sat for hours in the bathroom with my round brush, practicing my "and now for our local weather" voice.

Next up were my high school years. It was in that season of life that I realized I had a flair for teaching. My former third-grade teacher permitted me to "teach" a few lessons every week for a short period of time when I was her teacher's aide. It was then that I found my calling. I proceeded down the road of elementary education and started striving to set my life plans in order.

At eighteen years of age, I began college. I was determined to get my degree, a job, followed by marriage, then have children and enjoy summers off for family vacations. Well, I did end up with a fun job teaching first grade. I truly loved it, but I was still missing several parts of my plan—husband, children, and family vacations!

Fortunately, while in college, I had the privilege of being discipled! Through that experience, I realized that single or married, God had called me to be intentional in investing my life in others. I began striving to do that whenever God opened a door. I went on many youth trips as a counselor, spent summers working for BREAKAWAY Ministries, mentored girls at the Big Oak Girls Ranch, and found complete joy in living out 2 Timothy 2:2. I absolutely loved being able to teach and disciple others what God had so graciously taught me through those who had discipled me.

But, I was still lonely for my life mate. I remember praying and crying many nights and telling God, despite the loneliness, "I choose You!" I watched friend after friend get married and have children. Some days the loneliness seemed unbearable. And yet, it pushed me to the feet of Jesus and made me cling to His Word for hope and security. I learned I had to be intentional in my walk with the Lord, and so I sought to strive to do whatever I could not to fall prey to the ways of the world.

As time went on, God truly proved His faithfulness in my life. I laugh at the fact that I can quote nearly all the verses in the Bible on "waiting." I will tell you now that without a doubt, God's timing is Worth the Wait! I met the most amazing man at thirty-six years of age and married him one month before my thirty-eighth birthday. Now, in my forties, I am a mother to the cutest, most adorable little boy ever, and I can confidently say that God's timing is perfect! He is trustworthy, faithful, and He knows the plans He has for you!

INTENTIONAL LIVING AS WIFE AND MOM

by Angela Porada

I want to be INTENTIONAL about my role as a wife and mom. Intentional is defined as "done with intention or purpose; pointing beyond self." Therefore, I want our home to be a SAFE place, a place where my husband and children are filled up to go out and face the world. I want to take the word SAFE and use each letter to express the ways in which I desire to be intentional in my home.

S-SPIRITUALLY SAFE

- A home where everyone is free to ask questions
- A home where there is always time for conversation
- A home of unselfishness, not about me or my time

A-ACCEPTED

- A home where everyone is accepted regardless of his/her behavior; the person is accepted not the bad behavior
- A home where making fun of one another is not tolerated
- A home where differences are appreciated and accepted

F-FUN

- A home filled with laughter, music, games, and lots of noise
- A home where outdoor play is continual
- A home where spending time together is valued
- A home where cleaning is set aside, if need be, in order to have time as a family

E-ENGAGED/EDUCATIONAL

- A home where each family member is engaged in the lives of one another
- A home where dates as a couple are a priority
- A home where individual time is scheduled with each child
- A home where going to sporting events and outside activities to support one another is expected
- A home where teaching the children God's Word is first and foremost
- A home where education is valued and self-discipline and individual effort is expected whether in homeschooling (if God has called you to this), or attending public or private school

SEVERAL WAYS GOD HAS SHOWN ME
How to be Intentional

1. Obedience to God's Word—I have to rise early and spend time in the Word

2. I am to take every thought captive to the obedience of Christ

3. Submit to whatever it is God is asking me to do

4. Pray it; don't say it!

5. Turn off the television

6. Let the little things go

7. Allow the Lord to show me how I can meet the needs of my husband and family

8. Don't criticize my husband to my friends or my family

9. Praying and preparing before approaching my husband about sensitive or difficult subjects, and doing it with a calm, loving, and gentle spirit

Intentional Living Will Make My Home, and Your Home, a Safe Place for All Who Live There!

READING RESOURCES

WOMEN'S BOOKS:

A Loving Life by Paul E. Miller

A Praying Life by Paul E. Miller

A Young Woman After God's Own Heart by Elizabeth George

A Young Woman's Guide to Making Right Decisions by Elizabeth George

A Young Woman's Walk with God: Growing More Like Jesus by Elizabeth George

Before You Meet Prince Charming: A Guide to Radiant Beauty by Sarah Mally

Calm My Anxious Heart by Linda Dillow

Chance to Die—The Life and Legacy of Amy Carmichael by Elizabeth Elliott

Conversation Peace by Mary A. Kassian

Courtesy and Kindness for Young Ladies by Emilie Barnes

Desiring God by John Piper

Discerning the Voice of God by Priscilla Shirer

Everybody Always by Bob Goff

Every Young Woman's Battle: Guarding Your Mind by Shannon Ethridge and Stephen Arterburn

Fervent by Priscilla Shirer

Girls Gone Wise in a World Gone Wild by Mary A. Kassian

Grace by Max Lucado

Grace for the Good Girl by Emily P. Freeman

Graceful by Emily P. Freeman

His Princess—Love Letters from the King by Sheri Rose Shepherd

Kisses from Katie by Katie Davis Major

Lady in Waiting—Becoming God's Best While Waiting for Mr. Right by Jackie Kendall and Debby Jones

Let Me Be a Woman by Elizabeth Elliott

Lies Young Women Believe by Nancy DeMoss Wolgemuth

Live a Praying Life by Jennifer Kennedy Dean

Love Does by Bob Goff

Mothers and Daughters: Growing Into Wise Women Together by Nancy Wilson (Audio Book on CD)

Nothing to Prove by Jennie Allen

One in a Million by Priscilla Shirer

One Thousand Gifts by Ann Voscamp

Praying for Your Future Husband: Preparing Your Heart for His by Robin Jones Gunn

Restless by Jennie Allen

So Long Insecurity by Beth Moore

The Armor of God by Priscilla Shirer

The Hiding Place by Corrie ten Boom

The Red Sea Rules by Robert J. Morgan

The Resolution for Women by Priscilla Shirer

The Wise Woman and Other Stories by George MacDoanld

True Woman 101—Divine Design by Mary A. Kassian and Nancy DeMoss Wolgemuth

Twelve Extraordinary Women by John MacArthur

Unglued by Lysa TerKeurst

MARRIAGE BOOKS:

A Lifelong Love by Gary L. Thomas

As Long as We Both Shall Live by Gary Smalley and Ted Cunningham

Boundaries in Marriage by Dr. Henry Cloud and Dr. John Townsend

Cherish by Gary L. Thomas

Created to Be His Help Meet by Debi Pearl

Devotions for a Sacred Marriage by Gary L. Thomas

Every Man's Marriage by Stephen Arterburn

Have a New Husband by Friday by Dr. Kevin Leman

Hidden Keys of a Loving and Lasting Marriage by Gary Smalley

His Needs—Her Needs by Willard F. Harley, Jr.

Intended for Pleasure by Ed Wheat, M.D.

Intimacy Ignited by Joseph Dillow

Intimate Issues by Linda Dillow

Love and Respect for a Lifetime by Dr. Emerson Eggerichs

Love and War by John Eldredge

Marriage on the Rock by Jimmy Evans

Momentary Marriage by John Piper

Night Light: A Devotional for Couples by Dr. James Dobson and Shirley Dobson

Passages of Marriage by Mary Alice Minirth

Pray Big for Your Marriage by Will Davis

Quiet Times for Couples by H. Norm Wright

Romantic Lovers: The Intimate Marriage by David Hocking

Sacred Marriage by Gary L. Thomas

Sheet Music by Dr. Kevin Leman

The Act of Marriage by Tim LaHaye

The Book of Virtues by William Bennett

The Excellent Wife by Martha Peace

The Five Love Languages by Gary Chapman

The Four Seasons of Marriage: Secrets to a Lasting Marriage by Gary Chapman

The Love Dare by Alex Kendrick

The Power of a Praying Wife by Stormie Omartian

The Power of a Praying Husband by Stormie Omartian

What Did You Expect?: Redeeming the Realities of Marriage by Paul David Tripp

What's It Like to Be Married to Me? by Linda Dillow

When God Writes Your Love Story by Eric and Leslie Ludy

Young and In Love by Ted Cunningham

IN-LAW RELATIONSHIPS:

Boundaries by Dr. Henry Cloud

Grandmas and Mother-in-Laws: Onto the Next Thing by Nancy Wilson (Audio Book-CD)

In-Laws: Married with Parents by Wayne Mack

In-Law Relationship: The Chapman Guide to Becoming Friends with Your In-Laws by Gary Chapman

Peacemaking for Families by Ken Sande

The Message of Ruth by David J. Atkinson

The Mother-in-Law Dance: Can Two Women Love the Same Man and Still Get Along? by Annie Chapman

What's a Mother-in-Law to Do?: Essentials to Building a Loving Relationship with Your Son's New Wife by Jane Angelich

PARENTING:

Am I Messing Up My Kids? By Lysa TerKeurst

Boundaries with Kids by John Townsend

Bringing Up Boys by James Dobson

Bringing Up Girls by James Dobson

Cheers to the Diaper Years by Erin Brown Hollis

Christ-Centered Parenting by Russell Moore and Phillip Bethancourt

Faith of a Child by Art Murphy

Gospel-Powered Parenting: How the Gospel Shapes and Transforms Parenting by William P. Farley

Grace Based Parenting by Tim Kimmel

Have a New Kid by Friday by Kevin Leman

It Starts at Home by Kurt Bruner and Steve Stropp

Little Steps, Big Faith by Dawn Rundman

Parenting with Loving Correction by Sam Crabtree

Praying Circles Around Your Children by Mark Batterson

Shepherding a Child's Heart by Tedd Tripp

Siblings without Rivalry by Adele Faber

The Duties of Parents: Parenting God's Way by J.C. Ryle

The Family You Always Wanted to Be—5 Ways You Can Make It Happen by Gary L. Chapman

The 5 Love Languages of Children by Gary Chapman and Ross Campbell

The New Birth Order Book by Kevin Leman

TIME IN THE KITCHEN
RECIPES

Whole Wheat Yeast Rolls

- 2 envelopes rapid-rise active yeast
- 1¾ cups warm water
- ¼ cup sugar plus 2 tablespoons
- 2 teaspoons salt
- ½ cup butter, melted and divided
- 1 large egg, beaten
- 2¼ cups whole wheat flour
- 2¼ to 2½ cups all-purpose flour

Preheat oven to 400°F. Combine yeast, warm water, and 2 tablespoons sugar in a 2-cup liquid measuring cup, let stand for 5 minutes. Combine yeast mixture, remaining sugar, salt, ¼ cup melted butter, egg, and whole wheat flour in a large mixing bowl; beat on medium speed until well blended. Gradually add all-purpose flour to make soft dough. Turn dough out onto a well-floured surface; knead until smooth and elastic, approximately 5 to 10 minutes. Place in a well-greased bowl, turning to grease top. Cover and let rise in a warm place free from all drafts for 30 minutes or until doubled. Punch dough down, and divide in half; shape each into desired roll shape—crescent, cloverleaf, etc. Place in well-greased pan. Cover let rise in a warm place for approximately 20 minutes until doubled. Bake for 8 to 10 minutes until golden brown. Brush with remaining butter. Yields: 2 dozen.

Yeast Doughnuts

- ¼ cup warm water
- 2 tablespoons rapid-rise yeast
- 1½ cups warm milk
- ⅔ cup sugar
- 1¼ teaspoons salt
- 2 large eggs, beaten
- ⅓ cup shortening
- 5 cups all-purpose flour

In mixing bowl, whisk warm water and yeast together. Let stand 4 to 5 minutes making sure yeast is dissolved. Whisk in milk, sugar, salt, and eggs until blended. Add shortening and most of the flour, and blend. Knead dough with a dough hook on low speed until smooth; do not overmix. Remove dough from hook and coat with nonstick spray. Place back in bowl and cover bowl with clear plastic wrap. Let dough rise for 50 to 60 minutes until doubled. Turn dough onto floured surface and gently deflate. Roll to half-inch thickness and using a doughnut cutter, cut into doughnuts. Place on cookie sheet allowing room to rise. Cover loosely with plastic wrap and let rise 20 to 40 minutes. Heat oil in skillet to 350°F. Slide in doughnuts one at a time, frying 1 minute per side. Remove to wire rack set atop parchment paper. Cool.

TOP WITH GLAZE:

½ cup unsalted butter

1 ounce semisweet chocolate, melted

1½ teaspoons pure vanilla

2 cups confectioners' sugar

4 to 6 tablespoons hot water

Melt butter and chocolate on low heat. Remove and add vanilla and sugar. Stir in water as needed to desired thickness.

Sweet Cream Chocolate Cake

1 (4 ounce) unsweetened chocolate, melted

¾ cup unsalted butter

1½ cups sugar

3 large eggs, room temperature

2 egg yolks, room temperature

1 tablespoon pure vanilla

¼ cup strong coffee

1 cup whipping cream

½ cup ice water

2 cups all-purpose flour

¼ cup cocoa powder

2 teaspoons baking powder

1 teaspoon baking soda

½ teaspoon salt

Preheat oven to 325°F. Generously spray 2 (9-inch) pans and place on a parchment paper-lined baking sheet. Melt chocolate in microwave and allow to cool. In mixing bowl, cream butter and sugar until well blended. Fold in eggs, yolks, vanilla, and coffee. Blend well, 2 to 3 minutes, scraping bowl often to ensure nothing is stuck in well of mixer bowl. Blend in melted chocolate and then fold in whipping cream, water, flour, cocoa, baking powder, baking soda, and salt. Mix well on low speed until smooth. Pour batter into 9-inch prepared pans and bake for 45 to 50 minutes. Let cake cool on a rack in their pans.

Chocolate Cream Icing

1 stick butter, softened

4 (1 ounce) squares chocolate, melted

3 teaspoons cocoa

2 teaspoons pure vanilla

⅓ cup half and half

4½ to 5 cups confectioners' sugar

In mixing bowl, cream butter, melted chocolate, and cocoa. Add vanilla and half & half. Gradually blend in confectioners' sugar to spreading consistency. Ice cooled cake.

Whole Wheat Orange Muffins

½ cup butter, melted
2 ¼ cups sugar
2 tablespoons honey
4 large eggs, room temperature
½ cup canola oil
1 cup buttermilk
1 teaspoon pure vanilla
½ teaspoon each lemon and orange extract
½ cup bran
5 cups all-purpose flour
¼ teaspoon baking soda
1 tablespoon baking powder
½ teaspoon salt

Preheat oven to 350°F. Line muffin pan with paper liners. Place on a baking sheet lined with parchment paper. Cream butter with sugar and honey. Add eggs and oil. Blend well. Stir in buttermilk, vanilla, flavorings, bran, and remaining ingredients making a soft batter. Using a cookie scoop, scoop batter into prepared muffin cups, filling until almost full. Bake for 25 to 30 minutes until done.

Sour Cream Blueberry Muffins

2¼ cups sugar
½ cup butter, melted
½ cup canola oil
4 large eggs, room temperature
1 teaspoon pure vanilla
4-5 cups all-purpose flour
¼ teaspoon baking soda
1 tablespoon baking powder
½ teaspoon salt
1 cup buttermilk
½ cup sour cream
2 cups blueberries
Sugar to dust tops

Preheat oven to 425°F. Place paper liners in muffin tin and place atop a parchment-lined cookie sheet. Blend sugar, butter, and oil. Whisk in eggs and vanilla. Fold into batter 4 cups flour, baking soda, baking powder, and salt. Mix well before blending in buttermilk and sour cream. Batter may be thin. If needed, add in additional flour. Gently fold in blueberries with spatula, try not to break berries apart turning the batter blue. Using cookie scoop, scoop a very large amount into prepared muffin cups, load as full as possible. Dust tops with sugar. Bake 15 minutes at 425°F then reduce temperature to 350°F and bake until golden brown, 12 to 16 minutes. Let cool.

Six-Ingredient Granola Bars

2 cups old-fashioned oatmeal

½ cup brown sugar

¾ cup raisins, dried cherries, or cranberries

½ cup raw honey

½ cup crunchy peanut butter/optional

1 stick butter, softened

Preheat oven to 350°F. Spray a 9x13 pan with nonstick cooking spray. Mix all ingredients in a large bowl. Press into prepared pan and bake for 15 to 18 minutes, until lightly brown. Cool for five minutes, cut into rectangles or squares, and cool completely before serving. Store in airtight container. Makes 18 bars. Note: Peanut butter, almond butter, or butter can be used interchangeably.

Christine's Fabulous Coconut Smoothie

1 cup coconut milk, chilled

1 scoop high-quality protein powder

2 tablespoons ground flax seed meal

1 large banana

1 teaspoon coconut flavoring

10 ice cubes

Combine all the above ingredients in a blender and puree until smooth. Top with toasted, unsweetened coconut. For other fruit flavors, simply replace the coconut with peaches, mango, strawberries, or blueberries.

Peanut Butter Coconut Power Balls

1 cup dry old-fashioned oatmeal

1 cup Toasted Coconut, lightly toasted

½ cup natural peanut butter

¼ cup ground flax seed

¼ cup wheat germ

½ cup dark chocolate chips

¼ cup raw honey

1 teaspoon pure vanilla

Mix together all ingredients in a large mixing bowl until well blended. Chill for 1 hour. Once chilled, roll into balls the desired size and place on cookie sheet; chill 30 minutes. Store in an airtight container for up to 1 week. Makes 20 to 25 balls. Ground flax seed and wheat germ can be found in the cereal/health food sections of the local grocery.

Toasting Coconut: Preheat oven at 350°F. Spread coconut evenly onto large cookie sheet. Bake for 10 minutes and then remove from oven. Using a fork, stir coconut and place back in oven for 5 more minutes until golden brown. Cool and store in zipper bag until needed.

Whole Wheat Pita Chips

10 whole-wheat pita rounds, cut into wedges

1½ tablespoons olive oil

1½ teaspoons paprika

1½ tablespoons dried oregano

Preheat oven to 400°F. Toss pita wedges with oil, paprika, and oregano in large bowl. Spread on a baking sheet and bake until golden brown, about 20 to 25 minutes. Store in airtight container.

Cheesy Almond Spread

1 (8 ounce) package cream cheese, softened

1½ cups (6 ounce) Swiss cheese, shredded

½ cup almonds, sliced

⅓ cup mayonnaise

2 green onions, chopped

¼ teaspoon ground nutmeg

¼ teaspoon pepper

Garnish: Almond slices, toasted

Preheat oven to 350°F. Combine first 7 ingredients, stir well. Spread mixture into a 9-inch pie plate. Bake uncovered for 15 minutes until bubbly. Garnish with almond slices. Serve with pita chips.

Pan-Seared Cod

½ cup panko bread crumbs

½ cup pecans, finely chopped

⅓ cup flour

1 teaspoon baking powder

1 teaspoon salt

1 teaspoon black pepper

1 teaspoon paprika

½ cup buttermilk

1½ pounds Cod fillets

4 tablespoons butter

1 lemon, cut in wedges for serving

In shallow dish, combine panko crumbs and pecans. In another dish, combine flour, baking powder, salt, pepper, and paprika. In a third dish, add buttermilk. Taking one filet at a time, dust in flour mixture and shake off excess. Dip filet in buttermilk to evenly coat, drain excess. Dredge in pecan mixture, coating thoroughly. In a large skillet, heat butter over medium heat; and cook on each side for 2-3 minutes, or until fish is golden, flakes with a fork and reaches a safe internal temperature of 145°F. Serve with fresh lemon wedges, refrigerate any leftovers.

Creamy Salmon Fillets

¼ cup shallots

2 tablespoons butter, melted

½ cup white wine vinegar

½ cup water

4 Salmon fillets

Sea salt and pepper to taste

½ cup heavy cream

3 tablespoons fresh parsley, chopped

In skillet with lid over medium heat, heat shallots in butter, white wine vinegar, and water for 3-4 minutes. Season salmon with salt and pepper. Place atop shallots, cover and cook over low heat for 10 minutes, turning after 5 minutes. Cook to desired texture. Remove and keep warm. Add heavy cream to skillet; stir and cook over high heat until reduced by half. Add chopped parsley and pour over salmon fillets. Serve warm.

Trout Amandine

3 tablespoons butter

¼ cup sliced almonds

½ cup milk

1 egg yolk

½ teaspoon hot sauce

1 cup all-purpose flour

1 teaspoon salt

1 teaspoon pepper

6 (12 ounce) Rainbow Trout fillets

Olive oil

Lemon Cream Sauce

Melt butter in a large skillet over low heat. Add almonds and sauté until golden brown. Remove almonds from skillet and drain on paper towels. Set aside. In small bowl, whisk together milk, egg yolk, and hot sauce. In additional bowl, stir together flour, salt, and pepper. Dredge fillets in flour mixture; dip in egg mixture. Dredge an additional time in the flour mixture. Pour oil in skillet; heat to 375°F. Cook fillets 3 to 4 minutes on each side until golden brown. Spoon Lemon Cream sauce over each fillet and top with sautéed almonds.

LEMON CREAM SAUCE:

½ cup butter

2 tablespoons flour

1 (14½ ounce) can chicken broth

2 garlic cloves, minced

1 tablespoon lemon juice

⅓ cup whipping cream

¼ cup white wine Worchester sauce

½ teaspoon salt

½ teaspoon hot sauce

Over medium heat melt butter in skillet; whisk in flour. Cook and whisk for one minute. Add broth, garlic, lemon juice; whisk and bring to a boil. Reduce heat and simmer, whisking constantly for approximately five minutes. Whisk in cream and remaining ingredients, and cook for additional five minutes until thick.

LEADER GUIDE REFERENCE LIST

Alvanti, Christine. *Skinny Chicks Eat Real Food.* (Emmaus, Rodale Publishing, 2012), 147–148.

Blankenship, Sherry. *Draw Near.* (Tate Publishing, 2007). 199.

Chappa, Deborah R. *Words for When There Are no Words: Writing a Memorable Condolence Note* (Haverford, Infinity Publishing, 1999).

Dean, Jennifer Kennedy. *Live a Praying Life.* (New Hope Publishers, 2010).

Elliot, Elisabeth. *A Chance to Die.* (Revell Publishing, 1987).

Ewer, Cynthia. "Pantry Recipes for Homemade Cleaning Products." *www.organized.com/recipesforhomemadecleaningproducts.com*

Felton, Sandra. *The Messies Manual* (Revell Publisher Grand Rapids, Michigan 2005).

Halvorson, Christine. *Arm & Hammer Baking Soda, Over 100 Helpful Household Hints.* 1998. Lincolnwood: Publishers International, Ltd.

Home Furnishings. "Room arrangements," *www.homefurnish.com/livingroomdecor/homedecor/roomarrangements.aspx*

How to Beat House-work. Lincolnwood: Eureka Vacuum Cleaners Publication International, Ltd. 1988. Lansky, Vicki.

Baking Soda: Over 500 Fabulous, Fun, and Frugal Uses You've Probably Never Thought Of. 2004. Minnetonka: Book Peddlers.

Lockyear, Herbert. *All the Women of the Bible.* 1988. Grand Rapids: Zondervan Publishing.

May, Iva. *W3: Women, Worldview, and the Word.* Chronological Bible Discipleship, 2007. Revised 2010.

McNulty, JoAnne. "Age Appropriate Chores for Kids." *www.freeprintablebehaviorcharts.com*.

Mitchell, Nancy R. "Etiquette Rules!." 2017. New York, New York: Well Fleet Press.

Paper, Heather J. *Home Decorating* (Taunton Press, 2005).

Stanley, Charles. *The Charles F. Stanley Life Principles Bible: New King James Version.* 2005. Nashville: Thomas Nelson Publishing.

The Taste of Home Cookbook (Reiman Media Group Inc. 2009).

West, Kay. *How to Raise a Gentleman—A Civilized Guide to Helping Your Son Through His Uncivilized Childhood.* 2001. Nashville: Rutledge Hill Press-Division of Thomas Nelson Publishers, Inc.

West, Kay. *How to Raise a Lady—A Civilized Guide to Helping Your Daughter Through Her Uncivilized Childhood.* 2001. Nashville: Rutledge Hill Press-Division of Thomas Nelson Publishers, Inc.

Wimmer Cookbooks. *Why Didn't I Think of That?* 1993. Memphis: Wimmer Cookbooks.

About

THE AUTHOR

Dianne Dougharty was married to her high school sweetheart for forty-five years. After an extended illness, Mark went to be with Jesus on July 31, 2018. She is the mother of two daughters and Mimi to seven grandchildren. Dianne graduated from Trevecca Nazarene University with a degree in Elementary Education. For over twenty years, she has led women's Bible studies, spoken at conferences, authored curriculum, and contributed written work to several blogs. She faithfully served for years beside her husband in full-time vocational ministry.

Dianne has a desire to see older women fulfill the mandate given them in Titus 2:3-4, "These older women must train the younger women to love their husbands and their children, to live wisely and be pure, to work in their homes, to do good, and to be submissive to their husbands. Then they will not bring shame to the word of God." NLT

Her heart is for young women to become seekers of Christ, students of God's Word, and lovers of their home, husband, family, and calling. She has a passion to see women live purposefully—making investments in the lives of other women.

God led Dianne to develop the Secrets Savored Ministry, a fun hands-on approach to developing community among women who desire to create a spirit of hospitality and Christlikeness within their lives, homes, and relationships—for the glory of God! Once a week, small groups meet within home settings and learn to apply biblical principles for living a godly life in an often God-less world.

Check out the ministry at secretssavored.org.
Follow her on Facebook, Twitter, and Pinterest.

SECRETS Savored

CREATING COMMUNITY
THROUGH SIMPLE HOSPITALITY

Secrets Savored is a Titus 2 discipling tool. Women across generations discover the treasure of community as they practice simple hospitality and apply Biblical truths in a home setting. This in-depth Bible study is growing women into a deeper faith and building Christ-like character within them.

Follow Us: @SECRETSSAVORED